Models and Metaphors

Models and Metaphors

STUDIES IN LANGUAGE
AND PHILOSOPHY

Max Black

PROFESSOR OF PHILOSOPHY
CORNELL UNIVERSITY

Cornell University Press

ITHACA, NEW YORK

First published 1962
Second printing 1963
Third printing 1966
Fourth printing 1968

Library of Congress Catalog Card Number: 62-9128

PRINTED IN THE UNITED STATES OF AMERICA
BY VALLEY OFFSET, INC.
BOUND BY VAIL-BALLOU PRESS, INC.

TO *Susanna* AND *David*

Ist es doch nicht eine der geringsten Aufgaben des Logikers, auf die Fallstricke hinzuweisen, die von der Sprache dem Denkenden gelegt werden.

—*Gottlob Frege*

Preface

ALL the essays that follow have been written since the appearance of my last collection, *Problems of Analysis* (1954). Although the range of topics is wide, I hope there may be a certain unity of treatment arising from a steady interest in the bearing of language upon philosophical problems.

My greatest debt is to students and colleagues, whose searching criticisms have been invaluable.

For permission to reprint, I have to thank the editors of the journals and books in which most of these papers originally appeared. (Further details are contained in "Additional Notes and References" at the end of the book.) Mr. John Steadman and Mr. Melvin Standig have been kind enough to help me in preparing the book for the press.

MAX BLACK

Ithaca, New York
November, 1961

Contents

I

Language and Reality

BERTRAND RUSSELL once said, "The study of grammar, in my opinion, is capable of throwing far more light on philosophical questions than is commonly supposed by philosophers. Although a grammatical distinction cannot be uncritically assumed to correspond to a genuine philosophical difference, yet the one is *primâ facie* evidence of the other, and may often be most usefully employed as a source of discovery" (*The Principles of Mathematics*, Cambridge, 1903, p. 42).

The grammatical distinctions that Russell proceeds to use as guides to philosophical discoveries are the familiar ones between nouns, adjectives, and verbs. But he says that he hopes for "a classification, not of words, but of ideas" (*loc. cit.*) and adds, "I shall therefore call adjectives or predicates all notions which are capable of being such, even in a form in which grammar would call them substantives" (*ibid.*). If we are ready to call adjectives nouns, in defiance of grammar, we can hardly expect the grammatical distinction between the two parts of speech to guide us toward what Russell calls a "correct logic" (*ibid.*). If grammar is to teach us anything of philosophical importance, it must be treated with more respect.

My object in this paper is to clarify the character of philosophical inferences from grammar. By "grammar" I shall understand a classification of meaningful units of speech (i.e., "morphology"), together with rules for the correct arrangement of such units in sentences (i.e., "syntax"). The conclusions of the kinds of inferences I have in mind will be propositions commonly called "ontological"; they will be metaphysical statements about "the ultimate nature of reality," like "Relations exist," or "The World is the totality of

[1]

facts, not of things," or "There exists one and only one substance."

1

In seeking ontological conclusions from linguistic premises, our starting point must be the grammar of some actual language, whether living or dead. From the standpoint of a language's capacity to express what is or what might be the case, it contains much that is superfluous, in grammar as well as in vocabulary. Grammatical propriety requires a German child to be indicated by a neuter expression *("das* Kind"), a liability from which French children are exempt. If we are willing to speak ungrammatical German or French, so long as the fact-stating resources of the language are unimpaired, we can dispense with indications of gender. For to be told that the word *"Kind"* is neuter is to be told nothing about children that would have been the case had the German language never existed. The indifference of the English language to the gender of nouns sufficiently demonstrates the superfluity of this particular grammatical feature. For the purpose of eventual metaphysical inference, gender is an accidental, a nonessential, grammatical category.

In order to have any prospects of validity, positive philosophical inferences from grammar must be based upon essential, nonaccidental, grammatical features, that is to say on features whose deletion would impair or render impossible the fact-stating functions of language. The essential grammatical features, if there are any, must therefore be present in all actual or possible languages that have the same fact-stating powers. They must be invariant under all possible transformations of a given language that conserve fact-stating resources. The system of all such invariant grammatical features would constitute a universal or philosophical grammar. Metaphysical inferences from grammar must be founded upon the constitution of a hypothetical universal grammar, in abstraction from the idiomatic peculiarities of the grammars of given languages.

[2]

There is little reason to suppose that the universal grammar, if there is such a thing, will closely resemble any conventional grammar. Contemporary linguists have made plain the "formal" character of conventional grammatical classifications and the "arbitrariness" of conventional rules of syntax. We shall need something other than grammarians' tools to uncover the universal grammar.

I assume, however, that philosophical grammar will still resemble conventional grammar in consisting of a morphology together with a syntax. I shall suppose throughout that we are considering the prospects of a certain kind of classification, coupled with a system of rules for admissible combinations of the things classified. I shall use the conveniently noncommittal expression, "linguistic features," to refer to the things classified.

Were it possible to construct a philosophical grammar, or any fragment of it, it would be very tempting to say that something would thereby have been revealed about the nature of ultimate reality. For what could be the reason for the presence of some grammatical feature in all conceivable fact-stating languages except the correspondence of every such language with reality? There is an inclination to say with the author of the *Tractatus* that the essence of language must be "the essence of the World" (*Tractatus*, 5.4711). Or, with a more recent writer, "The universe is not a vain capricious customer of ours. If the shoe fits, this is a good clue to the size of the foot. If a language is adequate to describe it, this indicates something about its structure" (I. M. Copi, in *The Review of Metaphysics*, vol. 4 [1951], p. 436).

Of course, if metaphysical inferences from grammar are not to be circular, the construction of a universal grammar must proceed without prior ontological commitments. We shall need to consider whether the search for a universal grammar can be undertaken from a position of ontological neutrality.

It is obviously easier to show that some linguistic feature does not belong to universal grammar than the reverse; most

[3]

of the examples I shall consider will have this negative character, that is to say, will be instances in which we argue that some feature of a given language is not essential to the fact-stating powers of the language. The corresponding ontological inference is the negative one that nothing in ultimate reality corresponds to the rejected linguistic feature.

2

In the *Tractatus,* Wittgenstein says, "In the proposition there must be exactly as much distinguishable (*gleich soviel zu unterscheiden*) as in the state of affairs that it represents" (4.04). Let us read this to mean: "In the particular utterance, there must be exactly as many different symbols as there are constituents in the state of affairs represented." Following Wittgenstein, I shall assign two physically similar word-tokens to different symbols, when they have different senses or references.

Let us try to apply this plausible principle of invariance of the number of constituents to a concrete instance. Suppose I am riding in an automobile with somebody who is learning to drive, and I need some pre-arranged signals to tell him to start the car or to stop it. It is natural, and adequate, to use the words "Stop" and "Go"; but, of course, a tap on the shoulder would do just as well. Here we have a system of orders, not statements of fact; but similar considerations will apply in both cases, since the logical structure of the orders will be the same as that of the factual statements specifying the actions performed in response to those orders. An adherent of Wittgenstein's principle of isomorphism might point out that here the two actions to be performed are represented by exactly the same number of distinct symbols, "Stop" and "Go." He might add that it would be logically impossible for the learner-driver to understand the two different orders, unless he were supplied with different and distinct symbols for the two cases. And he might add that every set of symbols that could serve the same purpose would necessarily exhibit the

[4]

same duality. Whether the instructor spoke German, or Swahili, or anything else, he must necessarily use two symbols: here seems to be a perfect example of an essential feature, necessarily manifested in all the mutually equivalent notations.

But suppose the instructor used a whistle to signal "Start" as well as to signal "Stop." This device would be just as effective as the conventional words, and we need not suppose the whistle blasts to be substitutes for the English sounds: their meanings might have been taught directly, by demonstration and training. Have we not here an exception to Wittgenstein's principle—one symbol (the blown whistle), but two represented actions?

The retort is obvious: A whistle blown when the car is at rest means one thing ("Go"), but means another ("Stop") when the car is in motion. So the full symbol is whistle-plus-condition-of-car: there are two relevant states of the car, hence two symbols after all. But is this conclusive? Surely it would be just as easy to argue as follows: The whistle is one symbol, not two; but it also represents one action, not two: each time it means a *change-of-state*, whether from motion to rest or vice versa. To be consistent, an advocate of this view must be willing to say that the familiar orders "Stop" and "Go" mean one and the same thing; but a determined searcher for a depth grammar must accept consequences at least as strange as this.

In order to determine whether Wittgenstein's principle applies to the case in hand, we need criteria of identity for actions and criteria of identity for the corresponding symbols. We have to say whether starting the car and stopping it are to count as the same or as different actions; and we have to say whether blowing the whistle is to count as having the same or different meanings on various occasions. There are no definite criteria for identity in these cases. In ordinary life, in a particular setting, we might understand sufficiently well a request to say something different, or to do something different; but here we are not in an ordinary setting. We want to know whether there are *really* two actions and two symbols,

[5]

and have no way of finding out. We are free to decide whether the symbols are the same or different; the relevant fragment of philosophical grammar must be stipulated. The philosophical questions lack determinate sense and depend for their answers upon how we choose to describe the relevant utterances.

It may be said that this disappointing outcome arises from the artificiality of the example. I shall therefore turn to other cases having greater intrinsic interest.

3

Nowadays, it is often said that the copula, that figures so prominently in traditional logic, is superfluous. Listen to this, for instance: "There might certainly be various relations that the copula stood for, if it stood for any relation at all. But in fact no link is needed to join subject and predicate. . . . The grammatical copula is logically significant only when it serves as a sign of tense" (P. T. Geach, in *Mind*, vol. 59 [1950], p. 464).

But here is a traditionalist speaking: "The mode of connection of the subject and the predicate is symbolized in the standard formulation by the word 'is,' which is called the 'copula' because it links subject and predicate together; . . . some mode of connection requires symbolization, and this function is performed by the copula" (C. A. Mace, *The Principles of Logic*, London, 1933, pp. 77–78).

The dispute is clearly about philosophical grammar: the question is whether the copula is, or is not, an essential feature of language. On the one side, a strong case can be presented for the dispensability of the copula. There are languages, like Hebrew or Japanese, which manage very well without a copula; and we ourselves do without it in such constructions as "Peter loves Mary," in which the predicate, "loves Mary," is attached to its subject, "Peter," without benefit of any verbal link. Strongest of all is the argument that we could jettison the copula without in any way impairing the fact-stating resources of our language. Were we to say "Peter happy" as the Chinese are said to do, we would lose nothing in expressive and descriptive power. In any case, *some* words and expressions must be able to "hang together" in a sentence without a symbolic link, for otherwise no completed sentence would be possible. So why not dispense with the copula altogether?

A defender of the copula's significance might reply as follows: "You are right in claiming that we don't need the *word* 'is' or any other word between the subject and the predicate of a sentence. But this is trivial and was never in dispute. Consider the pidgin English sentence 'Peter happy,' that you offered as an adequate substitute for the conventional form. What is significant in this sentence is not merely the occurrence of the word-tokens 'Peter' and 'happy,' but the *relationship* between them. Separating the two words by others or by a sufficiently wide interval will disintegrate your sentence. It is the relationship of juxtaposition that here performs the function of linking subject and predicate. Similarly, in the conventional form, 'Peter is happy,' the union is effected by a relationship generated by writing the three words in correct order and in sufficiently close proximity. What is essential to the copula is not at all deleted by the translation into pidgin English. *Floreat copula!*"

What are we to say of this rebuttal? Its plausibility is undeniable, yet once again nothing compels us to accept it. For one thing, we may feel some reluctance to recognize "juxtaposition" as a genuine relation. Do we really need to *bring* the words into any relationship? Isn't it enough that we use them both in making the statement in question? Here again, consideration of some nonverbal notation might rid us of certain initial prejudices. Could we not, perhaps, use a red disk to mean that Peter is happy, with the disk standing for the man and its color for his condition of felicity? And what then would become of the alleged relationship between subject and predicate? Somebody might still insist, like W. E. Johnson in his *Logic,* that there would have to be a *characterizing relation* between the disk and its color. But anybody

[7]

who can confidently assert this must already be in a position to analyze reality directly, and has no need of the detour through language.

But indeed, an advocate of the no-copula view can reaffirm his position without invoking a hypothetical notation of qualified objects. *His* analysis of the sentence-fact "Peter happy" might well be in terms of an "object," the word-token "Peter" qualified by a certain property, that of having the word-token "happy" in immediate proximity. If he conceives of properties as "incomplete," i.e., as having the power to unite with objects without need of intermediaries, he will *see* the linguistic predicate in the same light. For such a neo-Fregean, learning how to *use* a predicate *is* learning how to attach it to subjects in complete statements, and there is no separate rule to be learned about the symbolic significance of the alleged relation of juxtaposition. For such a philosopher, a question about the relationship between subject and predicate of a statement is as otiose as a question about the relationship between a hand and the object it points at. Specification of the hand and the object indicated defines the gesture, without need for further specification; similarly, choice of a subject and an appropriate predicate uniquely determines a statement, without need for a further choice of a relationship between them.

Once again, we have a dispute which is inconclusive and threatens to be undecidable. What turns on the outcome? What difference will it make whether or not we recognize a characterizing relation? Well, a relation is conceived to hold between *terms,* so the traditional recognition of the copula goes with a classification of properties as special kinds of *things.* Admission of a characterizing relation allows questions to be asked about properties, so that predicates or their surrogates are sometimes permitted to function as subjects. The opposite point of view, that treats properties and their representing predicates as incomplete, forbids questions and assertions to be made about properties as subjects. The dis-

[8]

pute about the copula, trifling as it may seem at first sight, is a focus of contention for full-blown alternative grammars.

4

I pass on now to consider whether the ancient distinction between subject and predicate should be regarded as an essential feature of language that belongs to universal grammar.

How do we identify the subject and predicate of a given statement? A contemporary answers as follows: "A predicate is an expression that gives us an assertion about something if we attach it to another expression that stands for what we are making the assertion about" (P. T. Geach, *Mind,* vol. 59 [1950], pp. 461–462).

In order to apply this prescription to a particular instance, we have first to determine what a given assertion is "about." Should the assertion contain an expression standing for what the assertion is about, that expression will be the subject. According to the prescription, the remainder of the sentence will be the attached predicate.

This works well when applied to such a sentence as "Peter is happy," in which there is reference to a person. It is natural to say that a statement using that sentence is about Peter; hence the word "Peter" may be said to be a subject standing for Peter, and the remainder of the sentence, the expression "is happy," counts as the predicate.

But even in this paradigm case of the application of the distinction, an objection can be lodged. It may be plausibly argued that the statement in question is about happiness, no less than about Peter: the assertion, some would say, can be understood as a claim that happiness is instantiated in Peter. If it is permissible to say that the word "happy" stands for happiness, the rule we have adopted would lead us to say that "happy" is the subject and "Peter is" the predicate. The philosopher who formulated the rule I have cited would want to reject this inference.

Or, take the case of the statement "Happiness is desired by all men." Here, it is still more plausible to say that the statement is about happiness, referred to by the word "happiness." But the author of our rule refuses to recognize "happiness" as a subject, preferring to construe the sentence in question as being composed of two predicates.

I do not wish to suggest that a preference for this mode of analysis is willful or capricious; yet I believe there is no rational method for persuading somebody who rejects it. The dispute, like others already reported in this paper, can be resolved only by fiat. It is an error to suppose that we can determine what a statement is "about" by inspection of some extralinguistic realm. No amount of observation or reflection about nonverbal "things" will show whether a given statement is about a person or about a quality. The answer must be sought in language itself.

We know that the statement "Peter is happy" is about Peter, because we recognize "Peter" as a proper name, without knowing whether there is such a person as Peter. The starting point of the intended philosophical distinction between subject and predicate is conventional grammar, relying only upon formal criteria. But conventional grammar leaves us in the lurch as soon as we are asked to decide whether a statement using the word "happiness" is really about happiness.

5

I propose now to test the thesis of the universality of the subject-predicate form, by applying it to the report of a move in chess. The case may be thought to have special peculiarities, but will serve to reveal the chief points in dispute.

A full verbal report of a chess move, such as might be found in nineteenth-century manuals, has the form "The King's pawn moved to the King's fourth square." Here, there is no difficulty in identifying the grammatical subject, i.e., the expression "The King's pawn." Hence, the remainder of the formula, the expression "moved to the King's fourth square" must be the predicate, and the report can be certified as being of the subject-predicate form.

Nowadays, English-speaking chess players commonly use the concise notation, "P-K4." Reading this as a conventional abbreviation of the full English sentence previously cited, it is easy enough to discern a subject and a predicate in this fragment of symbolism: we might say that in "P-K4" the "P" is the subject, and the rest of the formula the predicate.

But other and equally adequate notations are in common use. In the so-called "Continental notation," a move is specified by giving only co-ordinates of the initial and terminal squares; thus the move already cited would be reported as "e2-e4." In this version, there is no component homologous with the subject recognized in the other form of report. A last-ditch defender of the omnipresence of the subject-predicate form might still argue that in the formula "e2-e4" the first complex symbol, "e2," indirectly specifies the chessman moved. However, it would be equally correct to treat the initial symbol, "P," of the English notation as being really an indirect specification of the square from which the move started. Somebody familiar only with the Continental notation can treat the English notations as having the square-to-square structure of his own paradigm; while a devotee of the English notation can treat the alternative symbolism as a disguised version of his own.

It becomes progressively harder to perceive the subject-predicate form in every conceivable chess notation as alternative notations are imagined. A given chess move might be represented by drawing a line on a square divided into 64 compartments, or by a set of two integers between 1 and 64, or by a single number less than 4096 ($= 64^2$), or by Morse code, or by suitably modulated electrical waves. Some of these possibilities might be handled by human beings, others might perhaps serve only to inform chess-playing computers; but all alike would have the requisite structure for representing

[11]

every possible move in a game of chess. All of them, to use Wittgenstein's word, would have the same "multiplicity" (*Tractatus*, 4.04). Now a determination to view all of these equivalent symbolic forms as having the subject-predicate structure would be quixotic in the extreme. Absurd loyalty to a preconception about logical form would be needed in order to view a line drawn on a chessboard as having a subject and a predicate. Long before this point was reached, most of us would prefer to abandon the dogma of the omnipresence of subject-predicate form.

The example may prepare us to expect similar conclusions about languages that are not restricted to the representation of an invented game. We are told, on good authority, that "Chinese, which is fully equipped for every sort of civilized communication, makes no use of the formal categories devised for the Indo-European languages" (W. J. Entwistle, *Aspects of Language*, London, 1953, p. 162). Another writer, after surveying the variety of grammars known to contemporary linguists, concludes that "no grammatical concept seems to be *per se* sacred or universal, far less indispensable" (Mario Pei, *The Story of Language*, New York, 1949, p. 129). In some languages, we are told, "An isolated word is a sentence; a sequence of such sentence words is like a compound sentence . . . [and] the terms verb and noun in such a language are meaningless" (B. L. Whorf, *Language, Thought and Reality*, Boston, 1956, pp. 98–99). If Whorf was right, the hope of finding the subject-predicate distinction exemplified in such "polysynthetic" languages is doomed to frustration. For that distinction presupposes a way of distinguishing between nouns and other parts of speech. Yet, "polysynthetic" languages may be just as rich in fact-stating resources as our own relatively analytical English. I conclude that the subject-predicate distinction, valuable as it may be for analyzing Indo-European languages, ought to find no place in a universal philosophical grammar.

[12]

6

The three examples I have discussed sufficiently illustrate the difficulties that beset any serious effort to construct a universal grammar. We are now in a position to diagnose the source of these difficulties. In each case, we were assuming that the logical structure of certain statements ("Stop," "Go," "Peter is happy") must be identical with the structure of the situations or states of affairs represented. The search for what is presumed to be invariant in all statements having the same meaning, that is to say, those representing the same state of affairs, is a search for some way of presenting the common logical structure. In order to do this, we must be able to do at least the following: decide which perceptible features of words or other signs can be treated as nonsignificant, recognize one and the same symbol behind its alternative manifiestations (that is to say, recognize when signs mean the same thing), and assign different symbols to the same logical category or type, on the basis of identity of function. In order for the procedure to provide any ground for ontological inference, such recognition, individuation, and classification of symbols must be performed without recourse to ontological premises, or to methods assuming the truth of such premises.

The chief difficulty arose from the need to count nonlinguistic contextual features of statements as significant. So long as we confine ourselves to analysis of conventional verbal statements, in isolation from their settings, traditional grammar provides us with means of segmentation and classification that can subsequently be elaborated and refined in the service of philosophical insight. There is no question but that "Stop" and "Go" are different words; "Peter" is clearly a noun and a grammatical subject in "Peter is happy." But immediately we recognize the nonverbal setting in which the words are pronounced as significant, we face formidable difficulties in identifying, distinguishing, counting and classifying the symbols that interest us. Are the situations in which a car is at rest

[13]

and in motion to count as the same or as different? Are the actions of stopping and starting a car the same or different? These are not questions to be answered by looking at cars or their drivers. They are questions of philosophical grammar for which there are no decision procedures. We have criteria for deciding whether words are to be treated as the same or different; for rules to this end (superficial rules of grammar) are part of the language we speak and understand. But there are no adequate criteria for deciding whether contextual situations are to be counted as the same or different, for the purpose of determining identities and differences of meaning. It might be thought that we ought to examine the semantical rules governing the sounds and written marks in question. But this maneuver achieves nothing. Were we assured that the rule governing "Stop" must count as different from the rule governing "Go," we would be entitled to conclude that there were indeed two symbols in question. But since the words "Stop" and "Go" or their synonyms will appear in expressions of those semantical rules, individuation of the rules will raise the same troublesome questions. Nor will the case be altered by speaking about "uses" instead of about "rules." For the purposes of philosophical grammar, descriptions in terms of "symbols," "rules," and "uses" are mutually equivalent and generate the same problems. We can choose as we please, and our decisions about the points of philosophical grammar at issue will be determined by the choices we have made, not by any imposed analysis of the statements inspected.

Similarly in our illustrations of the copula and the subject-predicate form. At the level of surface grammar, there are crude criteria for deciding whether an expression is expendable without loss of meaning. But when we try to push on to a would-be "deeper" level of analysis, we are embarrassed again by lack of criteria. Is the relation between "Peter" and "happy" really significant? Is there really a relationship there at all? It all depends upon how you choose to look at the statement. Nothing imposes an answer except the determination of the philosophical analyst to adhere to one mode of logical

[14]

parsing rather than another. Seen through one pair of grammatical spectacles, there plainly is a significant relation of juxtaposition between subject and predicate; but we can wear another pair of lenses and see nothing but subject and predicate, "hanging in one another like the links of a chain." When we recognize that the fact-stating functions of language can be adequately performed by nonverbal symbolisms, the problems of detecting invariant logical structure become insuperable. If we represent states of affairs by configurations of physical objects, the task of discerning logical structure demands a capacity to determine the logical structure of certain physical facts. But if we can ever do this, we don't need the detour via language. If we can analyze a fact, we can in principle discover the logical structure of reality without prior recourse to language. On the other hand, if we face some obstacle of principle in dissecting reality, we shall meet the very same difficulties in trying to dissect language. For language, though it represents reality, is also a part of reality.

7

In the light of the foregoing considerations, the prospects for a universal philosophical grammar seem most unpromising. I believe the hope of finding *the* essential grammar to be as illusory as that of finding the single true co-ordinate system for the representation of space. We can pass from one systematic mode of spatial representation to another by means of rules for transforming co-ordinates, and we can pass from one language to another having the same fact-stating resources by means of rules of translation. But rules for transformation of co-ordinates yield no information about space; and translation rules for sets of languages tell us nothing about the ultimate nature of reality.

It might perhaps be said that common logical structure is shown in an invariant web of entailment relations. It is certainly part of our concept of synonymity that statements of the same meaning shall have parallel consequences: if one statement has an entailment that is not synonymous with

[15]

some entailment of a second statement, that proves that the two original statements have different meanings. To put the matter differently, we shall not regard two languages as having the same fact-stating resources unless we can trace corresponding patterns of transformation rules in both. But we shall never arrive at a philosophical grammar by this road: correspondence of sets of entailments is compatible with the widest divergences of morphology and of syntax.

If we abandon the vain hope of finding the true philosophical grammar, we may still hope to use its by-products. Schoolroom grammar is coarse-grained for philosophical purposes, and the refinements of latter-day linguists are impressive without being philosophically useful. We shall do well to continue classifying words and expressions according to their uses and functions, inventing whatever labels will help us to remember our discoveries. It is not my intention to deprecate the received grammatical categories of "quality," "relation," "function," "class," and the rest, or the finer classifications invented by contemporaries. I would urge, however, that our atitude to such grammatical sieves should be pragmatic. If reality leaves us free to choose our grammar as convenience and utility dictate, we shall properly regard them as speculative instruments to be sharpened, improved, and, where necessary, discarded when they have served their turn.

To anybody who still feels that there must be an identity of logical form between language and reality, I can only plead that the conception of language as a mirror of reality is radically mistaken. We find out soon enough that the universe is not capricious: the child who learns that fire burns and knife-edges cut knows that there are inexorable limits set upon his desires. Language must conform to the discovered regularities and irregularities of experience. But in order to do so, it is enough that it should be apt for the expression of everything that is or might be the case. To be content with less would be to be satisfied to be inarticulate; to ask for more is to desire the impossible. No roads lead from grammar to metaphysics.

[16]

II

Explanations of Meaning

"WHEN Caesar said 'Veni, vidi, vici' he meant that he had won the battle." This is an example of what I propose to call a *meaning formula*. That is to say, I shall use "meaning formula" to stand for any statement of the form, "*S* meant *a* by *x*," in which "*S*" is replaced by a reference to some person, "*x*" by a specification of some gesture or utterance produced by him on a particular occasion, and "*a*" by any expression that makes the whole formula sensible. "Sensible" is here an antonym for "nonsensical." It will be convenient to call the expression that stands in the place of "*a*" the *accusative* of the meaning formula.

I shall also allow the shorter statement, "*S* meant *a*," to count as a meaning formula if the context identifies the intended gesture or utterance. On the other hand, a dictionary entry such as " 'Loch' means a narrow lake" will not be a meaning formula, since it does not refer to a particular speaker and a particular occasion.

Consider, first, a case in which the meaning of a gesture is explained by performing an action. Suppose that while I am waiting in my car a policeman regulating traffic gestures at me in a way that I do not understand. My friend in the car answers my question, "What did he mean by that?" by leaning forward and dimming the headlights. Meanwhile, he looks at me—"meaningfully," as we say—so that I understand what he is doing. He was not himself obeying the policeman's order to the driver but was *showing* what had to be done: he explained the gesture by *acting out* the correct response. The same can be done whenever an utterance calls for some overt response.

An imperative gesture is an instrument for producing a determinate response by a willing and competent receiver.

And the use of many an instrument can be explained by showing its intended effect. One way to explain the use of a potato slicer is to show the sliced potato it is intended to produce. Then I may know what the kitchen tool is used *for*, though perhaps not how to use it.

The passenger's demonstration was an *instance* of the standard response to the gesture, and was not connected with that response by an arbitrary convention. The case is similar when the meaning of a color word is explained by showing a color patch having the color in question. Just as the color sample is an "icon" of the color demonstrated, so the passenger's acted performance is an "icon" of the intended response. Here, we might speak of an *ostensive explanation* of meaning.

Consider, next, an explanation in words. This time, the driver's question evokes the reply "He meant 'Dim the lights.' " If the passenger had merely said "Dim the lights" in an imperative tone of voice, he himself would have been giving an order. Instead, he used the same expression to show what the order was: he might be said to be acting it out or miming it.

It is as if he had said: " 'Dim the lights!'—you recognize that order, don't you? Well, *that* is what the policeman wanted." The explanation given was able to be less explicit than this, since the hearer was already familiar with the linguistic practice of giving-and-receiving orders. The speaker was understood to be engaged in the *secondary* linguistic practice of explaining an order: all he needed to do was to supply the missing item of information by means of the accusative.

The explainer's action in saying "Dim the lights" is an icon of the action of uttering the same words to give an order: he shows the use of the gesture by imitating the giving of an equivalent verbal order. Of course, the explainer's action is not iconic of the policeman's action. For to imitate what the latter did, he would have had to produce the same or a similar gesture, and would then have explained nothing. But the use of the English imperative sentence is the same as that of the

[18]

gesture, since gesture and sentence express parallel intentions, demand parallel responses, and, more generally, play corresponding parts in the linguistic practice to which they belong. The explainer draws attention to the very same use, though he replaces a gesture by words. Similarly, the use of a nonverbal instrument might be shown by using another instrument having a similar use. I might explain to a child the use of a mechanical pencil sharpener by using a knife to sharpen a pencil.

When a meaning formula is printed, it is customary to use quotation marks at each end of the accusative, so that we have "He meant 'Dim the lights' " rather than "He meant Dim the lights." Now since a common use of quotation marks is for mentioning the word or expression that appears between the marks, we might suppose that the accusative of a meaning formula mentions a verbal expression. But this is easily shown to be wrong.

Mention of an expression can be made explicit by inserting the words "the expression" at the appropriate place in the sentence. Thus the mention of an expression in the statement, " 'Dim the lights' consists of three words," is made explicit by transforming the statement into "The expression, 'Dim the lights,' consists of three words." But the corresponding operation upon a meaning formula results in nonsense. In the situation imagined, the statement, "He meant the expression 'Dim the lights,' " would be unintelligible.

I conclude that the accusative is not a device for mentioning an expression. Since "mention" is opposed to "use," we must say that the accusative is used in a meaning formula, though in a peculiar way to which the quotation marks draw attention. For the hearer is required to pay attention to the physical character of the spoken accusative in order to determine which command is in question—just as it is necessary to examine the color of a color sample in order to determine which color is in question.

The original meaning formula might be replaced by the longer formula, "He meant what would be meant by saying

'Dim the lights.' " Since the longer formula clearly is a statement about an expression and could serve the same purpose as the original explanation, there might be some inclination to say that the latter was after all "really" about words.

But this would be a mistake. The statement "This is red" is also replaceable by, and in some way equivalent to, the longer statement "This has the color usually called 'red.' " But while the latter statement clearly mentions the word "red," it by no means follows that the original statement does. And the same can be said of our original example. We are therefore entitled to repeat that the meaning formula does not mention, but rather uses, the words of which its accusative is composed.

Although I have been using examples of explanations of imperatives, there is no difficulty in conceiving the use of meaning formulas for declarative utterances along the same lines. For the contention that the meaning formula *shows* a use, in the sense explained, does not depend upon any specification of the kind of use in question.

There remains the question whether the accusative may not designate something other than a verbal expression. To settle this, we can appeal to a general criterion, composed of two parts: Whenever *"E"* designates a *K*, it must be permissible to assert that *E* is a *K*, and also to replace *"E"* by " a *K*" in its original occurrence. Thus we can pass from "He pointed to Smith" to the two true statements, "Smith is a man" and "He pointed to a man," thereby confirming that "Smith" as so used does indeed designate a man.

Let us apply these tests to the meaning formula. The only simple predicate that can plausibly be attached to the expression "Dim the lights" is the predicate "is an order." Hence, the accusative might be expected to designate an order, if it is to designate anything at all. But the second part of the general criterion for designation leads to the statement, "He meant an order," which must be rejected. The correct version of what might be intended by these words is "He *gave* an order," and "gave" is not a synonym for "meant": we cannot

[20]

sensibly say "He gave 'Dim the lights.' " And so we must reject
the view that the accusative of a meaning formula designates
an order.

But could we not say that the accusative designates the
"use ' of the imperative expression? (For "use" is close to what
others have in mind when they speak of the "meaning" of the
imperative expression; and it is quite natural to want to say
that an expression stands for its meaning.) Well, what is the
"use" of the expression in question? The answer would have
to run somewhat as follows: "The expression 'Dim the lights'
is primarily used by a suitably trained speaker to order a suitably trained hearer to dim the lights." It is necessary to include the word "primarily," since the same expression is used
in other ways—e.g., to explain its own meaning. A shorter
but sufficiently adequate version of the statement of use is:
"The expression 'Dim the lights' is used to order somebody
to dim the lights."

It will be noticed that in both the longer and the shorter
versions the use is identified by means of an infinitive phrase
of the form "to so-and-so." And in general, a standard way of
specifying the use of anything is by means of such an infinitive
phrase, as when we say "The use of a hammer is *to* drive home
nails." Hence, if the accusative of a meaning formula designated the use of an imperative we would have to be able to
say "He meant to order somebody to dim the lights." To be
even plausible, this has to be amended by a reference to the
particular use made on the particular occasion, so that we
obtain "He meant *you* to dim the lights." This makes sense,
to be sure, but only because "meant" has now become a
synonym for "intended" and no longer means what it did in
the original meaning formula. For in the situation described
we cannot say "He intended 'dim the lights' " without being
unintelligible. So the attempt fails, and we must reject the
hypothesis that the accusative designates a use, or the particular use, of the gesture being explained.

We can choose to say, if we like, that the meaning formula
does indicate or identify the use of the order in question. For

one way of explaining the gesture would have been to say "He wanted you to dim the lights," and this might be taken to indicate the use that was made of the gesture. But to indicate in this loose sense is different from having the accusative designate a use, in the strict sense of "designate" to which I am adhering.

It will have been noticed that the two statements of the use of the expression "Dim the lights" cited above had the interesting peculiarity that the expression itself was used in the statement of its own use. We had to say " 'Dim the lights' is used to order somebody to *dim the lights"*—as if we had to use a hammer in stating the use of the hammer. This unavoidably reflexive use of the order-expression in specifying its own use agrees with the view here being defended of the "mimetic" use of accusatives. Even in a statement of use the order-expression seems to occur in the peculiar way already discussed.

I believe it will be found that the foregoing considerations can be generalized, so that the correct conclusion is that the accusative of a meaning formula designates nothing—or, rather, does not designate at all. Against this, a counterexample might sometimes be produced. In the meaning formula, "He meant 'Men are mammals,' " the accusative can be replaced by the expression "a proposition"; and it is certainly correct to say, " 'Men are mammals' is a proposition." So it seems that we sometimes ought to say that the accusative does designate something—that is to say, a proposition.

My answer is that "proposition," as so used, is a philosopher's word, invented to stand for the supposed designation of declarative sentences. Since the word was invented to permit reference to a supposed common objective counterpart of mutually synonymous sentences, it is not surprising to find it used in this way. It would be easy enough to provide a designation for imperatives by the same trick, since all that would be needed would be a technical term, say "imperation," to stand for the supposed entity designated by mutually synonymous imperatives. But such a use of the invented word would be pointless and unilluminating: its introduction

[22]

would serve merely to express a determination to construe meaning formulas on the inapplicable model of genuinely relational statements. I therefore reject the idea that declarative accusatives designate propositions, not on the ground that it is wrong to say so (for it must be right by the definition of "proposition") but because it is pointless and unilluminating to talk in this way.

It follows from what has been said that it would be misleading to treat the word "meant" as standing in the meaning formula for a relation. For it is part of our conception of a relation that it should relate two *things,* i.e., that the word for the relation should be accompanied in the relational statement by two designations. Now in "He meant 'Dim the lights,'" the subject undoubtedly designates a person, but we have seen that the object, the "accusative," does not designate at all. To think of meaning as a relation is just as misleading as to think of *the* meaning as an object.

When we want to state the meaning of an utterance we can do no better than use a meaning formula. An expansion of the formula, supplied to anybody who might find it cryptic, would eventually lead to a detailed account of the uses of such formulas in the secondary linguistic practices of explaining. We could provide as detailed an account as desired of the situations in which such formulas are used, the proper responses to them, their certifying conditions, the logical transformations appropriate, and so on. But nowhere in such a detailed elaboration would we find it necessary to try to designate something identifiable as *the* meaning of the explicandum.

When a philosopher asks, "Are linguistic meanings different from words? If different, are they ideas in Plato's sense or are they in the mind? And if in the mind, are they images or imageless concepts?" [1] he commits an initial mistake that probably dooms his inquiry to futility. For behind the question "What are meanings?" is the supposition that there are such things as meanings to be categorized. It is supposed that

[1] A. P. Ushenko, *The Field Theory of Meaning* (Ann Arbor, 1958), p. 1.

[23]

the accusatives of meaning formulas designate (refer to, stand for) entities: we are then invited to decide whether the entities in question are linguistic expressions, Platonic ideas, or perhaps something else again. But if the arguments I have outlined are sound, the initial supposition is mistaken. Although words and gestures *have* meanings, there are no meanings that can be designated, and hence no philosophical problems of assigning such supposedly designated entities to the appropriate categories. But of course, this does not exempt us from the task of trying to clarify how the word "meaning" and its cognates are used. My remarks about meaning formulas have been intended as a contribution to this task.

III

Metaphor

Metaphors are no arguments, my pretty maiden.
—*The Fortunes of Nigel*, Book 2, Chapter 2

TO DRAW attention to a philosopher's metaphors is to belittle him—like praising a logician for his beautiful handwriting. Addiction to metaphor is held to be illicit, on the principle that whereof one can speak only metaphorically, thereof one ought not to speak at all. Yet the nature of the offence is unclear. I should like to do something to dispel the mystery that invests the topic; but since philosophers (for all their notorious interest in language) have so neglected the subject, I must get what help I can from the literary critics. They, at least, do not accept the commandment, "Thou shalt not commit metaphor," or assume that metaphor is incompatible with serious thought.

1

The questions I should like to see answered concern the "logical grammar" of "metaphor" and words having related meanings. It would be satisfactory to have convincing answers to the questions: "How do we recognize a case of metaphor?" "Are there any criteria for the detection of metaphors?" "Can metaphors be translated into literal expressions?" "Is metaphor properly regarded as a decoration upon 'plain sense'?" "What are the relations between metaphor and simile?" "In what sense, if any, is a metaphor 'creative'?" "What is the point of using a metaphor?" (Or, more briefly, "What do we *mean* by 'metaphor'?" The questions express attempts to become clearer about some uses of the word "metaphor"—

[25]

or, if one prefers the material mode, to analyze the notion of metaphor.)

The list is not a tidy one, and several of the questions overlap in fairly obvious ways. But I hope they will sufficiently illustrate the type of inquiry that is intended.

It would be helpful to be able to start from some agreed list of "clear cases" of metaphor. Since the word "metaphor" has some intelligible uses, however vague or vacillating, it must be possible to construct such a list. Presumably, it should be easier to agree whether any given item should be included than to agree about any proposed analysis of the notion of metaphor.

Perhaps the following list of examples, chosen not altogether at random, might serve:

(i) "The chairman plowed through the discussion."
(ii) "A smoke screen of witnesses."
(iii) "An argumentative melody."
(iv) "Blotting-paper voices" (Henry James).
(v) "The poor are the negroes of Europe" (Chamfort).
(vi) "Light is but the shadow of God" (Sir Thomas Browne).
(vii) "Oh dear white children, casual as birds,
    Playing amid the ruined languages" (Auden).

I hope all these will be accepted as unmistakeable *instances* of metaphor, whatever judgments may ultimately be made about the meaning of "metaphor." The examples are offered as clear cases of metaphor, but, with the possible exception of the first, they would be unsuitable as "paradigms." If we wanted to teach the meaning of "metaphor" to a child, we should need simpler examples, like "The clouds are crying" or "The branches are fighting with one another." (Is it significant that one hits upon examples of personification?) But I have tried to include some reminders of the possible complexities that even relatively straight-forward metaphors may generate.

Consider the first example—"The chairman plowed through the discussion." An obvious point to begin with is

[26]

the contrast between the word "plowed" and the remaining words by which it is accompanied. This would be commonly expressed by saying that "plowed" has here a metaphorical sense, while the other words have literal senses. Although we point to the whole sentence as an instance (a "clear case") of metaphor, our attention quickly narrows to a single word, whose presence is the proximate reason for the attribution. And similar remarks can be made about the next four examples in the list, the crucial words being, respectively, "smoke screen," "argumentative," "blotting-paper," and "negroes."

(But the situation is more complicated in the last two examples of the list. In the quotation from Sir Thomas Browne, "Light" must be supposed to have a symbolic sense, and certainly to mean far more than it would in the context of a textbook on optics. Here, the metaphorical sense of the expression "the shadow of God" imposes a meaning richer than usual upon the subject of the sentence. Similar effects can be noticed in the passage from Auden—consider for instance the meaning of "white" in the first line. I shall have to neglect such complexities in this paper.)

In general, when we speak of a relatively simple metaphor, we are referring to a sentence or another expression in which *some* words are used metaphorically while the remainder are used nonmetaphorically. An attempt to construct an entire sentence of words that are used metaphorically results in a proverb, an allegory, or a riddle. No preliminary analysis of metaphor will satisfactorily cover even so trite an example as "In the night all cows are black." And cases of symbolism (in the sense in which Kafka's castle is a "symbol") also need separate treatment.

2

"The chairman plowed through the discussion." In calling this sentence a case of metaphor, we are implying that at least one word (here, the word "plowed") is being used metaphorically in the sentence, and that at least one of the remaining words is being used literally. Let us call the word "plowed" the *focus* of the metaphor, and the remainder of the sentence in which that word occurs the *frame*. (Are *we* now using metaphors—and mixed ones at that? Does it matter?) One notion that needs to be clarified is that of the "metaphorical use" of the focus of a metaphor. Among other things, it would be good to understand how the presence of one frame can result in metaphorical use of the complementary word, while the presence of a different frame for the same word fails to result in metaphor.

If the sentence about the chairman's behavior is translated word for word into any foreign language for which this is possible, we shall of course want to say that the translated sentence is a case of the *very same* metaphor. So, to call a sentence an instance of metaphor is to say something about its *meaning*, not about its orthography, its phonetic pattern, or its grammatical form.[1] (To use a well-known distinction, "metaphor" must be classified as a term belonging to "semantics" and not to "syntax"—or to any *physical* inquiry about language.)

Suppose somebody says, "I like to plow my memories regularly." Shall we say he is using the same metaphor as in the case already discussed, or not? Our answer will depend upon the degree of similarity we are prepared to affirm on comparing the two "frames" (for we have the same "focus" each time). Differences in the two frames will produce *some* differences in the interplay [2] between focus and frame in the two cases. Whether we regard the differences as sufficiently striking to warrant calling the sentences *two* metaphors is a matter for arbitrary decision. "Metaphor" is a loose word, at

[1] Any part of speech can be used metaphorically (though the results are meagre and uninteresting in the case of conjunctions); any form of verbal expression may contain a metaphorical focus.

[2] Here I am using language appropriate to the "interaction view" of metaphor that is discussed later in this paper.

best, and we must beware of attributing to it stricter rules of usage than are actually found in practice.

So far, I have been treating "metaphor" as a predicate properly applicable to certain expressions, without attention to any occasions on which the expressions are used, or to the thoughts, acts, feelings, and intentions of speakers upon such occasions. And this is surely correct for *some* expressions. We recognize that to call a man a "cesspool" is to use a metaphor, without needing to know who uses the expression, or on what occasions, or with what intention. The rules of our language determine that some expressions must count as metaphors; and a speaker can no more change this than he can legislate that "cow" shall mean the same as "sheep." But we must also recognize that the established rules of language leave wide latitude for individual variation, initiative, and creation. There are indefinitely many contexts (including nearly all the interesting ones) where the meaning of a metaphorical expression has to be reconstructed from the speaker s intentions (and other clues) because the broad rules of standard usage are too general to supply the information needed. When Churchill, in a famous phrase, called Mussolini "that *utensil*," the tone of voice, the verbal setting, the historical background, helped to make clear *what* metaphor was being used. (Yet, even here, it is hard to see how the phrase "that utensil" could ever be applied to a man except as an insult. Here, as elsewhere, the general rules of usage function as limitations upon the speaker's freedom to mean whatever he pleases.) This is an example, though still a simple one, of how recognition and interpretation of a metaphor may require attention to the *particular circumstances* of its utterance.

It is especially noteworthy that there are, in general, no standard rules for the degree of *weight* or *emphasis* to be attached to a particular use of an expression. To know what the user of a metaphor means, we need to know how "seriously" he treats the metaphorical focus. (Would he be just as content to have some rough synonym, or would only *that*

[29]

word serve? Are we to take the word lightly, attending only to its most obvious implications—or should we dwell upon its less immediate associations?) In speech we can use emphasis and phrasing as clues. But in written or printed discourse, even these rudimentary aids are absent. Yet this somewhat elusive "weight" of a (suspected or detected [3]) metaphor is of great practical importance in exegesis.

To take a philosophical example: Whether the expression "logical form" should be treated in a particular frame as having a metaphorical sense will depend upon the extent to which its user is taken to be conscious of some supposed analogy between arguments and other things (vases, clouds, battles, jokes) that are also said to have "form." Still more will it depend upon whether the writer wishes the analogy to be active in the minds of his readers; and how much his own thought depends upon and is nourished by the supposed analogy. We must not expect the "rules of language" to be of much help in such inquiries. (There is accordingly a sense of "metaphor" that belongs to "pragmatics" rather than to "semantics"—and this sense may be the one most deserving of attention.)

3

Let us try the simplest possible account that can be given of the meaning of "The chairman plowed through the discussion," to see how far it will take us. A plausible commentary (for those presumably too literal-minded to understand the original) might run somewhat as follows: "A speaker who uses the sentence in question is taken to want to say *something* about a chairman and his behavior in some meeting. Instead of saying, plainly or *directly*, that the chairman dealt summarily with objections, or ruthlessly suppressed irrelevance, or something of the sort, the speaker chose to use a word ('plowed') which, strictly speaking, means something

---

[3] Here, I wish these words to be read with as little "weight" as possible!

[30]

else. But an intelligent hearer can easily guess what the speaker had in mind." [4] This account treats the metaphorical expression (let us call it "*M*") as a substitute for some other literal expression ("*L*," say) which would have expressed the same meaning, had it been used instead. On this view, the meaning of *M*, in its metaphorical occurrence, is just the *literal* meaning of *L*. The metaphorical use of an expression consists, on this view, of the use of that expression in other than its proper or normal sense, in some context that allows the improper or abnormal sense to be detected and appropriately transformed. (The reasons adduced for so remarkable a performance will be discussed later.)

Any view which holds that a metaphorical expression is used in place of some equivalent *literal* expression, I shall call a *substitution view of metaphor*. (I should like this label to cover also any analysis which views the entire sentence that is the locus of the metaphor as replacing some set of literal sentences.) Until recently, one or another form of a substitution view has been accepted by most writers (usually literary critics or writers of books on rhetoric) who have had anything to say about metaphor. To take a few examples: Whately defines a metaphor as "a word substituted for another on account of the Resemblance or Analogy between their significations." [5] Nor is the entry in the Oxford Dictionary (to jump to modern times) much different from this: "Metaphor: The figure of speech in which a name or descriptive term is transferred to some object different from, but analogous to, that to which it is properly applicable; an instance of this, a metaphorical expression." [6] So strongly entrenched is the view

---

[4] Notice how this type of paraphrase naturally conveys some implication of *fault* on the part of the metaphor's author. There is a strong suggestion that he ought to have made up his mind as to what he really wanted to say—the metaphor is depicted as a way of glossing over unclarity and vagueness.

[5] Richard Whately, *Elements of Rhetoric* (7th rev. ed., London, 1846), p. 280.

[6] Under "Figure" we find: "Any of the various 'forms' of expression, deviating from the normal arrangement or use of words, which are

expressed by these definitions that a recent writer who is explicitly arguing for a different and more sophisticated view of metaphor, nevertheless slips into the old fashion by defining metaphor as "saying one thing and meaning another." [7]

According to a substitution view, the focus of a metaphor, the word or expression having a distinctively metaphorical use within a literal frame, is used to communicate a meaning that might have been expressed literally. The author substitutes M for L; it is the reader's task to invert the substitution, by using the literal meaning of M as a clue to the intended literal meaning of L. Understanding a metaphor is like deciphering a code or unraveling a riddle.

If we now ask why, on this view, the writer should set his reader the task of solving a puzzle, we shall be offered two types of answer. The first is that there may, in fact, be no literal equivalent, L, available in the language in question. Mathematicians spoke of the "leg" of an angle because there was no brief literal expression for a bounding line; we say "cherry lips," because there is no form of words half as convenient for saying quickly what the lips are like. Metaphor plugs the gaps in the literal vocabulary (or, at least, supplies

---

adopted in order to give beauty, variety, or force to a composition; e.g., Aposiopesis, Hyperbole, Metaphor, etc." If we took this strictly we might be led to say that a transfer of a word not adopted for the sake of introducing "beauty, variety, or force" must necessarily fail to be a case of metaphor. Or will "variety" automatically cover every transfer? It will be noticed that the O.E.D.'s definition is no improvement upon Whately's. Where he speaks of a "word" being substituted, the O.E.D. prefers "name or descriptive term." If this is meant to restrict metaphors to nouns (and adjectives?) it is demonstrably mistaken. But, if not, what is "descriptive term" supposed to mean? And why has Whately's reference to "Resemblance or Analogy" been trimmed into a reference to analogy alone?

[7] Owen Barfield, "Poetic Diction and Legal Fiction," in *Essays Presented to Charles Williams* (Oxford, 1947), pp. 106–127. The definition of metaphor occurs on p. 111, where metaphor is treated as a special case of what Barfield calls "tarning." The whole essay deserves to be read.

the want of convenient abbreviations). So viewed, metaphor is a species of *catachresis*, which I shall define as the use of a word in some new sense in order to remedy a gap in the vocabulary; catachresis is the putting of new senses into old words.[8] But if a catachresis serves a genuine need, the new sense introduced will quickly become part of the *literal* sense. "Orange" may originally have been applied to the color by catachresis; but the word is now applied to the color just as "properly" (and unmetaphorically) as to the fruit. "Osculating" curves do not kiss for long, and quickly revert to a more prosaic mathematical contact. And similarly for other cases. It is the fate of catachresis to disappear when it is successful.

There are, however, many metaphors where the virtues ascribed to catachresis cannot apply, because there is, or there is supposed to be, some readily available and equally compendious literal equivalent. Thus in the somewhat unfortunate example,[9] "Richard is a lion," which modern writers have discussed with boring insistence, the literal meaning is taken to be the same as that of the sentence, "Richard is brave." [10] Here, the metaphor is not supposed to enrich the vocabulary.

When catachresis cannot be invoked, the reasons for sub-

[8] The O.E.D. defines catachresis as: "Improper use of words; application of a term to a thing which it does not properly denote; abuse or perversion of a trope or metaphor." I wish to exclude the pejorative suggestions. There is nothing perverse or abusive in stretching old words to fit new situations. Catachresis is merely a striking case of the transformation of meaning that is constantly occurring in any living language.

[9] Can we imagine anybody saying this nowadays and seriously meaning anything? I find it hard to do so. But in default of an authentic context of use, any analysis is liable to be thin, obvious, and unprofitable.

[10] A full discussion of this example, complete with diagrams, will be found in Gustaf Stern's *Meaning and Change of Meaning* (Göteborgs Högskolas Arsskrift, vol. 38, 1932, part 1), pp. 300 ff. Stern's account tries to show how the reader is led by the context to *select* from the connotation of "lion" the attribute (bravery) that will fit Richard the man. I take him to be defending a form of the substitution view.

[33]

stituting an indirect, metaphorical, expression are taken to be stylistic. We are told that the metaphorical expression may (in its literal use) refer to a more concrete object than would its literal equivalent; and this is supposed to give pleasure to the reader (the pleasure of having one's thoughts diverted from Richard to the irrelevant lion). Again, the reader is taken to enjoy problem-solving—or to delight in the author's skill at half-concealing, half-revealing his meaning. Or metaphors provide a shock of "agreeable surprise" and so on. The principle behind these "explanations" seems to be: When in doubt about some peculiarity of language, attribute its existence to the pleasure it gives a reader. A principle that has the merit of working well in default of any evidence.[11]

Whatever the merits of such speculations about the reader's response, they agree in making metaphor a *decoration*. Except in cases where a metaphor is a catachresis that remedies some temporary imperfection of literal language, the purpose of metaphor is to entertain and divert. Its use, on this view, always constitutes a deviation from the "plain and strictly appropriate style" (Whately).[12] So, if philosophers have something more important to do than give pleasure to their readers, metaphor can have no serious place in philosophical discussion.

[11] Aristotle ascribes the use of metaphor to delight in learning; Cicero traces delight in metaphor to the enjoyment of the author's ingenuity in overpassing the immediate, or in the vivid presentation of the principal subject. For references to these and other traditional views, see E. M. Cope, *An Introduction to Aristotle's Rhetoric* (London, 1867), Book III, Appendix B, Ch. 2, "On Metaphor."

[12] Thus Stern (*op. cit.*) says of all figures of speech that "they are intended to serve the expressive and purposive functions of speech better than the 'plain statement'" (p. 296). A metaphor produces an "enhancement" (*Steigerung*) of the subject, but the factors leading to its use "involve the expressive and effective (purposive) functions of speech, not the symbolic and communicative functions" (p. 290). That is to say, metaphors may evince feelings or predispose others to act and feel in various ways—but they do not typically *say* anything.

[34]

4

The view that a metaphorical expression has a meaning that is some transform of its normal literal meaning is a special case of a more general view about "figurative" language. This holds that any figure of speech involving semantic change (and not merely syntactic change, like inversion of normal word order) consists in some transformation of a *literal* meaning. The author provides, not his intended meaning, m, but some function thereof, $f(m)$; the reader's task is to apply the inverse function, f^{-1}, and so to obtain $f^{-1}(f(m))$, i.e., m, the original meaning. When different functions are used, different tropes result. Thus, in irony, the author says the *opposite* of what he means; in hyperbole, he *exaggerates* his meaning; and so on.

What, then, is the characteristic transforming function involved in metaphor? To this the answer has been made: either *analogy* or *similarity*. M is either similar or analogous in meaning to its literal equivalent L. Once the reader has detected the ground of the intended analogy or simile (with the help of the frame, or clues drawn from the wider context) he can retrace the author's path and so reach the original literal meaning (the meaning of L).

If a writer holds that a metaphor consists in the *presentation* of the underlying analogy or similarity, he will be taking what I shall call a *comparison view* of metaphor. When Schopenhauer called a geometrical proof a mousetrap, he was, according to such a view, *saying* (though not explicitly): "A geometrical proof is *like* a mousetrap, since both offer a delusive reward, entice their victims by degrees, lead to disagreeable surprise, etc." This is a view of metaphor as a condensed or elliptical *simile*. It will be noticed that a "comparison view" is a special case of a "substitution view." For it holds that the metaphorical statement might be replaced by an equivalent literal *comparison*.

Whately says: "The Simile or Comparison may be con-

[35]

sidered as differing in form only from a Metaphor; the resemblance being in that case *stated,* which in the Metaphor is
implied." [13] Bain says that "the metaphor is a comparison
implied in the mere use of a term" and adds, "It is in the
circumstance of being confined to a word, or at most to a
phrase, that we are to look for the peculiarities of the metaphor—its advantages on the one hand, and its dangers and
abuses on the other." [14] This view of the metaphor, as condensed simile or comparison, has been very popular.

The chief difference between a substitution view (of the
sort previously considered) and the special form of it that I
have called a comparison view may be illustrated by the stock
example of "Richard is a lion." On the first view, the sentence
means approximately the same as "Richard is brave"; on the
second, approximately the same as "Richard is *like* a lion
(in being brave)," the added words in brackets being understood but not explicitly stated. In the second translation, as
in the first, the metaphorical statement is taken to be standing
in place of some literal equivalent. But the comparison view
provides a more elaborate paraphrase, inasmuch as the original statement is interpreted as being about lions as well as
about Richard.[15]

[13] Whately, *loc. cit.* He proceeds to draw a distinction between "Resemblance, strictly so called, i.e., *direct* resemblance between the objects themselves in question, (as when we speak of '*table*-land', or
compare great waves to *mountains*)" and "Analogy, which is the resemblance of Ratios—a similarity of the relations they bear to certain
other objects; as when we speak of the '*light* of reason', or of 'revela-
tion'; or compare a wounded and captive warrior to a stranded ship."

[14] Alexander Bain, *English Composition and Rhetoric* (enl. ed., London, 1887), p. 159.

[15] Comparison views probably derive from Aristotle's brief statement
in the *Poetics:* "Metaphor consists in giving the thing a name that belongs to something else; the transference being either from genus to
species, or from species to genus, or from species to species, or on
grounds of analogy" (1457b). I have no space to give Aristotle's discussion the detailed examination it deserves. An able defence of a view
based on Aristotle will be found in S. J. Brown's *The World of Imagery*
(London, 1927, esp. pp. 67 ff.).

[36]

The main objection against a comparison view is that it suffers from a vagueness that borders upon vacuity. We are supposed to be puzzled as to how some expression (*M*), used metaphorically, can function in place of some literal expression (*L*) that is held to be an approximate synonym; and the answer offered is that what *M* stands for (in its literal use) is *similar* to what *L* stands for. But how informative is this? There is some temptation to think of similarities as "objectively given," so that a question of the form, "Is *A* like *B* in respect of *P*?" has a definite and predetermined answer. If this were so, similes might be governed by rules as strict as those controlling the statements of physics. But likeness always admits of degrees, so that a truly "objective" question would need to take some such form as "Is *A* more like *B* than *C* on such and such a scale of degrees of *P*?" Yet, in proportion as we approach such forms, metaphorical statements lose their effectiveness and their point. We need the metaphors in just the cases when there can be no question as yet of the precision of scientific statement. Metaphorical statement is not a substitute for a formal comparison or any other kind of literal statement, but has its own distinctive capacities and achievements. Often we say, "*X* is *M*," evoking some imputed connection between *M* and an imputed *L* (or, rather, to an indefinite system, $L_1, L_2, L_3, \ldots$) in cases where, prior to the construction of the metaphor, we would have been hard put to it to find any literal resemblance between *M* and *L*. It would be more illuminating in some of these cases to say that the metaphor creates the similarity than to say that it formulates some similarity antecedently existing.[16]

[16] Much more would need to be said in a thorough examination of the comparison view. It would be revealing, for instance, to consider the contrasting types of case in which a formal comparison is preferred to a metaphor. A comparison is often a prelude to an explicit statement of the grounds of resemblance whereas we do not expect a metaphor to explain itself. (Cf. the difference between *comparing* a man's face with a wolf mask by looking for points of resemblance—and seeing the human face *as* vulpine.) But no doubt the line between *some* metaphors and *some* similes is not a sharp one.

5

I turn now to consider a type of analysis which I shall call an *interaction view* of metaphor. This seems to me to be free from the main defects of substitution and comparison views and to offer some important insight into the uses and limitations of metaphor.[17]

Let us begin with the following statement: "In the simplest formulation, when we use a metaphor we have two thoughts of different things active together and supported by a single word, or phrase, whose meaning is a resultant of their interaction." [18] We may discover what is here intended by applying Richard's remark to our earlier example, "The poor are the negroes of Europe." The substitution view, at its crudest, tells us that something is being indirectly said about the poor of Europe. (But what? That they are an oppressed class, a standing reproach to the community's official ideals, that poverty is inherited and indelible?) The comparison view claims that the epigram presents some comparison between the poor and the negroes. In opposition to both, Richards says that our "thoughts" about European poor and American negroes are "active together" and "interact" to produce a meaning that is a resultant of that interaction.

I think this must mean that in the given context the focal

17 The best sources are the writings of I. A. Richards, especially Chapter 5 ("Metaphor") and Chapter 6 ("Command of Metaphor") of his *The Philosophy of Rhetoric* (Oxford, 1936). Chapters 7 and 8 of his *Interpretation in Teaching* (London, 1938) cover much the same ground. W. Bedell Stanford's *Greek Metaphor* (Oxford, 1936) defends what he calls an "integration theory" (see esp. pp. 101 ff.) with much learning and skill. Unfortunately, both writers have great trouble in making clear the nature of the positions they are defending. Chapter 18 of W. Empson's *The Structure of Complex Words* (London, 1951) is a useful discussion of Richards' views on metaphor.

18 *The Philosophy of Rhetoric*, p. 93. Richards also says that metaphor is "fundamentally a borrowing between and intercourse of *thoughts*, a transaction between contexts" (p. 94). Metaphor, he says, requires two ideas "which co-operate in an inclusive meaning" (p. 119).

[38]

word "negroes" obtains a new meaning, which is not quite its meaning in literal uses, nor quite the meaning which any literal substitute would have. The new context (the "frame" of the metaphor, in my terminology) imposes extension of meaning upon the focal word. And I take Richards to be saying that for the metaphor to work the reader must remain aware of the extension of meaning—must attend to both the old and the new meanings together.[19]

But how is this extension or change of meaning brought about? At one point, Richards speaks of the "common characteristics" of the two terms (the poor and negroes) as "the ground of the metaphor" (*The Philosophy of Rhetoric*, p. 117), so that in its metaphorical use a word or expression must connote only a *selection* from the characteristics connoted in its literal uses. This, however, seems a rare lapse into the older and less sophisticated analyses he is trying to supersede.[20] He is on firmer ground when he says that the reader is forced to "connect" the two ideas (p. 125). In this "connection" resides the secret and the mystery of metaphor. To speak of the "interaction" of two thoughts "active together" (or, again, of their "interillumination" or "co-operation") is to *use* a metaphor emphasizing the dynamic aspects of a good reader's response to a nontrivial metaphor. I have no quarrel with the use of metaphors (if they are good ones) in talking about metaphor. But it may be as well to use several, lest we are misled by the adventitious charms of our favorites.

Let us try, for instance, to think of a metaphor as a filter. Consider the statement, "Man is a wolf." Here, we may say, are *two* subjects—the principal subject, Man (or: men) and the subsidiary subject, Wolf (or: wolves). Now the metaphorical sentence in question will not convey its intended mean-

[19] It is this, perhaps, that leads Richards to say that "talk about the identification or fusion that a metaphor effects is nearly always misleading and pernicious" (*ibid.,* p. 127).

[20] Usually, Richards tries to show that similarity between the two terms is at best *part* of the basis for the interaction of meanings in a metaphor.

[39]

ing to a reader sufficiently ignorant about wolves. What is needed is not so much that the reader shall know the standard dictionary meaning of "wolf"—or be able to use that word in literal senses—as that he shall know what I will call the *system of associated commonplaces*. Imagine some layman required to say, without taking special thought, those things he held to be true about wolves; the set of statements resulting would approximate to what I am here calling the system of commonplaces associated with the word "wolf." I am assuming that in any given culture the responses made by different persons to the test suggested would agree rather closely and that even the occasional expert, who might have unusual knowledge of the subject, would still know "what the man in the street thinks about the matter." From the expert's standpoint, the system of commonplaces may include half-truths or downright mistakes (as when a whale is classified as a fish); but the important thing for the metaphor's effectiveness is not that the commonplaces shall be true, but that they should be readily and freely evoked. (Because this is so, a metaphor that works in one society may seem preposterous in another. Men who take wolves to be reincarnations of dead humans will give the statement "Man is a wolf" an interpretation different from the one I have been assuming.)

To put the matter in another way: Literal uses of the word "wolf" are governed by syntactical and semantical rules, violation of which produces nonsense or self-contradiction. In addition, I am suggesting, literal uses of the word normally commit the speaker to acceptance of a set of standard beliefs about wolves (current platitudes) that are the common possession of the members of some speech community. To deny any such piece of accepted commonplace (e.g., by saying that wolves are vegetarians—or easily domesticated) is to produce an effect of paradox and provoke a demand for justification. A speaker who says "wolf" is normally taken to be implying in some sense of that word that he is referring to something fierce, carnivorous, treacherous, and so on. The idea of a wolf is part of a system of ideas, not sharply de-

[40]

lineated, and yet sufficiently definite to admit of detailed enumeration.

The effect, then, of (metaphorically) calling a man a "wolf" is to evoke the wolf-system of related commonplaces. If the man is a wolf, he preys upon other animals, is fierce, hungry, engaged in constant struggle, a scavenger, and so on. Each of these implied assertions has now to be made to fit the principal subject (the man) either in normal or in abnormal senses. If the metaphor is at all appropriate, this can be done —up to a point at least. A suitable hearer will be led by the wolf-system of implications to construct a corresponding system of implications about the principal subject. But these implications will *not* be those comprised in the commonplaces *normally* implied by literal uses of "man." The new implications must be determined by the pattern of implications associated with literal uses of the word "wolf." Any human traits that can without undue strain be talked about in "wolf-language" will be rendered prominent, and any that cannot will be pushed into the background. The wolf-metaphor suppresses some details, emphasizes others—in short, *organizes* our view of man.

Suppose I look at the night sky through a piece of heavily smoked glass on which certain lines have been left clear. Then I shall see only the stars that can be made to lie on the lines previously prepared upon the screen, and the stars I do see will be seen as organized by the screen's structure. We can think of a metaphor as such a screen and the system of "associated commonplaces" of the focal word as the network of lines upon the screen. We can say that the principal subject is "seen through" the metaphorical expression—or, if we prefer, that the principal subject is "projected upon" the field of the subsidiary subject. (In the latter analogy, the implication-system of the focal expression must be taken to determine the "law of projection.")

Or take another example. Suppose I am set the task of describing a battle in words drawn as largely as possible from the vocabulary of chess. These latter terms determine a sys-

[41]

tem of implications which will proceed to control my description of the battle. The enforced choice of the chess vocabulary will lead some aspects of the battle to be emphasized, others to be neglected, and all to be organized in a way that would cause much more strain in other modes of description. The chess vocabulary filters and transforms: it not only selects, it brings forward aspects of the battle that might not be seen at all through another medium. (Stars that cannot be seen at all, except through telescopes.)

Nor must we neglect the shifts in attitude that regularly result from the use of metaphorical language. A wolf is (conventionally) a hateful and alarming object; so, to call a man a wolf is to imply that he too is hateful and alarming (and thus to support and reinforce dyslogistic attitudes). Again, the vocabulary of chess has its primary uses in a highly artificial setting, where all expression of feeling is formally excluded: to describe a battle as if it were a game of chess is accordingly to exclude, by the choice of language, all the more emotionally disturbing aspects of warfare. (Similar by-products are not rare in philosophical uses of metaphor.)

A fairly obvious objection to the foregoing sketch of the "interaction view" is that it has to hold that some of the "associated commonplaces" themselves suffer metaphorical change of meaning in the process of transfer from the subsidiary to the principal subject. And these changes, if they occur, can hardly be explained by the account given. The primary metaphor, it might be said, has been analyzed into a set of subordinate metaphors, so the account given is either circular or leads to an infinite regress.

This might be met by denying that *all* changes of meaning in the "associated commonplaces" must be counted as metaphorical shifts. Many of them are best described as extensions of meaning, because they do not involve apprehended connections between two systems of concepts. I have not undertaken to explain how such extensions or shifts occur in general, and I do not think any simple account will fit all cases. (It is easy enough to mutter "analogy," but closer examina-

[42]

tion soon shows all kinds of "grounds" for shifts of meaning with context—and even no ground at all, sometimes.)

Secondly, I would not deny that a metaphor may involve a number of subordinate metaphors among its implications. But these subordinate metaphors are, I think, usually intended to be taken less "emphatically," i.e., with less stress upon their implications. (The implications of a metaphor are like the overtones of a musical chord; to attach too much "weight" to them is like trying to make the overtones sound as loud as the main notes—and just as pointless.) In any case, primary and subordinate metaphors will normally belong to the same field of discourse, so that they mutually reinforce one and the same system of implications. Conversely, where substantially new metaphors appear as the primary metaphor is unraveled, there is serious risk of confusion of thought (compare the customary prohibition against "mixed metaphors").

But the preceding account of metaphor needs correction, if it is to be reasonably adequate. Reference to "associated commonplaces" will fit the commonest cases where the author simply plays upon the stock of common knowledge (and common misinformation) presumably shared by the reader and himself. But in a poem, or a piece of sustained prose, the writer can establish a novel pattern of implications for the literal uses of the key expressions, prior to using them as vehicles for his metaphors. (An author can do much to suppress unwanted implications of the word "contract," by explicit discussion of its intended meaning, before he proceeds to develop a contract theory of sovereignty. Or a naturalist who really knows wolves may tell us so much about them that *his* description of man as a wolf diverges quite markedly from the stock uses of that figure.) Metaphors can be supported by specially constructed systems of implications, as well as by accepted commonplaces; they can be made to measure and need not be reach-me-downs.

It was a simplification, again, to speak as if the implication-system of the metaphorical expression remains unaltered by the metaphorical statement. The nature of the intended ap-

[43]

plication helps to determine the character of the system to be applied (as though the stars could partly determine the character of the observation-screen by which we looked at them). If to call a man a wolf is to put him in a special light, we must not forget that the metaphor makes the wolf seem more human than he otherwise would.

I hope such complications as these can be accommodated within the outline of an "interaction view" that I have tried to present.

6

Since I have been making so much use of example and illustration, it may be as well to state explicitly (and by way of summary) some of the chief respects in which the "interaction" view recommended differs from a "substitution" or a "comparison" view.

In the form in which I have been expounding it, the "interaction view" is committed to the following seven claims:

(1) A metaphorical statement has two distinct subjects—a "principal" subject and a "subsidiary" one.[21]

(2) These subjects are often best regarded as "systems of things," rather than "things."

(3) The metaphor works by applying to the principal subject a system of "associated implications" characteristic of the subsidiary subject.

(4) These implications usually consist of "commonplaces" about the subsidiary subject, but may, in suitable cases, consist of deviant implications established *ad hoc* by the writer.

(5) The metaphor selects, emphasizes, suppresses, and organizes features of the principal subject by implying state-

---

[21] This point has often been made. E.g.: "As to metaphorical expression, that is a great excellence in style, when it is used with propriety, for it gives you two ideas for one" (Samuel Johnson, quoted by Richards, *ibid.*, p. 93).

The choice of labels for the "subjects" is troublesome. See the "note on terminology" (n. 23, below).

ments about it that normally apply to the subsidiary subject.

(6) This involves shifts in meaning of words belonging to the same family or system as the metaphorical expression; and some of these shifts, though not all, may be metaphorical transfers. (The subordinate metaphors are, however, to be read less "emphatically.")

(7) There is, in general, no simple "ground" for the necessary shifts of meaning—no blanket reason why some metaphors work and others fail.

It will be found, upon consideration, that point (1) is incompatible with the simplest forms of a "substitution view," point (7) is formally incompatible with a "comparison view"; while the remaining points elaborate reasons for regarding "comparison views" as inadequate.

But it is easy to overstate the conflicts between these three views. If we were to insist that only examples satisfying all seven of the claims listed above should be allowed to count as "genuine" metaphors, we should restrict the correct uses of the word "metaphor" to a very small number of cases. This would be to advocate a persuasive definition of "metaphor" that would tend to make all metaphors interestingly complex.[22] And such a deviation from current uses of the word "metaphor" would leave us without a convenient label for the more trivial cases. Now it is in just such trivial cases that "substitution" and "comparison" views sometimes seem nearer the mark than "interaction" views. The point might be met by classifying metaphors as instances of substitution, comparison, or interaction. Only the last kind are of importance in philosophy.

For substitution-metaphors and comparison-metaphors can be replaced by literal translations (with possible exception for

[22] I can sympathize with Empson's contention that "The term ['metaphor'] had better correspond to what the speakers themselves feel to be a rich or suggestive or persuasive use of a word, rather than include uses like the *leg* of a table" (*The Structure of Complex Words*, p. 333). But there is the opposite danger, also, of making metaphors too important by definition, and so narrowing our view of the subject excessively.

the case of catachresis)—by sacrificing some of the charm, vivacity, or wit of the original, but with no loss of *cognitive* content. But "interaction-metaphors" are not expendable. Their mode of operation requires the reader to use a system of implications (a system of "commonplaces"—or a special system established for the purpose in hand) as a means for selecting, emphasizing, and organizing relations in a different field. This use of a "subsidiary subject" to foster insight into a "principal subject" is a distinctive intellectual operation (though one familiar enough through our experiences of learning anything whatever), demanding simultaneous awareness of both subjects but not reducible to any comparison between the two.

Suppose we try to state the cognitive content of an interaction-metaphor in "plain language." Up to a point, we may succeed in stating a number of the relevant relations between the two subjects (though in view of the extension of meaning accompanying the shift in the subsidiary subjects implication system, too much must not be expected of the literal paraphrase). But the set of literal statements so obtained will not have the same power to inform and enlighten as the original. For one thing, the implications, previously left for a suitable reader to educe for himself, with a nice feeling for their relative priorities and degrees of importance, are now presented explicitly as though having equal weight. The literal paraphrase inevitably says too much—and with the wrong emphasis. One of the points I most wish to stress is that the loss in such cases is a loss in cognitive content; the relevant weakness of the literal paraphrase is not that it may be tiresomely prolix or boringly explicit (or deficient in qualities of style); it fails to be a translation because it fails to give the insight that the metaphor did.

But "explication," or elaboration of the metaphor's grounds, if not regarded as an adequate cognitive substitute for the original, may be extremely valuable. A powerful metaphor will no more be harmed by such probing than a musical masterpiece by analysis of its harmonic and melodic structure.

[46]

METAPHOR

No doubt metaphors are dangerous—and perhaps especially so in philosophy. But a prohibition against their use would be a willful and harmful restriction upon our powers of inquiry.[23]

[23] (*A note on terminology*): For metaphors that fit a substitution or comparison view, the factors needing to be distinguished are: (i) some word or expression E, (ii) occurring in some verbal "frame" F, so that (iii) $F(E)$ is the metaphorical statement in question; (iv) the meaning $m'(E)$ which E has in $F(E)$, (v) which is the same as the literal meaning, $m(X)$, of some literal synonym, X. A sufficient technical vocabulary would be: "metaphorical expression" (for E), "metaphorical statement" (for $F(E)$), "metaphorical meaning" (for m') and "literal meaning" (for m).

Where the interaction view is appropriate, the situation is more complicated. We may also need to refer to (vi) the principal subject of $F(E)$, say P (roughly, what the statement is "really" about); (vii) the subsidiary subject, S (what $F(E)$ would be about if read literally); (viii) the relevant system of implications, I, connected with S; and (ix) the resulting system of attributions, A, asserted of P. We must accept at least so much complexity if we agree that the meaning of E in its setting F depends upon the transformation of I into A by using language, normally applied to S, to apply to P instead.

Richards has suggested using the words "tenor" and "vehicle" for the two "*thoughts*" which, in his view, are "active together" (for "the two *ideas* that metaphor, at its simplest, gives us"—*The Philosophy of Rhetoric*, p. 96, my italics) and urges that we reserve "the word 'metaphor' for the whole double unit" (*ibid.*). But this picture of two *ideas* working upon each other is an inconvenient fiction. And it is significant that Richards himself soon lapses into speaking of "tenor" and "vehicle" as "things" (e.g. on p. 118). Richards' "vehicle" vacillates in reference between the metaphorical expression (E), the subsidiary subject (S) and the connected implication system (I). It is less clear what his "tenor" means: sometimes it stands for the principal subject (P), sometimes for the implications connected with that subject (which I have not symbolized above), sometimes, in spite of Richards' own intentions, for the *resultant* meaning (or as we might say the "full import") of E in its context, $F(E)$.

There is probably no hope of getting an accepted terminology so long as writers upon the subject are still so much at variance with one another.

[47]

IV

Presupposition and Implication

1

FREGE once said, "If anything is asserted, there is always an obvious presupposition that the simple or compound proper names used have reference."[1] Frege uses as examples, the sentences

(a) Kepler died in misery

and

(b) He who discovered the elliptic form of the planetary orbits died in misery.

He might have used instead any sentence whose grammatical subject is either a proper name or a definite description. I shall call the assertions made by using such sentences *primary assertions*. A presupposition, in Frege's sense, of the primary assertion, (a), is that there was once somebody whose name was "Kepler"; a presupposition of the primary assertion, (b), is that there was somebody who first discovered the elliptic form of the planetary orbits; and, in general, a presupposition associated with a given primary assertion will be that the object ostensibly referred to by the sentence used in making that assertion really exists.

Consider now the assertions that could be made by saying:

(p) "Kepler" designates something

---

[1] "Wenn man etwas behauptet, so ist immer die Voraussetzung selbstverständlich, dass die gebrauchten einfachen oder zusammengesetzten Eigennamen eine Bedeutung haben." In "Ueber Sinn und Bedeutung," *Zeitschrift für Philosophie und philosophische Kritik,* vol. 100, 1892, p. 40. For the English translation see *Translations from the Philosophical Writings of Gottlob Frege* (Peter Geach and Max Black, eds.), Oxford, 1952, p. 69.

[48]

or again

(q) There was somebody who first discovered the elliptic form of the planetary orbits.

I shall call these the corresponding *secondary* assertions.

Frege's chief point is that the secondary assertion does not follow from, is not entailed by, the associated primary assertion. Or, to use his own terminology, the sense (*Sinn*) of the secondary assertion is not a *part* of the sense of the primary assertion. Here Frege's view is in sharp conflict with Russell's theory of descriptions, according to which any assertion about the so-and-so does entail that the so-and-so exists.

When the secondary assertion is true, Frege and Russell agree that the primary assertion is legitimate, though they would disagree about its analysis. The difference between the two views appears most clearly in a case where the secondary assertion happens to be false. Russell says that the primary assertion is then simply false. But Frege's answer has to be that in such a case no primary assertion can be made. For the sentence needed to make the assertion is neither true nor false. In order to be either, the whole sentence must have reference (*Bedeutung*), which it cannot do unless each of its component designations has reference. Now if the secondary assertion is false, the grammatical subject of the sentence needed for the primary assertion stands for nothing, and the whole sentence therefore fails to stand either for the false or the true.

The only formal argument used by Frege is the contention that if the sense of the secondary assertion were part of the sense of the primary assertion, the negation of (a) would have to run:

(a') Either Kepler did not die in misery, or the name "Kepler" has no reference.

This he seems to regard as a *reductio ad absurdum*.[2]

---

[2] A puzzling feature of (a') is the recurrence of the original sentence, (a), as a subclause. Perhaps we might say that on the view Frege is attacking, (a) would have to be construed as:

Frege does not explain what he means by the word "presupposition." His contention that when it is asserted that Kepler died in misery there is a presupposition that there was once somebody called "Kepler" might be interpreted in any of the following ways:

(i) Anybody making the assertion assumes, or takes for granted, that there was once somebody called "Kepler."

(ii) Anybody hearing the assertion is entitled to make the same assumption.

(iii) No assertion is made unless there was once somebody called "Kepler."

I have chosen the third of these interpretations (though for all I know Frege may have had all three in mind). On this interpretation, the meaning of the sentence used in making the assertion depends upon a matter of fact (i.e., whether in fact anybody was ever called "Kepler"). And this may explain why Frege regarded the reliance of ordinary language on such presuppositions as a "fault" (*Mangel*) and an "imperfection" (*Unvollkommenheit*). In a well-constructed language, he believed, whether a given sentence can be either true or false ought not to depend upon matters of extralinguistic fact. He saw to it that his own artificial ideography (*Begriffsschrift*) should be free from such blemishes.[3]

(a_1) The person whose name was "Kepler" died in misery.
Since this still contains a name, viz., the name of a word, "Kepler," it ought in turn to be replaced by:
(a_2) The person whose name was the name referred to by " 'Kepler' " died in misery.
In this way we are led into an infinite regress that prevents us from ever producing a "correct" version of (*a*), or fully expressing its sense.

Alternatively, we might argue that, on the view to be refuted, the negation of (*a'*) would not be (*a*), but some other sentence, so that double negation would not be equivalent to affirmation.

[3] Frege's substitute for a definite description is a symbol of the form "$\backslash \varepsilon' \phi(\varepsilon)$" that designates the object falling under $\phi(\xi)$ if $\phi(\xi)$ applies to just one thing, and otherwise designates the value-range of ϕ. Thus a

I am, accordingly, equating Frege's "presupposition" with "necessary condition for having reference." On Frege's view, the presupposition is also a necessary condition for the sentence in question to be wholly meaningful. For he counts reference as part of the meaning ("*Bedeutung*" equals "meaning" in nontechnical German). When the presupposition is not the case, we have no assertion, but only the utterance of a form of words needing supplementation in order to have truth value.

On my interpretation, then, a presupposition, in Frege's sense, is expressed by a certain "that"-clause (e.g., "that there was somebody called 'Kepler' "). The presupposition is something that is the case or else is not the case. And a presupposition is therefore not an assertion, though of course there will always be a corresponding assertion to the effect that the presupposition is satisfied, i.e., that the state of affairs in question obtains.

2

Views similar to those of Frege have been energetically advocated by Mr. P. F. Strawson.[4] Thus, one of Strawson's main points is that what he calls a "statement" has no truth value if one of its "presuppositions" is not satisfied.[5] This leads

---

symbol of this form always stands for something ("hat immer eine Bedeutung"). An analogue for ordinary language would be to construe "the king of France" as meaning the same as "either the one thing that is a king of France, if there is one and only one such, or the class of things that are kings of France otherwise." Cf. Frege's *Grundgesetze*, no. 11.

[4] See his "On Referring," *Mind*, vol. 59 (1950), pp. 320–344; *Introduction to Logical Theory*, London, 1952; and "A Reply to Mr. Sellars," *Philosophical Review*, vol. 63 (1954), pp. 216–231. I shall cite these as "Referring," *Introduction*, and "Reply." See also his paper on "Truth" (symposium with J. L. Austin), *Aristotelian Society*, suppl. vol. 24 (1950), pp. 129–156. A similar view about definite descriptions is contained in P. T. Geach's "Russell's Theory of Descriptions," *Analysis*, vol. 10 (1950), pp. 84–88.

[5] See, for instance, *Introduction*, p. 175.

him to reject Russell's theory of descriptions,[6] and to attack some influential views concerning the analysis of subject-predicate propositions.[7]

If Strawson meant by "statement" what Frege meant by "assertion," we could say both agreed that a man making a statement or assertion does not *assert* that the presuppositions of his statement are satisfied.[8] This is the main plank of Strawson's theory. Both would also agree, I think, that if the presupposition is not satisfied, the question of truth-or-falsity of the original statement "fails to arise."[9]

Yet, there is a difference between the two views which might be important. Consider Strawson's formal definition of his (special) sense of "presupposition." It runs:

"S presupposes S'" is defined as follows: "The truth of S' is a necessary condition for the truth or falsity of S."[10]

Here, a shift has occurred. On my interpretation of Frege, a presupposition of the assertion, "The king of France is wise," is that one and only one man reigns over France, i.e., some-

6 See "Referring," pp. 324–325, and *Introduction*, pp. 184–190. On p. 187, Strawson calls Russell's theory a "jejune existential analysis."

7 See *Introduction*, pp. 165 ff. Strawson holds that the "rules of the traditional system" apply and are intended to apply when and only when the existential presuppositions of subject-predicate statements are satisfied.

8 "When a man uses such an expression [as 'The king of France'], he does not *assert*, nor does what he says *entail*, a uniquely existential proposition" ("Referring," p. 331).

9 [Suppose someone says "All John's children are asleep" but John has no children]: "Then is it true or false that all John's children are asleep? Either answer would seem to be misleading. But we are not compelled to give either answer. We can, and normally should, say that, since John has no children, the question does not arise" (*Introduction*, pp. 173–174).

"When a question does not arise, the only proper way of answering is to say so and explain the reason; the 'plain' affirmative or negative answer, though grammatically possible, is *out of place*" (Geach, *op. cit.*, p. 85).

10 "Reply," p. 216. The same definition is in *Introduction*, p. 175.

thing that either is, or is not, the case. For Strawson, however, if we are to follow his formal definition, the presupposition is always a *statement*, i.e., something that may itself be true or false, genuine or spurious. It follows that a presupposition might itself have presuppositions, that presuppositions might be asserted, accepted, rejected, and so on. Now none of these remarks apply to "presuppositions" in what I have taken to be Frege's sense of *necessary condition for reference*. (E.g., it is nonsensical to call a necessary condition true or false, genuine or spurious, or the like.) [11]

Let us see how the difference shows itself in the crucial case in which a presupposition is false. Consider the sentences:

(c) The present king of Siam is a bachelor

and

(r) There is at present one and only one king of Siam.

And suppose that in fact there is no king of Siam. Frege's verdict is: a necessary condition for reference fails, so (c) formulates nothing that can be true-or-false and has no reference, though it still has a sense (*Sinn*). Strawson's position is not quite the same. He cannot say that the falsity of (r) entails that *no* statement can be made by using (c); for then his definition would have to run:

"S presupposes S' " means the same as "The truth of S' is a necessary condition for S to be a *statement*."

This would involve a shift in his conception of "statement." It would then be *necessary* that a statement should have a truth value, and one point of disagreement between Strawson and Russell would disappear. Strawson is therefore committed to holding that we still have a statement even when its presuppositions are falsified. In such a case he calls the

[11] We might use "precondition" for Frege's sense of *Voraussetzung*. In what follows, I shall try to use "presupposition" in the sense intended to be fixed by Strawson's formal definition.

[53]

statement "spurious." [12] A spurious statement must, therefore, still count as a statement; a man making a spurious statement must still *state* something.

But what does he state? We might be inclined to compare making a statement with hanging a label on an actual individual. Then, if there is no individual to be labeled, the attempt to say something about him fails, and *no* statement results. Making a spurious statement would then be like tying a string round a nonexistent parcel. A case of this sort occurs if I point to a place where there is nobody, and say *"He* looks happy." The natural comment is that I have made no statement. But Strawson, as we have seen, is committed to rejecting this line.

Why should we not say that a man who says "The king of Siam is a bachelor" is saying that the king of Siam is a bachelor, even when there is no king of Siam? We might seem to be risking self-contradiction, for when *we* use the phrase "the king of Siam," we normally commit ourselves to there being one and only one king of Siam. But any appearance of self-contradiction can easily be canceled by adding a supplementary phrase. *We* can say "He said that the king of Siam is a bachelor, though of course there isn't any king of Siam," or, again "He said that Bourbaki is a fine logician, though we know there isn't any such person." In either case, we report what was said, without committing ourselves to the existence of the person to whom reference was originally intended.

I suggest, accordingly, the following view of the situation that arises when a presupposition is falsified. Our language contains rules for seeking and finding things and rules for making remarks about such things after they have been located. Because we know such rules, an expression like "the present king of Siam" tells us how to set about looking for

12 [If, when a man utters a sentence] "he is not talking about anything, then his use is not a genuine one, but a spurious or pseudo-use: he is not making either a true or a false assertion, though he may think he is" ("Referring," p. 329).

[54]

the person answering to the identifying expression. And similarly for the case of "Bourbaki." Recognizing it as a personal name, we know what steps to take in order to identify a man who, if he exists, has this name. So we can understand a statement about "Bourbaki" before we have met anybody having that name—before we even know that Bourbaki exists. We take the speaker to be identifying a man according to procedures established by our general rules for using personal names, and we take him to be attributing a designated property to the man in question. Our report of what was "said," in a case where the subject of the assertion does not exist, consists in reporting the identifying procedure for that subject, together with a report of the ascription supposedly attaching to the person supposedly identified.

The foregoing account is very close to Frege's view that words have two distinguishable dimensions or aspects of meaning—sense (*Sinn*) as well as reference (*Bedeutung*)—so that even when the reference is missing, through failure of a presupposition, we can still use words in reported speech to stand for what would normally be their sense. (I would myself, however, not count the *Bedeutung* as part of the "meaning.")

Now, some of Strawson's remarks indicate that he either accepts or is very close to accepting some such view as I have just outlined. (E.g., "For a singular referring expression to have a meaning, it suffices that it should be possible in suitable circumstances to use it to refer to some one thing, person, place, etc. Its meaning is the set of linguistic conventions governing its correct use to refer," *Introduction,* p. 188.) If so, there is very little difference between Strawson, Frege, and myself. For though I have chosen to talk about "identifying rules," I have been making substantially the same point as Frege does when he says an expression can have sense without reference. The chief merit of Strawson's formulation is that it draws our attention to certain neglected relations between two statements, both of which are *part of the language.*

[55]

According to the view I have outlined, the relation between a statement S and its presupposition, S', begins to look like a *logical* relation. Because there are conventional rules for the identifying uses of proper names and descriptions, the use of such designations *commit* their user to the satisfaction of the rules. There is, as Strawson says, a "kind of logical absurdity" in affirming a statement while in the same breath denying its presupposition; it is *logically* absurd to say "All John's children are asleep, but John has no children," [13] and we recognize this "logical absurdity" as soon as we understand both clauses. If a man were to use the paradoxical sentence, believing that John had no children, while all the time John really was a parent, Frege might have to say that an assertion had been made. But whether John is *in fact* a parent or not, the compound sentence still violates the rules of discourse. There has to be a connection between S and S' independent of the *actual* truth value of S'.

Consider what might be meant by saying that the truth of S' is a "necessary condition" for S to be either true or false. We might first consider the imputed relation between S' and S as external to S. When a man makes a promise, there is no doubt some necessary condition for that promise to count as either legally valid or legally invalid in a court of law. But it is no part of our conception of what the promise means that it should have an attached presupposition of legal validity; the very same promise might have been subject to other conditions for legal validity. But the case of S and S' is different. It is not merely a contingent fact about S that unless S' is true, S will have no truth value. We cannot say that the very same statement S might have had a different presupposition: that S has that presupposition is part of our conception of S, and statements with different presuppositions must be different statements.

Contrast making a statement with shooting at a target. A necessary condition for a marksman's either hitting or missing is the existence of a target for him to fire at. If the marksman

[13] *Introduction*, p. 175.

thinks there is a target, but we know there is not, it is improper for *us* to say either that he hit or that he missed. But since firing is not stating, there is no question of the marksman "committing himself" to the target's existence, or of our having "the right to assume" that there is a target. There can be no right here, because no rule is violated. A man who pretends to fire at a target, and shoots at nothing, may trick us into thinking he was aiming at something, but he has violated no convention.

So, talking about something with the help of names or descriptions differs in one important respect from aiming at a target. In using the words, the speaker necessarily makes himself responsible for the truth of the presupposition. The man who pretends to shoot at a nonexistent target can disclaim any responsibility for our mistaken inferences; but a speaker may not adopt the motto of *caveat auditor*. There is a logical—or, "quasi-logical"—connection between a statement and its presuppositions.

Can we say anything more about this connection? Strawson supplies a useful hint when he says "To say, 'The king of France is wise' is, in some sense of 'imply,' to imply that there is a king of France." [14] And one way to become clearer about presupposition would be to become clearer about this notion of implication. I cannot see that "this is a very special and odd sense of 'imply.' " [15] It seems to me, on the contrary, a very common and familiar sense of the word. Admittedly, a statement may imply something that is not a presupposition of that statement in Strawson's sense of that word—as when a man who asserts that p implies that he believes p.[16] Yet presupposing is so tightly connected with implying that clarifica-

[14] "Referring," p. 330.

[15] *Ibid.* Of course, if Strawson was thinking of a sense of "imply" in which the speaker is not committed to what he implies, I would agree that that sense of "imply" was odd.

[16] Confusion between presupposing (in Strawson's sense) and implying led Professor Sellars to misunderstand the doctrine under discussion. Cf. *Philosophical Review*, vol. 63 (1954), p. 203, where Sellars takes belief that p to be a presupposition of the statement that p.

tion of the latter may be expected to throw light upon the former. In any case, the notion of "implication" deserves some independent examination, to which I should now like to address myself. For lack of time, I shall have to content myself with a mere sketch, that would need extensive elaboration in order to be adequate.

3

In what follows, I want to exclude uses of "imply," or its grammatical variants, in which one statement is said to imply another when the first *entails* the second, i.e., when the truth of the second *follows from* the truth of the first. The ordinary uses I have in mind are not those of logicians and philosophers; I shall not be concerned with the sense in which one proposition is said to "materially imply" another nor that in which Lewis talked about "strict implication."

Typical examples of the uses I wish to consider are those in which either a *speaker* (or writer) is said to imply something, or, again, certain *words* are said to imply something. An instance of the former is:

. . . his ability to imply in one flat, elliptic sentence everything that a more literary performer would require a lengthy speech or two to say [*The New Yorker*, Nov. 3, 1956, p. 68].

An example of the second type is:

Here the particle *also* implies that the writer, after what he has said before, feels justified in taking the thing for granted [F. Max Müller, translator's preface to Kant's *Critique of Pure Reason*, 1907, p. xxix].

An obvious feature of such uses of "imply" is a contrast between "implying" and "saying outright" or "saying in so many words." "Imply" belongs to the same family as "suggest," "hint," "insinuate," all of which evoke a picture of a meaning below the surface, partly concealed and not in plain view. It is always proper to use some such formula as, "He didn't *say* such-and-such, but he *did* imply it." Here, as is

[58]

often the case, the use of "but" suggests [17] both similarity *and* dissimilarity. It is as if the formula ran: "He didn't *exactly* say it, didn't pronounce words whose conventional use guaranteed the expression of his meaning, yet, after all, *did* imply it—as good as said it." So what the speaker implies is treated as a part of his whole communication or *message,* though regarded as occupying a subordinate position in the whole.

What a speaker implies can, at least upon some occasions, properly be taken as part of what he is intending to convey. So we sometimes respond to an implication as we would to an explicit statement, by agreeing, objecting, answering, drawing conclusions, and so on.[18] Again, we often pin down the speaker's implication by using the formula *"Am I to understand* that such-and-such" and we say "Did you *mean* such-and-such?" In some cases, at least, the implications are intended to be understood; and sometimes the implication is the focus of the communication, so that the normal pattern of relative subordination is displaced.

Since the basic contrast is with what is said in so many words (said explicitly, said expressly) we might hope to advance by making the latter notion more precise.

What normally counts as an answer to the question, "What did so-and-so actually say?" What does it mean to "say in so many words"? A clear case is that in which a full sentence is cited. If a man uses the words "I shall come tomorrow," there can be no question but that he said he would come tomorrow. But if he had replied to the question "Will you come tomorrow?" by using the words "You can count on it," it is not so clear that he said he would come tomorrow.

The narrowest sense of "say" calls for direct quotation of the words that were used. But even so, we have no provision

[17] Or: implies.

[18] "I'm thirsty." "All right—let's go." Here the speaker responds as if to an invitation. It would be absurd, sometimes, to pretend that no invitation had been given. A kind of converse case is one in which an implication is rendered prominent by a prior question. "Do you *expect* him to win?" "He will win." Here it would be pedantic to insist that the question had not been answered.

[59]

for "quoting" the tone of words used, or the significant emphasis given to parts of the utterance. So, much that is unmistakably communicated or conveyed does not count as actually having been "said" in this sense of "say." It will hardly do to draw the lines around "saying explicitly" so tightly that we shall have to say that a man answering "Yes" to the question, "Will you come tomorrow?" has not said that he would, but merely implied it. Nevertheless, a paradigm for "saying explicitly" seems to be the case in which a full sentence is used. We stretch the conditions somewhat by also allowing cases in which the context (e.g., a prior question) allows the use of a recognizable substitute, for which a full sentence can be immediately substituted without possibility of error or dispute.

In wider senses of "say," we allow ourselves to paraphrase "what a man said" by using indirect speech. But whatever latitude we allow for the use of the expression, "what the speaker said," there are ultimate bounds upon our freedom to use it. We cannot treat silence (to take an extreme case) as part of what the speaker "said explicitly." Yet silence can be significant, and deliberate refusal to speak may, as people say, "speak louder than words." Nor can we, in general, count ellipsis, stress, intonation, sentence construction, choice of words, or allusion, as part of what is "said explicitly." This is connected with the fact that we have to report what is "said" by means of a "that"-clause, within which there is provision only for formal statement. We report the paraphrasable content of a speaker's remarks and have no devices for citing anything but the gross linguistic features, as it were, of the remarks reported. We cannot report an implication by implying something ourselves; if we want to talk about tone, emphasis, and the like, we have to describe them, not report them.

Implications are, of course, expressed. They are not transmitted from speaker to hearer by some occult telepathy. On the contrary, it always makes sense to ask, "What showed that A was implying such-and-such?" and "How could you tell that

[60]

he was implying *X?"*; and an answer will always be forth-coming with sufficient trouble.[19] Implications are expressed by identifiable linguistic features. The contrast between what is said "in so many words" and what is implied is a con-trast between two modes of expression. Parts of the commu-nication that can be identified by direct quotation of words, or by plausible paraphrases of the words used, count as being said explicitly; all the rest of what can be accepted as "what the speaker meant" or "what he intended to be understood" counts as implication. It is just because our notion of what is said "outright" is so narrow (and tends, under pressure, to move in the direction of greater "strictness") that the notion of the implicit communication is so important for an adequate conception of language.

A picture that seems to fit the relation between the explicit and the implicit communication is that of a "foreground" and a "background." A portrait painter presents his sitter against a setting, and normally we would say that the person depicted is the principal subject. The background may be only vaguely indicated, but it is presented, no less than the human figure. Similarly, we might think of the explicit statement as pre-sented against a "background" of more or less clearly de-lineated, unstated, but still expressed, implications. The im-plications are, as it were, merely sketched in and normally presented as subordinate to the principal theme—the stated communication.

Consequently, the speaker is allowed to disclaim some re-sponsibility for his implications.[20] Or, to be more precise, in proportion as the implication is less precisely determined by

[19] Often an implication works by signaling the hardening of bound-aries between words that are generally more fluid. For instance, the general contrast between "some" and "all" does not make them sharp opposites ("some" can mean "some, and perhaps all"). But if I stress *"some"* when I speak, it is as if I said, "This time, I mean some *but not* all." Contextual reduction of vagueness is, of course, not the only mechanism for implications.

[20] The witness swears to tell the whole truth. He does not swear to imply nothing but the truth.

[61]

conventional rules for implication, the speaker has correspondingly greater license to avow or repudiate the implication. We are allowed to say "I do not intend to imply such-
and-such." [21] or "I am here implying such-and-such"; and
where we do not either formally avow or repudiate an implication, it is to some extent within our hearer's discretion to
draw or not to draw the implication. (So we make him, as it
were, a collaborator in the communication—as in a game in
which the opponent may, if he chooses, make extra moves
for us, which then count as if we had made them.)

To the extent, however, that the speaker uses formal linguistic signals of implications, he forfeits the option of disclaiming the implication. He cannot say, "In saying 'After
the performance was over . . .' I did not mean to imply that
there had been a performance." He had no choice but to
imply it: his *words* implied it, whether he so intended or
not.[22] Now in proportion as the implication is fixed by conventional rules, the differences between implication and
formally stated communication may come to seem less important. Attempts to reject the implication by explicit denial
can now hardly be distinguished from flat logical contradiction. If a man says "John's children are clever, but he has only
one child," should we say that he is contradicting himself, or
not? Well, it might be urged that the speaker had not said
that John had more than one child, but only implied it, so
that by proceeding to reject the implication, he had merely
rendered his first statement null and void (without truth
value). But would it not be just as plausible to hold that the
speaker "as good as said" that John has more than one child,
i.e., that the use of the plural is so invariable and definite

21 But such formal disavowal is often self-stultifying. In stating the
implication to be rejected, the speaker may reinforce the disavowed
suggestions. Cf. the effect of the form of words, "I do not imply that
he is a liar or a cheat."

22 Much more needs to be said about the connection between "what
the speaker implies" and "what *the words* imply." The criteria for the
two by no means coincide.

that the speaker is hardly in a position to treat the implication as *mere* background? From this standpoint, the sharp line drawn by Strawson between what is "said" and what is "presupposed" seems not so much mistaken as oversimplified.[23]

Strawson's theory of presuppositions is part of an attempt to replace the theory of descriptions by a model that more closely reflects the actual rules of usage in ordinary language. But ordinary language is apt to be more complicated than even its closest observers realize. If something like the account of implication outlined above is correct, it may appear that Strawson's account is still somewhat remote from the actual patterns of connection between stated and implied communication. And if we are to operate with simplified models of language, as we must in formal logic, it will be an open question whether Russell's model may not be more serviceable than the more sophisticated, but still idealized, model by which Strawson seeks to replace it.

[23] Strawson has conceded this in his latest remarks on the subject, where he speaks of the "error" he made in "canonizing" tendencies and making them into fixed and rigid rules, whereas they have exceptions ("Reply," p. 229). I am inclined to think the exceptions outnumber the "rules."

V

Necessary Statements and Rules

I WANT to explore some relations between certain kinds of necessary statements and certain associated rules of language. If possible, I would like to clarify the nondeductive certification of necessary statements—for not all necessary statements can be certified as valid by deduction from necessary statements previously accepted as valid. We can always try to prove a given necessary statement, but the attempt may fail because the statement in question is in some fashion too "simple" or "fundamental" for proof to be feasible. If this is so, we are not driven to the dogmatic assertion of the necessary statement without supporting grounds; nor need we await the dubious blessing of some supposed act of infallible intuition. There are nondeductive ways of certifying necessary statements that provide rational grounds for their assertion; where the resources of proof are exhausted, there remain other discursive tests to be applied.

Such certification, as it may be called, has less practical importance than recourse to proof. Scientists and mathematicians (not to speak of the "man in the street") have been trained to accept some simple necessary statements without hesitation or question; then problems about necessary statements are always problems of calculation. A philosopher, however, will probably be more perplexed about certification than about proof—though he is interested in both. For unless he can satisfy himself that he had a sufficiently clear understanding of how some necessary statements are certified, he will naturally regard the process of proof as showing merely how some necessary statements depend upon others.

I wish to argue that the process of certification may properly be regarded as one of checking a necessary statement against a corresponding rule of language. Or, rather, I shall argue

[64]

that this is so in the case of a special class of necessary statements. I want to show how, and in what ways, such necessary statements are based upon and function as surrogates for linguistic rules. But these expressions, "based upon," and "function as surrogates," are at present too imprecise for useful discussion; and the same might be said for the familiar word "rule." The success of the following sketch will depend largely upon the extent to which these expressions receive relatively more precise meanings.

(It will have been noticed that I have chosen to speak of the "validity" of necessary statements rather than of their "truth," and of their "certification" rather than their "verification." My purpose in so doing has been to emphasize from the outset the differences between necessary statements and contingent ones. If the theory to be outlined below is sound, it will become plain that the uses of necessary statements differ strikingly from those of contingent statements. So great are these differences that a good case might be made for rejecting the expression "necessary *statement*" altogether. Unfortunately, if we withhold the title of "statement," we shall have no good alternative label. "Axiom" might serve if it were not already pre-empted in special senses. The best we can do is to continue talking about "necessary statements," without allowing the label to control our thoughts.)

1

I wish to conduct the discussion by using a single example of a necessary statement that can be certified but not usefully proved. In order to develop my case as simply as possible, I want to exclude statements belonging to logic or pure mathematics—like "(p): $p \vee \sim p$" and "$1 + 1 = 2$"—and also statements in which particular words occur "vacuously" (like "A man is a man" or "If Tom is an Englishman, Tom is either an Englishman or a Frenchman").

Consider the following statement, which I shall call "S":

Monday is the day before Tuesday. $\hspace{1em}(S)$

I fear there may be some reluctance to accept this as an authentic necessary statement, on the ground that it refers to an artificial division of the week, and is therefore a mere "convention" or "definition." I think such objections are unsound for reasons that I do not now propose to discuss. But in any case I do not wish to argue about the choice of an example. I hope that what is to be said will apply equally well to the case of any other simple necessary statement that might be substituted for S. (However, the example ought to be one that would normally be called an "analytical" necessary statement, and not the sort that would commonly be called "synthetic.")

Given the necessary statement, S ("Monday is the day before Tuesday"), we can now construct what I shall call the *associated linguistic rule,* or "R" for short:

"Monday" may be replaced by "the day
before Tuesday" and vice versa.   (R)

If we are given any necessary statement whose verbal expression consists of some expression (or word) E_1, followed by the word "is" and then by an expression (or word) E_2, so that the whole necessary statement reads "E_1 is E_2," the associated linguistic rule will be to the effect that E_1 can be replaced by E_2, and also E_2 by E_1.

2

My chief contention will be that *one* way to certify S is to establish that R is indeed a rule in force in the English language. But now is there such a rule of synonymity concerning the word "Monday" and the expression "the day before Tuesday" in the English language as at present spoken? An affirmative answer would have the following important consequence: Anybody who substituted the word "Wednesday" for the expression "the day before Tuesday" would be criticized for making a mistake, would be called to account as soon as the substitution was noticed. Linguistic rules are normative; they state what is and is not to be done when the language is used; and so departures from or violations of the rules evoke complaint and demands for correction.

The same, however, can be said of some misstatements of facts. Anybody who said "London is the capital of the United States" would also be regarded as making a mistake and would be held to account as soon as his remark was noticed. So the fact that anybody who replaced the expression "the day before Tuesday" by the word "Wednesday" would be held to be wrong and called upon to retract, does not yet show that we are dealing with a rule of language. We have to decide what reason would be offered for or against such deviations from normality and the sanctions that would ultimately be invoked if the offence were repeated. If a man said, in apparently good faith, that London was the capital of the United States, we would suspect that he was speaking figuratively or, possibly, making some paradoxical statement with a hidden point to it. But if he were to insist upon repeating it, while maintaining that he meant just what he said, we could only assume that he himself did not believe his own words and was, for some obscure purpose, sowing confusion in his hearers. But if a man insisted on substituting "Wednesday" for the expression "the day before Tuesday" and proved equally refractory to attempted correction, our conclusion could only be that he was using some of the words in senses differing from our own. This kind of behavior, I am maintaining, in which the man in question insists on making unorthodox substitutions, is conclusive evidence that he is using some words in ways other than those prescribed in the English language. It is along these lines, I believe, that we can distinguish the case of a violation of a linguistic rule from that of an error about fact.

Consider the corresponding situation in connection with an explicit rule of definition that somebody adds to the language. If I introduce the expression "Old Year's Day" for the last day of the year and subsequently find somebody who is willing to substitute the expression "Old Year's Day" for, say, the first of December, that is conclusive proof that the other man cannot be using my label in the way I had intended. The situation with respect to "Monday" and the expression "the day before Tuesday" differs inasmuch as nobody known to us has introduced the word "Monday" into the English language and in that no unique stipulative definition of that word is available. But this is no reason for denying that there is a rule of synonymity governing the use of the two expressions.

I am going to take it as established in what follows that R is a rule of synonymity now in force in the English language, and I shall proceed to examine the relations between R and the necessary statement, S.[1]

3

The chief thing I wish to say about the relations between S and R is that a necessary and sufficient condition for the validity of the former is that the latter should be a rule now in force in the English language.

This view about the certification of necessary statements may seem reminiscent of theories that have been called "linguistic theories of the a priori" or "conventionalistic interpretations of necessary statements." Such theories have in the past been exposed to a number of powerful objections which I must try to meet in their proper place. But supposing the objections can be met (as I hope they can), what positive grounds can be offered in support of the contention? I can think of no better way of persuading somebody who is not already convinced than by asking him to consider what would

---

1 Some readers will demand a good deal of argument before they are satisfied that R is a rule now in force in the English language; others will perhaps need convincing that natural languages contain any normative rules or regulations. A discussion of the notion of a linguistic rule that might persuade these dissenters would require so large a digression that I have decided to reserve the topic for a separate paper (see the next essay).

[68]

be the relation between a statement of the form I have been discussing and the associated linguistic rule of synonymity, in case there should be such a rule in force. If we were to agree that the word "flubor" should in future count as a synonym for the expression "female fox," would not the statement "A flubor is a female fox" then be a necessary statement? If the answer is in the affirmative, the defense of my contention will then shift to the question of whether there are rules of synonymity that have not been introduced into the language by explicit definition. But about this I have already said all that I can at present.

(In any case we must remind ourselves that philosophical conclusions do not stand to their reasons as the conclusion of a deductive argument to its sufficient premises. The success of any philosophical investigation must be judged by the extent that it dispels initial perplexity and permits a perspicuous view of a complex territory. The value of any "theory" about necessary statements must be judged in the end by the light it throws upon the ways in which necessary statements are used, their modes of certification, their relations to contingent statements, and so on. The choice between the view I am trying to develop and, say, the "realist" interpretation will be settled in the end by such considerations as these and not by formal argument for or against one or the other view.)

4

I have claimed that S is certified, that is, shown to be valid, by establishing that the associated linguistic rule, R, holds in the English language. In other words, to certify S is to verify the contingent proposition, E, that R is a rule of the English language. It is to be noted, however, that I am not identifying the necessary statement, S, either with R or with the contingent statement E.

Other philosophers who have defended views about necessary statements similar to those I am here presenting, have

[69]

sometimes made the mistake of identifying a necessary statement with a convention, definition, resolution, or the like. Thus Professor A. J. Ayer once incautiously said of a necessary statement that it *"records our determination"* to use words in a certain way.[2] Professor C. D. Broad thought he could refute this by saying "If an analytic proposition states that the person who records it intends to use certain words in a certain way, it evidently makes a statement about the present experiences of the speaker, and about his future behaviour." [3] And he went on to say that this view treats all analytic propositions as empirical and synthetic. It is, however, a mistake to treat a resolution as the conjunction of a report about present experience and a forecast about future behavior. And so Broad's refutation of Ayer must be rejected. And yet it *would,* for all that, also be a mistake to say that a necessary statement *is* the same thing as a resolution (a "record of our determination" to use words in a certain way). Quite superficial considerations are enough to show that necessary statements are not used in the way that statements of resolutions are used. We can, for example, always ask of a given resolution who were its authors and when the resolution was made, yet these questions are nonsensical when applied to a necessary statement. No sense attaches to the question *"Who* resolved that two and two shall make four?" or the question *"When* was it resolved that two and two should make four?" Again a resolution about words must involve reference *to* the words, yet the corresponding necessary statement is not about the words but rather *uses* those words. ("I resolve to use 'two and two' and 'four' as synonyms" mentions the expressions "two and two" and "four"; the statement "two and two make four" *uses* those same expressions.)

It is easy enough to bring parallel considerations against any view that identifies necessary statements with definitions

2 *Language, Truth and Logic* (London, 1936), p. 104.

3 *Proceedings of the Aristotelian Society,* Supplementary Vol. XV (1936), 107.

or conventions or rules of language. Very little effort is needed to show that the grammar of "necessary statement" differs at crucial points from the grammar of "convention" or "definition" or the other terms by which it has been attempted to be replaced.

Yet it by no means follows that in *certifying* a necessary statement we cannot be establishing that an associated rule holds in the English language or, for that matter, verifying a corresponding empirical statement to the effect that the rule holds. Consider the following analogy. In order to make sure that a given check is good, we have to verify that the account on which it is drawn has sufficient funds to meet it, and this is a matter of fact. But it by no means follows that the check itself is the expression of a matter of fact, say an assertion to the effect that the account in question does contain sufficient funds for the draft to be honored. The check is an *order*, even though the determination of the worth or value of that order is a matter of empirical verification.

Or consider the case of an Act of Parliament. That the Act is valid or legitimate can be established by examining appropriate documents and, if necessary, settling questions of historical fact (whether the Bill was properly read, whether a proper Parliament was sitting at the time, and so on). But the Act itself is not a collection of historical statements; that the determination of the legitimacy of the Act is an empirical inquiry does not make it necessary for us to say that the Act itself is an empirical statement or a collection of empirical statements.

Now much the same can be said about many statements that are not themselves statements of fact. In many such cases the statement in question can be *appraised* as "correct" or "incorrect," "valid" or "invalid." And the statement of appraisal may itself be checked or "verified" by appeal to matters of fact. Yet it never follows, on this ground alone, that what is appraised is itself a statement of fact. Nor does it follow that the appraisal is a statement of fact.

[71]

5

The best way to make clear what the relation is of the necessary statement S to the associated linguistic rule, R, is, I think, to review some of the main uses of necessary statements. I propose to deal with this somewhat indirectly, by considering first some of the distinctive uses of rules in a system constituted by the presence of those rules. And instead of considering the uses of linguistic rules in language, I shall begin with the simpler case of the use of the rules of chess.

The rules of chess seem to be used in at least the following five ways:

(1) We formulate and pay explicit attention to the rules when learning or teaching the game.

(2) Once the rules have been learned, there are many of them that we never have occasion to consider explicitly. I doubt if any chess player ever has before his mind the rule that two pieces must not occupy the same square simultaneously; such a possibility, as we say, "never occurs to him." It seems that one effect of acceptance of the rules of the game is to reduce the indefinitely large number of physically possible maneuvers of the pieces to just that set which are characterized as "legal moves" in a given position. Thus no chess player ever takes account of the physical possibility that a piece will move right off the chessboard (indeed this would not count as a "move"); the effect of his having accepted the rules is that this physical possibility is excluded from his calculations. We may say that the rules create a *Spielraum*—an idealized space in which only "legal moves" can occur.

(3) But occasions may occur when the legality of a proposed move becomes problematic. Chess players sometimes doubt whether a king may castle by passing over a square controlled by an enemy piece (partly because occasions for the application of the rule are so rare that they tend to forget it and

partly because the rule seems more "arbitrary" than some of the others). A player uncertain whether he is allowed to perform the maneuver in question may still in some sense "know" the rule. By enunciating the rule explicitly he makes it clear to himself that the move would be illegal.

(4) A similar situation arises when an opponent makes an illegal move. Then the relevant rule is recited to convince the offender that an infringement has in fact occurred.

(5) Explicit reference *to* the rules is needed if a theory *of* the game is to be constituted. For example, if I want to show that the maximum number of queens on the board at any time is eighteen, I shall have to state the rules in order to draw certain inferences.

These uses of the rules of chess can be briefly but not too misleadingly summarized as follows: The rules in their entirety define the game of chess—to play chess is to play in conformity with, and with due recognition of, the authority of those rules. So, explicit formulation of the rules occurs, as we should expect, in learning or teaching the game (case 1) or in move behavior not already sufficiently fixed by the original teaching procedure (case 3) or in challenging actual or alleged infringements of the rule (case 4) or in making preparation for explicit analytic talk *about* the game (case 5). We might add, somewhat paradoxically, that the rules are most effective when no explicit or conscious attention is paid to them, their influence being then shown only in the habits that their acceptance creates and sustains (case 2).

Now let us see how far what has been said about the rules of a game like chess will apply, with suitable changes, to a language. To the rules of chess there correspond now the rules of meaning that define a particular language. And we should expect that there would be occasion for the explicit enunciation of the rules when the language is being learned or taught (case 1) or when the appropriate linguistic behavior is not yet sufficiently determinate (case 3) or when an actual or suspected infringement of the rules occurs (case 4) or in

[73]

inquiries like the present essay in which analytical investigations are made into the theory of language. We must bear
in mind that infringement of the rules now means failure to
talk sense according to the conventions determining the
meaning of expressions in the particular language in question.
Speaking roughly, then, the function of the affirmation of
the rules is to render explicit to ourselves or to others the
meanings of expressions in the language we are using. As in
the parallel case of the game, we have good reason to invoke
the rules only in the cases where there is some indication or
risk that the language is not being used correctly. The distinctive use of the rules of language is to inculcate, reinforce,
and exhibit the meanings of statements in that language.

6

I want to argue now that some of these distinctive functions
of linguistic rules can be facilitated by the use of "dummy
statements" and that necessary statements can be properly
regarded in this light. There is nothing corresponding to
this in the game of chess as it is played at present. As Frege
said, "It is true that the moves of the game are made in accordance with the rules; but no position of the chessmen, and no
move expresses a rule; for it is not at all the job of chessmen to
express anything; they are, rather to be moved in accordance
with rules." [4] Frege goes on to say that *if* positions expressed
rules, there would be danger of conflict between the arbitrary
manipulations of chess positions and the restrictions neces-
sitated by the need to transform positions expressing rules
only into those expressing *inferences* from the rules. But let
us consider how the present game of chess might be modified
by the introduction of what I shall call *"dummy pieces."*

(1) Imagine that a new piece, the "blocker," is introduced,
its powers being defined as follows: "There is only one blocker.

[4] *Translations from the Philosophical Writings of Frege,* Peter Geach
and Max Black, eds. (Oxford, 1952), p. 203.

[74]

At the outset of the game the blocker is placed on a certain square to be agreed upon by the two players; it then stays on that square for the duration of the game. The blocker can neither capture nor be captured." This would be a very inert kind of piece, and we should be strongly inclined to call it a "dummy." The word "dummy" suggests a waxwork man or a lay figure, resembling a living man in appearance, yet incapable of motion or action. More generally, we use the word to refer to a counterfeit object, a mere simulacrum or pretense. Now it is easy to see why the blocker should be so regarded: it may look like a piece (be made of wood like the others and have a distinctive conical shape) yet it neither moves, captures, nor is captured. We might add that it belongs to neither side. And we might compare it to the function of the dummy fourth player in dummy whist. But it would be an overstatement to say that it does *no* work, for it serves exactly the same function as would a certain rule, viz., "There is one square, to be agreed upon by both players at the outset of each game, which may at no time be occupied or traversed by any piece."

It might seem easier to introduce this rule than to add the peculiar dummy piece; yet our imagined "blocker" has at least a *mnemonic* function, for it is easier to stay off an occupied square than to remember an arbitrary agreement about keeping out of a square. The blocker is about as useful as the crosses that builders paint on windowpanes to remind themselves not to crash through the glass.

(2) If the game of chess were ever to be modified in the manner described, nobody would be likely to treat the added chessman as if it were *"really* a piece" of somewhat unusual powers of movement. But now consider still another way in which the game might be modified: this time suppose each player to have a piece, called the "king's companion" subject to the following regulations: "The king's companion *may* be placed on a square adjacent to the king immediately after the king has moved out of check, such placing of the king's

[75]

companion not to count as an extra move. The king's companion *must* be removed immediately before the player makes his next move, such removal not to count as an extra move. The king's companion may neither capture nor be captured."

Once again we have a "dummy piece" and, as in the last example, all that is achieved by the introduction of the new piece *could* be achieved by the addition of a rule suitably framed. The presence on the board of the "king's companion" acts as a restriction upon the freedom of movement of the other pieces on the board, the presence and position of the obstacle to movement varying with the character of the position and the will of the players. And it would be possible to frame a rule imposing the very same restrictions upon the moves at present allowed in ordinary chess. But I think everybody will agree that the "mnemonic value" of the new chessman in this case would be very much greater than in the case of the "blocker." I think it would be impossible *in practice* to observe a rule of the required complexity without the intermediary of the dummy piece. But just because this dummy piece, unlike the simpler "blocker," has several resemblances to "regular pieces," I think there would be correspondingly more inclination to regard it as a "regular" piece with "queer" powers.

(3) Finally, imagine new pieces whose use in the game was still mainly to "block" or to restrict the freedom of movement of other pieces, but now in far more complicated ways. We might imagine each side to have two "obstructors" whose relative positions on the board had to conform to complex specifications (for example, that two obstructors of the same color must always be on the same rank or file), we might suppose that the "obstructors" could force other obstructors temporarily *off* the board, but could not capture regular pieces, and so on. By the time this amount of complexity had been introduced, the practical utility of these "dummy pieces" as surrogates for the rules that *might* have been introduced instead would be very great. And the variety of ways in which

[76]

the new "obstructors" could appear on the board and the dependence of their positions upon the choice of the players would make it very plausible for them to be regarded as regular, though still somewhat "peculiar" pieces. For, after all, marked differences in function can be found in the pieces already in use (as is shown for instance by the privileged position of the king); and the peculiarities in the "moves" of the new pieces might not be regarded as too great to be tolerated in "genuine pieces."

Much of what has been said about the introduction of possible "dummy pieces" could be also said, with minor changes, about "dummy *moves.*" Consider "two-move chess," played exactly like the present game, except that each player makes two consecutive moves in turn. And now suppose when it is White's turn to move he causes a piece to pass to another square and then return back to its original square, so that the position of the pieces on the chessboard is unchanged by his action. I think that a "move" of this kind might properly be regarded as a pretense, or counterfeit, or dummy—and for the very same reasons as led us to apply the label of "dummy" to certain *pieces.* The rules of "two-move chess," as I have imagined them, permit moves the second part of which reverses the effect of the first. Now instead of calling these self-canceling operations "moves," we could define the very same game by agreeing (i) that only maneuvers resulting in a *change* of the position of at least one piece shall count as "moves," but (ii) a player shall have the privilege, when his turn comes, of choosing *not* to move. In other words, so far as the game goes, the effect of these "dummy moves" could be achieved by a mere change in the rules. This is not to say that there may not be practical utility in admitting dummy moves—as there was in admitting dummy pieces —for their introduction may lead to substantial simplification in the rules. Indeed, since a "dummy piece" may be regarded as one that makes only "dummy moves," much of what was said about the utility of such pieces will carry over, with but little modification, to the case of the dummy move.

One final remark about the game of chess as it is now played. Consider the setting up of the pieces at the beginning of the game. It is not usual to call this a move or a series of moves. Yet it involves the manipulation of pieces in ways which are specified by the rules; we could therefore, if we pleased, call it a "move." But we would immediately want to qualify this description by saying it is a "very peculiar kind" of move. It is "very peculiar" because instead of setting up the pieces in their initial configuration we could imagine a new set of rules that would achieve the same end. Suppose the game were to start with an empty chess board, each piece appearing on it only when it first "did some work" either by moving, obstructing, capturing, checking or being checked, and in such ways that just the moves that are *now* legal in the game should be admissible. I say it is conceivable that a set of rules should accomplish this end without there being any initial configuration, but of course the practical difficulties would be staggering. It seems likely that the game would become so difficult that no person of average intellectual powers would ever be able to play it correctly. The function of the "dummy move" that consists in placing all the pieces on their initial squares is to render possible a relative simplicity of the rules. I hope this final example will show very clearly the practical utility of what might otherwise seem the artificial expedient of introducing "dummy moves" and "dummy pieces" into a game.

7

Let us now see how the notions outlined in the last two sections can help us to understand the role of necessary statements. I have said that "the distinctive use of the rules of language is to inculcate, reinforce, and exhibit the meanings of statements in that language." Consider, for instance, the rule "Wherever 'father' occurs 'parent' may be substituted." This can be looked upon as a succinct way of allowing certain moves in the "game" of inference, for example, from the state-

[78]

ment "Tom is a father" to "Tom is a parent." [5] In this form the rule is clearly *about* permissible transitions from one statement to another and is not itself a statement, as rules of chess are about the moves of pieces and are not themselves pieces. But if we take the corresponding necessary statement "A father is a parent," we have something that might well be called a "dummy" statement. Counting it as a "statement" that may be used as a *premise* allows the rules of inferential deductive transformation to take a simpler form. Inasmuch as the necessary statement uses ordinary words combined in a familiar construction, we may well be inclined to accord it all the dignities that go with the title of "statement." But as we reflect that the rules of our language *dictate* the form of the necessary statement, so that *we* can convey no information by using it, we may perhaps feel inclined to qualify our description and to add "but it is a very peculiar kind of statement." I think necessary statements can be regarded as a "very peculiar kind of statement"—as dummy assertions whose chief function is to simplify the rules of inference.

That such simplification is produced by the use of the trivial necessary statement "A father is a parent" is not at all obvious. The full advantages of the quasi-statement form for necessary statements are most clearly seen when we calculate with necessary statements. Meanwhile, the kind of simplification we have in mind can be illustrated by the following simple example. Let us regard any necessary statement having the form "p or not-p" as a "dummy" assertion in the sense already explained. Suppose we already have a rule for the validity of the dilemma, that is, for an argument of the form

(a) a or b
If a then c
If b then d
∴ c or d.

[5] The actual rules connecting the uses of "parent" and "father" are quite complicated. We are not entitled to pass from "I saw the father of Mary" to "I saw the parent of Mary," for instance. But such additional complexity of detail will not hurt the argument.

Now let us suppose we have to determine the validity of an argument

(β) If a then c
If not-a then d
$\therefore$ c or d.

As presented, argument (β) does not have the logical form of (a) and the rule certifying the validity of the latter does not yet certify the validity of the former. Suppose, however, we add to (β) the dummy premise "a or not-a," thus obtaining

(a') a or not-a
If a then c
If not-a then d
$\therefore$ c or d.

Now (a') does have the same form as (a) and one and the same rule certifies both. We no longer need to find a separate rule for (β) and have reduced the number of types of arguments that need to be treated as separate or exceptional cases.

8

In the last section I treated assertions as if they corresponded to pieces and transitions from one assertion to another as if they corresponded to moves in the "game of inference." Another way of looking at the matter might be to regard an assertion itself as a move in the "game of using language." In that case certain grammatically well-formed statements might, from yet another standpoint, have to be regarded as dummy assertions. We have already considered a kind of "move" (in a game) that left the position unchanged, and was therefore called a "dummy" or quasi-move. In order to treat necessary statements as "dummy" assertions, it will be necessary to show how they can be regarded as making no difference to the "game" of assertion.

I shall lead up to this by considering a number of instances, rather like this one of the empty move, of what I shall call "self-canceling operations."

(1) Suppose we have a simple code for instructing a person to reach an indicated destination, the manner in which he reaches the end point being unimportant. Let the instruction "N5E2S1" mean that he is to proceed to a point, in whichever way he chooses, that *can* be reached by first going five miles north, then two miles east, and finally one mile south. Every instruction, accordingly, begins with the indication of a compass point, is followed by a number, continues alternately with compass points and numbers, and ends with a number. (The foregoing might be regarded as a concise way of specifying the syntax of the code.) With this understanding what are we to say of such an instruction as "N5W5S5E5"? In order to obey this, the receiver must go to a point which *could* be reached by going first five miles north, then five miles west, then five miles south, and finally five miles east—in other words, he is asked to "go" to his starting point. Shall we call this an "instruction" after all? Since the receiver can "conform" by doing nothing at all, the effect of understanding and "performing" this instruction, if we are to call it that, is the same as that of not having received an instruction at all. So we might be inclined to say it "really" is *no* instruction. But if we do so we shall have to reformulate the syntactical rules of the code in a very complex fashion, for the description of the combinations of letters and numbers that would not be admissible, though it could be given, would be very complicated. It is simpler in practice to allow a *redundancy* in the code—that is, to permit sequences such as "N5W5S5E5" to *count as* "instructions" and to be transmitted. For the receiver to understand this partially redundant language in which instructions are transmitted, it is clear that he must understand that the instruction "N5W5S5E5" makes no demands upon him. It is a dummy "instruction"—or, as we might prefer to say, a "limiting case" of an instruction.

[81]

(2) At a certain restaurant the clients order dinner by crossing out those items on the menu that they do not wish to have served. One evening it happens that a customer perversely chooses to cross out *all* the items of the menu; shall we say he has or has not "ordered" a meal? Clearly, this is a question of how we shall choose to *describe* what actually happened. The chef would probably say no order had been given, while a mathematician's predilection would be for saying that a "null order" or a "limiting order" had been given. The imaginary situation here described may be considered as involving a primitive "language" where "statements" are produced by striking lines through items on the list of articles available. The question whether an act of striking out *all* the items shall count as expressing a "statement" in this notation is therefore parallel to the question we were just discussing as to whether an utterance like "N5W5S5E5," which calls for no action, should count as an "instruction." It is like asking whether the words "Do anything you like" shall count as a command. We could choose to frame the regulations for giving dinner orders in such a way that the striking out of all the items was taken to be a *breach* of the regulations. Or, instead, we could also allow *all* the items to be struck out, though we would not then expect that such an order could be obeyed in the way that other orders are obeyed. (Of course the null order could here be construed as a command *not* to bring anything—but this is not an order for a dinner.)

(3) The last example recalls the mathematician's use of an expression like "point at infinity" or his custom of describing a straight line, say, as a circle "of infinite radius." When we say "parallel lines meet at a point at infinity" it would have been equally correct, though less convenient, to say "parallel lines do not meet at all." To transform one of these statements into the other is to change the meaning of the term "point" (and so to change the language of which that word is part). The peculiar status of the points "at which parallel

lines meet" is shown by the added words in the phrase "point at infinity." Such modes of expression are not introduced willfully into mathematics, merely to mystify the layman. Mathematical fictions have a use, but they must be recognized for what they are, if senseless questions are not to be generated.

One consideration that leads a mathematician to talk about "points at infinity" can be shown by the following example. Imagine in Figure 1 that the line b revolves anticlockwise

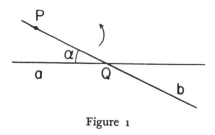

Figure 1

about the point P. As it does so, the angle between the lines a and b progressively diminishes, and the point of intersection, Q, moves progressively toward the right. By making the angle α sufficiently small, we can send Q as far as we like toward the right; and α can be made as small as we like. The *limiting position* is that in which the two lines have become parallel and the angle of inclination, α, has become zero. Now it is very tempting to add, as if it were a mathematical discovery,

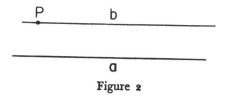

Figure 2

"and the point Q is then located infinitely far to the right." This addendum is, of course, nonsensical if "point" continues to be used in the old sense in which lines must *not* be parallel if they are to intersect in a point. The parallel lines simply do *not* meet and hence there is no point anywhere at which

[83]

they meet. But it is in just such a situation that the mathematician often finds it useful to *extend* his terminology in such a way as to include the limiting case. Nothing prevents him from saying "The lines *do* meet—at a point at infinity"; for "meeting at a point at infinity" now means what *"not* meeting" meant before.

Similar considerations apply to the renaming of a straight line as a "circle of infinite radius." We think now of a series of circles as shown in Figure 3, of constantly diminishing curva-

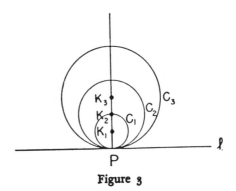

Figure 3

ture, and all touching a given line l at the same point P. As we take larger and larger circles, C_1, C_2, C_3, . . . , C_n, . . . , the curvature of the circles diminishes without limit toward zero—and the centers of the circles, K_1, K_2, K_3, . . . K_n . . . , are located farther and farther from P. Sometimes the mathematician will say that the line l, which is the geometrical limit to which the circles converge, *is* a circle of "infinite radius" and "zero curvature." This choice of terminology allows him to speak of what were previously called "circles" and what were previously called "straight lines" in a *single* theory. Such unification is one of the main results achieved by the introduction of mathematical fictions.

When the limits of series (whether of geometrical figures or other mathematical entities) are described by applying to them the language previously reserved for *members* of the series, certain anomalies result. (For example the analytic

[84]

equation of a straight line is of the first degree, while that of a circle is of the second degree.)

In general, the limit of a series of things all having a complex defining characteristic K, will *not* always have the property K: the limit of a series of intervals may be a *point*, the limit of series of rational numbers an irrational number, and so on. If the language is now so extended that the same term "K" is used henceforth to apply also to the *limit*, the difference between it and the terms of the series will reappear as an apparent difference in "properties." The limit will be regarded as a "peculiar kind of K"—or as "a K with peculiar properties." When the "properties" of the limit appear simpler than those of K's in general, it is sometimes called a "*degenerate* case." Thus we can regard a straight line as a degenerate case of a circle, or, again, zero can be regarded as a degenerate case of an integer. ("Degenerate" has the force of "abnormal," with an additional suggestion of regression to the relatively undifferentiated or more primitive. Thus zero follows special or abnormal rules for computation; again many arithmetical operations performed upon zero—doubling, squaring, and the like—merely lead back to zero again.)

9

Some necessary statements can be regarded as limiting or degenerate cases of *contingent* statements. Consider, for instance, the four statements:

(*a*) Tom is home and Dick is home.
(*b*) Dick is home.
(*c*) Tom is home or Dick is home.
(*d*) Tom is home or Tom is not home.

Of these, (*a*) entails but is not entailed by (*b*); (*b*) entails but is not entailed by (*c*); and (*c*) entails but is not entailed by (*d*). That is to say, it is logically impossible for (*a*) to be true but (*b*) false, though not vice versa; and similarly for the other two pairs. This set of relationships is sometimes de-

[85]

scribed by saying (*a*) is "logically stronger" than (*b*), (*b*) than
(*c*), and (*c*) than (*d*); or, again, by asserting that each statement "says more" than the one next to it in the series. These
modes of expression make it natural to say that (*d*) is the
"logically weakest" of the four, and "says less" than the other
three. Indeed, since there is no further statement that is
entailed by (*d*) but does not itself entail (*d*), it is very natural
to take the further step of asserting that (*d*) "says nothing at
all." The same line of thought leads us to say that all statements of minimum strength "say the same," that is, nothing
at all. As Wittgenstein puts it, "A tautology follows from all
propositions: it says nothing," [6] and again, "All propositions
of logic say the same thing. That is, nothing." [7]

This way of regarding necessary statements clearly treats
them as limiting or degenerate cases of statements proper
(that is, contingent statements). Among the reasons that lead
us to treat the sentence "Tom is at home or not at home" as
expressive of a "statement" are (i) that the sentence is well
formed and is clearly not "nonsense" in the pejorative sense
of that term, (ii) it has cognitive uses, (iii) it can be inserted
into a series of sentences expressing statements arranged
according to "strength" or "logical priority." Such considerations incline us to say that necessary statements are statements in good standing. But there are balancing considerations that incline us to regard them rather as *limiting* cases
of statements proper. For, seeing that necessary statements
cannot fail to be true, we feel inclined to say they do not
convey differential information and in this way resemble
the limiting or empty commands that make *no* demands upon
their recipients. From this point of view, the presence in our
language of necessary statements is due to the benign redundancy of our notation.

A necessary statement is naturally regarded as "degenerate,"
inasmuch as its logical relationships manifest abnormal simplicity: every proposition entails a tautology—and all tautologies entail one another. The seeming paradox in saying

[6] *Tractatus*, 5.142.   [7] *Ibid.*, 5.43.

that all tautologies say the same, that is nothing, is another characteristic sign of a degenerate case. If we use the word "say" as a way of indicating the *information* conveyed by statements, we should say not "tautologies say nothing" but, rather, "it is absurd to ask whether tautologies say anything." The queerness of saying all tautologies have the same subject matter arises from our determination to overlook the differences between necessary statements and contingent statements by calling all of them "statements."

Yet I do not think the view of necessary statements as "tautologies," illuminating as it is, will cover all cases of what we would normally wish to call necessary statements. Of course, if we use "tautology" as a mere synonym for "necessary statement," as some writers do, it will necessarily follow that all necessary statements are tautologies; but, by the same token, this will itself then be an unilluminating tautology of the form "*A* is *A*." It seems wiser to reserve the term "tautology" for a narrower usage, as referring to statements whose form is such that we can *prove* from definitions of the terms occurring that they are "self-canceling."

Wittgenstein, who introduced the term "tautology" and is to that extent responsible for the term's wide currency, was thinking in the first instance of the necessary statements of the propositional calculus. There, the various logical operations ("∨," "∼," and the others) are defined by means of truth tables, so that the demonstration that a particular formula is a tautology requires the calculation, on the basis of these given definitions, of the truth value of the whole formula. When this is done and the result is found to be always "truth," it is intuitively plausible to say that the various logical operations cancel one another and therefore "say nothing." But this method of calculating truth values is not generally available, even in the artificially simplified calculi of mathematical logic. When the only method for showing a formula in the functional calculus is to derive it from accepted axioms, it becomes less illuminating to regard the theorems or the formulae as "empty tautologies."

[87]

The more general mode of description is in terms of what I have called "dummy assertions." For tautologies can be regarded as limiting cases or degenerate cases of statements, can be counted as statements in order to simplify the rules of inference. But not all necessary statements can profitably be regarded as tautologies, while they *can* all be regarded as dummy assertions.

10

I have now said all that I usefully can, at this stage, about the distinctive ways in which necessary statements are *used*. I have regarded them, mainly, as *surrogates* for rules, formulae resembling (and yet, also, not resembling) contingent statements, that serve as supplements for the purpose of simplifying the patterns of valid inference. And now we shall do well, I think, to take up the question of how, in this view, the assertion of necessary statements can be justified.

The circumstances in which I shall conceive the demand for a direct justification to have arisen are as follows. One person, A, has affirmed some necessary statement, say "Nobody can be in two places at the same time" and his hearer, B, is *genuinely* in doubt about its truth and is seriously asking that reasons be supplied. (By stipulating that the doubt be "genuine" I mean to exclude cases when a philosophical doubt is raised, that is, when the protagonist is concerned with how *any* necessary statements could be defended, not with the defense of the particular necessary statement under consideration. Compare the difference between somebody who wants a reason for believing that he will see a bear in the woods and the skeptic who wants reasons for believing *anything* about what is not observed at the time of utterance.) The specification I have given requires that B, the doubter, shall understand the necessary statement that A has made, according to the normal English meaning that is customarily attached to the words that A has used. I am excluding a case when B fails to understand what A has said; the case in which

[88]

A is using words in some way other than that of the standard English usage is discussed later.

Granted that B understands A's statement, the view I have been defending requires A to direct B's attention to the rule (of the English language) to which reference is made in the assertive content of the necessary statement in question. In other words, A must show B, if a direct justification of the necessary statement is to be provided, that there *is* a rule in English providing that a statement of the form "X is now at Y and Z," when Y and Z are different places and X is a person, shall have *no use*.

Now there are two ways in which this could be shown. The first mode of direct justification makes the evidence for the truth of the necessary statement consist in certain complex facts about the behavior of typical members of those who would be regarded as speaking correct English. In some cases the evidence will be hard to get and when found may point in opposite directions; if this is so, the alleged necessary statement really will be problematic. But I think this is not so in the case in question. I think we know that persons who speak standard English would recognize that it was wrong to say "X is at Y and also at the same time at the other place Z"; and that, however puzzling it may seem to us in our philosophical moments, we have the complex evidence needed; we do in fact know it. This way of gathering evidence about the relevant rule might be called external: it might conceivably be followed by somebody not himself a member of the English speech community, just as the character of the rules of chess might be empirically determined from the behavior of chess players by somebody who could not himself play chess.

But the questioner B, by hypothesis, does know how to speak English and is therefore more intimately acquainted with the relevant rules than any external observer could be who himself had no command of the language. So A might most effectively ask B himself to reflect upon how *he* would use the phrase "X is at place Y and also at place Z." Such "reflection" might better be described as a rehearsal of usage. We ask B to describe the circumstances in which he, speaking undistorted English just as we do, would regard it as correct to apply the sentence. This might be called a search for internal justification. This seems to me the more important kind of justification and in some sense more primary.

The outcome of this process of reflection might take one of the following forms: (i) B, after thinking of all kinds of situations, decides it would never be correct to call any of them cases of "X being at place Y and also at place Z at one and the same time." He has then recognized that the relevant rule is in force and the necessary statement has received "direct" justification.

(ii) B describes some situations which he thinks it would be correct to describe in the manner indicated. The only question between A and B would then be whether B has changed or distorted standard English usage. But this is a trivial question for all except linguists. B is entitled, within reasonable limits of prudence and courtesy, to speak as he pleases; by indicating the situations when he would apply the formula in question he has made so far plain the rules governing *his* discourse.

(iii) B is unable to describe any situations in which he would apply the words in question but obstinately reiterates that all the same "a man *can* be in two places at once." This is now sheer dogmatism on his part; we cannot prevent him from uttering those words—nor would we be interested in physical coercion, anyhow—but we must say that he has given no sense to his utterance.

(iv) B recognizes the rule, viz., that "X is both at Y and at Z at the same time" shall not be used, but asks *why* the rule should be obeyed. Now it is no longer clear what he is re-

[90]

quiring or what will satisfy him. We might, of course, talk about the practical benefits of speaking the same language as others, but it may be presumed that this is not what he wishes to hear. There is no other sense of "justification" that he has made clear to us.

The details of the discussion above could be exactly paralleled by considering what could reasonably be done to satisfy a doubt that a given statement really did represent a rule of some game. The peculiarity of the case in which somebody wants a necessary statement (and not the rule of some conventional pastime) to be justified is that the question does not arise except for somebody who already speaks the language, that is, is already bound by and recognizes the relevant rules. And this is the source of the feeling we have that what is said in a necessary statement "could not be otherwise." To give anybody a direct justification of an unequivocally necessary statement is simply to put him in a position to recognize more clearly and more forcefully the rules to which in some sense he is already committed. But I am not saying that the necessity of the necessary statement has anything to do, logically speaking, with the feelings of those who use it. Its necessity, according to my argument, consists in its relation to an associated rule of language. And this account, right or wrong, does not offer any psychological criterion of necessity.

11

We can now see more clearly what the function of "intuition" and the *Gedankenexperiment* really are in establishing necessary statements. Let us consider the simplest possible case, since this will show what is involved just as clearly as a more complicated instance. It is not inconceivable for somebody to have been using the words "violet" and "lavender" to refer to the same shades of color, without ever having reflected upon the connections between the meanings of these words. Upon being asked for the first time whether violet and lav-

[91]

ender are the same he "imagines" something violet and something "lavender" and, as he says, "sees" for the first time that both are the same color.

Now this *Gedankenexperiment* can be even more effectively performed upon actual objects than upon images. Let us suppose, therefore, that our subject has been provided with a large number of uniformly tinted pieces of cardboard. First he hunts through the pile until he finds a piece, say K, which he recognizes as "violet." Next, he goes through the pile again until he finds a piece, say L, that he recognizes as "lavender." The crucial step, for our purpose, is that in which by "looking" at K and L he "sees" violet and lavender are "the same." If K and L, the specimens he actually chose, are the same color, this is an empirical fact, just as much so as is the fact, say, that they are both of the same temperature. In order to derive the necessary statement, we need as premises statements about the *colors*, not merely about the pieces of cardboard that have been inspected. The premises might be:

(i) This color is violet
(ii) This same color is lavender

from which, of course, it does follow that lavender and violet are the same. But the assertive content of (i) is not a fact about anything except linguistic usage. On my view the person who affirms (i) and (ii) is simply saying—so far as the assertive content of (i) and (ii) goes—" 'violet' and 'lavender' are both used correctly in this kind of situation." The effect of the color cards is to remind the speaker forcefully that he does use "violet" and "lavender" interchangeably. This is what he "sees" and not some alleged fact concerning the identity of a color with itself. There *is* no fact or truth to the effect that a color is identical with itself, and so there is nothing of this sort for even the most penetrating examiner to "see."

Now the assertion that two words are synonyms cannot be conclusively verified by a single instance of identity of application. The man who looks at the two colored pieces of cardboard must assume that he has representative instances before him, and it is conceivable that he might make a mistake about this. There might be other specimens that he would call violet and refuse to call lavender, or others that he would call lavender and refuse to call violet. Of course the affirmation of the necessary statement "Violet is lavender" itself renders it unlikely that this will occur; the affirmation of a problematic necessary statement has a tendency to make that statement true.

I will agree that the "flash of insight" that sometimes crowns the performance of a *Gedankenexperiment* may have considerable heuristic value; it may indeed be an excellent index of the truth of the necessary statement concerned (though it may also be deceptive, as countless instances attest). My central point is that the occurrence of such flashes of insight is not logically relevant to the truth of the necessary statement, being neither necessary nor sufficient for the truth of that necessary statement. If a man *does* follow the rule that "K" and "L" are interchangeable, the statement "K is L" when pronounced by him *is* necessary, whether or not he has the power to practice what has been sometimes called "intuitive induction." Conversely, if he has a flash of vision in which he "sees" that "K and L are the same," but in his practice does *not* use the two terms as synonyms, then the statement "K is L" is *not* a necessary truth when he utters it, no matter how much he protests that he has intuitive certainty to the contrary.

12

I hope the account I have given has managed to avoid some of the weaknesses of "conventionalism." The essential point of difference is that the view here presented does not regard the necessary statements themselves as "arbitrary." On the contrary, for the man who has already accepted the relevant linguistic rule (and only such a man can entertain the necessary statement) the truth of the necessary statement is already determined and not within the speaker's power to change. That many instances arise in which the associated rule is not unambiguously in force, I must certainly agree; and in such cases it is indeed for the speaker to choose the rules by which, if he so wishes, he will henceforward be governed. But these are not the cases I have regarded as typical for the certification of necessary statements. In proportion as the rules are not yet firmly established in the language there can, indeed, be no question of the "truth" of the corresponding necessary statements—nor, for that matter, will there be any necessary statements in any strict sense of "necessary."

To those who still desire a "ground" or "reason" for the linguistic rules themselves, I can offer no other than pragmatic considerations of convenience or usefulness. And if anybody objects that this leaves necessary statements without any justification at all "in the last analysis," I shall have to retort that they have been granted all the justification that can be reasonably demanded.

VI

The Analysis of Rules

THE WORD "rule" is used a good deal in contemporary philosophical discussion, but I cannot find any satisfactory examination of its meaning. Anybody who undertakes this task will have to decide a number of perplexing questions, some of which are discussed below. I shall attempt to deal with only a few of the more interesting features of the logical grammar of "rule" and its cognates.

1. RULES ARE STATED

If the word "rule" is to have any uses at all, it would seem necessary that it should have some *demonstrative* ones. It would seem there must be cases where, after suitable preparation, we can say *"That* is a rule." A familiar way of eliciting such a use is for somebody to ask to be given an "example" of a rule. (If the demand is not to be mysterious, we can imagine that the speaker explains his purpose as that of testing some theory about the analysis of the meaning of "rule.")

Should somebody ask me for an example of a rule, I might reply by saying "A pawn reaching the eighth rank must be exchanged for a piece." I have stated a rule—and, of course, in words. Would the case have been different if I had been asked to give an example of something other than a rule? In that case also, would I not have needed to use words in answering? Does the expression "stated in words" mean anything more than "referred to by means of words"?

Let us try to answer by thinking for a moment about admirals instead of rules. It would sound odd to be asked to "give an example of an admiral," but no doubt the demand would be interpreted to be the same as a demand to "name" an admiral or to "pick out" an admiral. This request could

[95]

be satisfied by saying "Nelson"—or, if memory failed, by saying "The man who defeated the French at Trafalgar." This time, as in the case of giving an example of a rule, words are used for the identification of an instance. The answer "Nelson" supplies a man's *name;* the expression "The man who defeated the French at Trafalgar," a man's *description.* Names and descriptions may be called *designations;* they are expressions suitable for use in *referring* to the things named or described. The request to give an example of an admiral was met by referring to Nelson. There seems to be no other way of "picking out" or identifying an admiral—if we exclude nonverbal means, such as pointing or showing a photograph —than by using a suitable designation.

Much the same can be said for a great variety of objects. I meet the request to "pick out" or "give an example" of a hurricane, or a champion Labrador, or an operatic aria, by supplying a suitable designation. And there is no other verbal way of meeting these requests.

Now I *can* satisfy the demand to give an example of a rule in the same way, e.g., by saying "The Golden Rule" or "The rule of eleven in bridge." For in these latter cases I do use designations to refer to the rules in question. But when I answered the request for an example of a rule by saying "A pawn reaching the eighth rank must be exchanged for a piece," I was not referring to a rule; I was neither naming the rule nor describing it.

The sentence beginning with the words "A pawn" is clearly not a name in the sense in which "Nelson" is a name. If I know somebody's name is Nelson, that piece of information tells me nothing more about him: I have yet to know whether he is alive or dead, an Englishman or a Frenchman. But when someone is told that a certain rule is "A pawn reaching the eighth rank must be exchanged for a piece" he knows what the rule is, not merely what its name is. He has been provided with the rule itself, not a pointer that will lead to it; and that is why he is now able to cite that rule. In stating a rule the speaker does not *name* it.

[96]

It is not quite so obvious that the words "A pawn reaching the eighth rank must be exchanged for a piece" are not a *description* of the rule. A description (in Russell's sense) is a set of words purporting to identify a single thing. Anybody understanding a given description knows how to identify the thing answering to that description; but he does not yet know whether there is any such thing. The fact that a speaker uses the expression "the man who defeated the French at Trafalgar" cannot guarantee that there was such a man. Similarly in the case of any description offered as satisfying the request to give an example of an *X*, where *X* is anything you please. It always makes sense to ask whether a unique thing answers to the description supplied. Hence, also, it makes sense to deny that anything answers to the description.

If I "give an example of a rule" by saying "Leibniz' rule of permutations," it certainly makes sense for a bystander to object "I don't believe there is any such rule." But there I was using what is admitted to be a designation of a rule. Would a similar objection make sense if I had said "A pawn reaching the eighth rank must be exchanged for a piece"? Could somebody properly say "I don't believe there is any such rule"?

Perhaps. The objector might be doubting whether the rule I had stated belonged to the official rules of chess, as that game is now played. He would then be raising a question of fact, which could be settled by appeal to an official book of rules. Here there seems to be a close parallel to a case in which an objection to a description of an admiral ("I don't believe there was any such man") is settled by investigation of historical facts.

But there are cases where the objection would be absurd. Suppose I had given an example of a rule by saying "A king can move two squares at a time after both queens have been captured." This rule is not one of "the official rules of chess," and is not followed by chess players, yet there can be no question of my having made a mistake. Although I know that there is no such rule of chess, and my hearer knows it, I

[97]

have satisfied the original request (upon one interpretation of that request). The rule is one that I invented, and although it be the case that nobody ever has or ever will play according to that rule, it is a rule for all that. It would be absurd for somebody to murmur "I wonder whether there is any such rule," for my answer supplied the rule. And it would be just as absurd for somebody to wonder whether my answer stated the rule correctly. My answer determines what the rule is and leaves no room for any independent investigation about the nature of the rule. The rule is necessarily what I say it is.

Consider an analogous case. On being asked for an example of a question, I reply by stating one in the words "Can termites sleep?" My reply supplies a question, whose nature is completely determined by that reply. No provision is made for an independent investigation into the nature of that question, and it is logically impossible that I should have made a mistake about it. (Of course, I could have said words I did not intend, by some slip of the tongue, but that is another story. So also when, on being asked to choose a color, I point to a place on a color chart. Here, too, there can be no question of a mistake, or of any further investigation to determine whether there really is a corresponding color.) A question is stated, not described, by an interrogative sentence of a suitable form; a rule is stated, not described, by a suitable set of words.

There remains to be considered the case in which (as I agreed above) a rule can be stated correctly or incorrectly. If I am asked for a rule of chess, I am not free to invent a rule; and so it might seem plausible to say that here we must treat the verbal expression of the rule as a description of it. But the following considerations, if I am not mistaken, are enough to refute this suggestion.

That Nelson defeated the French at Trafalgar is a contingent fact; it is logically possible that he might have lost the battle, though in fact he did not. Hence there is no contradiction in saying: The man designated by the expression "the man who defeated the French at Trafalgar" *might not* have defeated the French at Trafalgar. Let us call this true

[98]

statement, A. A statement paralleling A in the case of the rule of chess we have used as an example would be the following: The rule expressed in the words "A pawn reaching the eighth rank must be exchanged for a piece" might not have been the rule that a pawn reaching the eighth rank must be exchanged for a piece. Let us call this statement, B. The only way in which we could make sense of B would be to suppose that it said that the meanings of the English words used in stating the rule might have been different. But A had no reference to the contingent meaning of English words; it did not mean that the words "the man who defeated the French at Trafalgar" might have had some other meaning (if the English language had been other than it is); the meaning was, rather, that with the present meaning of the description, it is simply a matter of historical fact that Nelson (i.e., the man designated by the description in question) did indeed defeat the French at Trafalgar. To this no analogue can be found in B. It is absurd to suppose that the rule stated in the words "A pawn on reaching the eighth rank must be exchanged for a piece" might have been another rule.

But does not this argument prove too much? Consider the expression, "the first prime number after 20." This would commonly be counted as a description of a number (the number 23). Yet the statement "The number designated by the expression 'the first prime number after 20' might not have been the first prime number after 20" is clearly absurd. And the absurdity arises because all statements of "properties" of numbers are necessary statements. So all we have proved, it might be said, is that a rule, like a number, can be given a "necessary description," that is to say a description by means of an internal property.

By this time, the dispute shows signs of beginning to degenerate into trivial ones about words (e.g., should a "necessary description" be called a description; should we say that numbers can be "described" in the same sense as admirals can be?). Yet it is worth pointing out one final difference between the expression for a rule and the expression "the first prime

[99]

number after 20." As the latter is used in mathematics, it does not count as a definition of 23, though it does follow from the definition of that number (as the number equal to twice 10 plus 3) in conjunction with the principles of arithmetic. On the other hand, the expression used in stating a rule does not follow from a definition of a rule—it *is* the definition of the rule in question. Thus a simple analogue in arithmetic of the expression for a rule is the expression "The number that is greater than 3 by 1." This can hardly be called a description of 4, since it defines the number. And similarly for the rule.

2. RULE FORMULATIONS

There seems to be a particularly intimate connection between a rule and the set of words by which the rule is stated. The relation between the rule and its statement in words is not something external and contingent, as in the case of the relation between anything and its verbal designation: the rule is, in some way, constituted by its formulation. The same can be said, however, about a verdict, a promise, a command, a question, and many other things. Each of these can be stated in words, and the statement does not provide a description of the verdict, promise, command, or question. To be told that a man promised to give his money to the poor is not to be given a description of his promise but rather to be told *what* the promise is, and the same can be said about a rule.

It does not follow, however, that a promise *must* be formulated in words. We can and do talk about implied promises and about promises that nobody has ever made or even thought about. So it is prima facie not absurd to inquire into the possibility of implicit rules (rules that nobody has formulated) —or rules that perhaps never will be stated. Whether it makes sense to talk of an implicit rule is a question which I am anxious to answer in the course of this investigation.

Let us call a set of words used in stating a rule a *formulation* of that rule. Thus one formulation of the rule about

[100]

promoting pawns to which I have already referred several times is the sentence, "A pawn on reaching the eighth rank must be exchanged for a piece."

A single rule can have many different formulations. We can say that the rule in question is the rule "Pawns shall be promoted on reaching the end of the chessboard" or the rule "Pawns must be replaced by pieces whenever a further move would carry them off the chessboard" or the rule "Pawns reaching the last rank are replaced by pieces"; and these formulations are all different, though several words recur in more than one of them. Again, each of these formulations could be translated into German, or any other language containing names for chess pieces and their moves. In this way we could obtain many more equivalent formulations, still more obviously differing from any one of the English formulations, and yet all of them, still, formulating the same rule.

It follows from this that it would be a mistake to identify the rule about the promotion of pawns with any one of its formulations. For there is the one rule, but indefinitely many formulations of it. Again, we can ask of any particular formulation, as of any set of words, whether it contains five words or more, whether it consists of English words or words in some other language, whether it is a sentence or part of a sentence, and so on. But all these questions, which make sense when asked of a verbal expression, are nonsensical when applied to a rule. It is nonsense to ask how many words the Golden Rule contains—or whether the rule is an English, rather than a French, rule.

On the other hand, it does make sense, as we have seen, to speak of stating a rule in a sentence. And it also makes sense to speak of adopting a rule, following it, breaking it, and so on. And all these ways of speaking become nonsensical when applied to sentences. It is absurd to speak of stating a sentence in a sentence; and just as absurd to speak of adopting, following, or breaking a sentence.

Yet now that I have emphasized the distinction between a rule and any formulation of that rule, I must pay my respects to the versatility of language by admitting that talk about a "rule" is sometimes about what I have called the "formulation" (the set of words used in expressing the rule). Thus if a man were to ask how many words occurred in Occam's Rule (an intelligible question, though an eccentric one), he would probably be supposed to be asking a question about the Latin formula, "Entia non sunt multplicanda praeter necessitatem." I shall, however, never intentionally use "rule" in this way.

We saw that a number of formulations can state the same rule: they may be called *equivalent* formulations. Some logicians would be tempted at this point to say that a rule can be defined as a class of equivalent rule-formulations—with the expectation that what is to count as a "rule-formulation" or a case of "equivalence" between rule-formulations shall be independently stated (and without reference to the "problematic notion" of a rule). This might be supposed to have the advantage of bringing the notion of a rule "down to earth" by directing attention to the satisfyingly tangible notion of a class of rule-formulations.

Tempting or not, the attempt is mistaken. For the tests used in distinguishing rules from rule-formulations above will also serve to show that the logical grammer of "rule" is different in important respects from the logical grammar of "class of rule-formulations." It is, for example, absurd to speak of breaking a class of rule-formulations, though very far from absurd to speak of breaking a rule. Those who might wish to define a rule as a class of rule-formulations might explain that they were "reconstructing" the notion of rule by attaching a a new meaning to such expressions as "breaking a rule," "adopting a rule," and so on. But this undertaking of finding new meanings for common words, whatever its merits, is not the one in which we are at present engaged.

3. IS A RULE A MEANING?

A more plausible suggestion is that a rule is what each of its formulations *means*. On this view, the relation between a rule and any of its formulations is like that between a proposition and any of the sentences or "that"-clauses that "express" the proposition.

In defense of this suggestion it might be urged that if a man knows what a given formulation of a rule means, he necessarily knows what the rule is; and, furthermore, that there is no way of coming to know what a certain rule is except by understanding one of its formulations. If this should be what is meant by saying that a rule is the meaning of a certain form of words (a formulation of that rule), there is no occasion to disagree. It is true and important that a rule can be given only via a formulation of the rule; and that there is no independent way of becoming acquainted with the rule. (Of course, I might be able to infer a rule of chess by observing the behavior of chess players, but I would not know *what* the rule was until I had a formulation of it. Contrast this with the case in which I could get to know what a color was without knowing its name or having any other designation of it.)

On the other hand, this characterization of a rule as the meaning of a certain set of words (a formulation of a rule) is not illuminating. Anybody who is puzzled about "the nature of a rule" will not be helped by being presented with a specimen set of words, and told, "You know what those words mean—well, the rule in question is just that meaning."

For, in the first place, this sounds as if there were two things that I could inspect—the set of words, and also the meaning of that set of words—and as if I had only to attend to the second of these, the meaning, in order to see what the rule is. But the words "attend to the meaning" provide me with no instructions that I can follow. If I have been given the form of words ("Pawns are exchanged for pieces on reaching the last rank") and understand those words, but am still puzzled as to what kind of thing the rule formulated by those words may be, the suggestion that the rule *is* the meaning will not help me.

And, in any case, the suggestion that the rule *is* the meaning will certainly not do if interpreted literally. For it would

[103]

seem to imply that, if a rule R is formulated by the set of words W, the expression "the rule formulated by W" means exactly the same as the expression "the meaning of W," so that the one expression can always be substituted for the other without change of sense. Sometimes, indeed, this seems to be the case. For, "The rule formulated by W_1 is the same as the rule formulated by W_2" appears to mean the same as "The meaning of W_1 is the same as the meaning of W_2." On the other hand, it makes sense to say "I propose to adopt the rule formulated by W," yet it is nonsense to say "I propose to adopt the meaning of W." And similarly it makes sense to say "I always follow the rule you have just stated" but it is nonsense to say "I always follow the meaning you have just stated." In short, the expressions "rule formulated by W" and "meaning of W" have different logical grammars, though there are some similarities between those grammars.

Anybody who favored the suggestion that a rule could be identified with the meaning of certain kinds of verbal expressions might reply that he did not intend his suggestion to be taken so literally. "I did not mean to suggest," we can imagine him saying, "that the meaning of a set of words is something separable from the words that express it. Nor did I mean that whenever you speak of a rule you could equally well speak of the meaning of certain words. In drawing your attention to the meaning of the rule-formulation I intended merely to remind you that such formulations have *uses*. And I wish to say that if you are puzzled as to what a rule is, consider how rule-formulations are used. In reminding yourself of those uses, you will be finding the only sensible answer to your original problem. For in discovering how rule-formulations are used you will be discovering (or rather reminding yourself) what a rule is."

I have no quarrel with this advice and shall try to follow it. But I believe there are some special difficulties in following it that do not arise in similar but simpler cases.

Imagine, for the sake of contrast, a man impressed by the following features of our uses of the word "command": (1)

a command can be given in words (or gestures, or some other substitute for words); (2) to know a formulation of the command is to know what the command is; (3) there is no way of knowing what a command is except by being supplied with a form of words in which the command is stated; (4) so the command-formulation does not describe the command; (5) nor is the command identical with any of its formulations, nor with the class of all of its formulations. And suppose him to be sufficiently confused as to ask "What then is this mysterious thing called a command, that now seems to elude inspection?" Here, he might be advised to consider how command-formulations are *used*—or, more simply, to consider the circumstances in which it would be correct to say that a certain command had been given. To understand the activity that we call the "giving of commands" (and so also the logically related activities of obeying commands, ignoring them, and so on) is to understand all that there is to be understood about "the relation between a command and its formulation." Similarly, it might be urged, the best way to become clear about the relation between a promise and the form of words in which a promise is made is to become clear about the criteria for cases of promis*ing*.

Commanding and promising are relatively well-demarcated activities. But there is no correspondingly well-demarcated activity associated with rules. There is no activity called "ruling" related to a rule as promising is to a promise or commanding to a command or questioning to a question. (A judge's ruling is an authoritative decision and is not even a special case of the production of a rule.)

This does not mean that there are no characteristic activities involving the use of rule-formulations, whose nature can be expected to throw light upon our perplexities. It means, I believe, that there are *many* such connected activities, which have to be discussed separately. Or to put the matter in another way, the word "rule" is versatile in a way that "command" and "promise" are not. The word "command" is used in our language like a piece belonging to only

[105]

a single game—a pawn—while the word "rule" is like a playing card used in many different games.

4. SOME FEATURES OF RULE-FORMULATIONS

Before discussing the background "activities" in which rule-formulations play a part, I wish to record some features of rule-formulations that can be discovered without reference to these activities.

It is obvious, first, that some forms of words can *never* be used for formulating a rule: it is impossible to imagine any situation in which the words "I am hungry," for instance, could be used for stating a rule—unless, of course, the words were being used as a code. But if we ask which expressions *are* eligible for formulating rules, we find a host of available candidates.

A request for an example of a rule can be satisfied by producing a full sentence in the indicative ("The dealer at bridge always bids first"), a "that"-clause ("[The rule] that students enrolled in American colleges must have a high school diploma"), a verbal clause in the infinitive ("To show small capitals in proof, underline twice"), a full sentence in the imperative ("Do unto others as you would be done by"), an imperative phrase ("No smoking in classrooms")—and no doubt in many other ways. There is indeed no special form of words conventionally reserved for the formulation of rules—as there is in the case of questions. Any set of words that can sometimes be used in stating a rule can at other time be used for other purposes.

This can be quickly seen in the case of the expressions quoted in the last paragraph. The sentence, "The dealer at bridge always bids first" might very well be used to state a general truth about the behavior of bridge players, and would in that use not be functioning as the formulation of a rule. If you say, "I do not believe that students enrolled in American colleges must have a high school diploma," the "that"-clause expresses your belief, and does not here formulate a

[106]

rule. When I say "My advice is—to show small capitals, under-line twice," I am giving a piece of advice, not formulating a rule. The words "No smoking in classrooms," pronounced in a suitably emphatic manner, might very well be an *order*. And so on.

The absence of a simple *formula* for a rule (such as there is in the case of questions) is one reason why the formulation of a rule is in practice often prefixed by the words, "The rule. . . ." These words forestall an ambiguity that might other-wise occur, and make it clear that a rule and nothing else is in question. (But, of course, anybody who is puzzled about "the nature of rules" will get cold comfort from being told that a formulation of a rule is any set of words to which it is proper to affix the words "A rule." For he would like to under-stand better *when* it is proper to do this.)

Let us consider, next, the content of a rule formulation, i.e., the specific information about the character of the rule that anybody receives who understands a statement of the rule.

I think it will be found in every case that a rule-formu-lation identifies what I shall call a *class of human actions,* for want of a better expression. A rule may be about entering college, or parking overnight, or bidding at bridge, or smok-ing, or voting when absent from one's home town, or making good tea, or getting the answer to a quadratic equation right, or treating others as one wishes to be treated. And these are all kinds of things that men can do—they are what I am calling *actions.*

The rule must be about a kind of thing that *human beings* can do. A rule to the effect that butterflies shall not eat cab-bages would be an absurdity, in the same way that a command or an order addressed to butterflies would be an absurdity. If a rule to the effect that dogs shall not bark in corridors is to be counted as making sense, it must be construed as con-cerning the owners of the dogs. For seeing to it that dogs shall not bark is something that human beings can do.

Not everything that a man might be said to do can count

[107]

as an "action" in the sense intended. "What is he doing now?" "He is crying." But crying is not something that men can choose to do or not do—it is not something that can be done voluntarily by the normal person. And so it cannot count as an "action." Rules about crying are an absurdity unless intended for some special class of persons having the capacity to cry or to abstain from crying at will.

I hope these remarks will make sufficiently plain what I mean by saying that a rule is about a class of human actions.

In addition to identifying a class of human actions, the rule-formulation must indicate with respect to those actions whether they are *required, forbidden,* or *permitted.* (This is usually done by including such expressions as "must," "must not," "may," "are required to," "need not," and so on. But the meanings of such modal words, as we might call them, are not obvious.)

To the two conditions for a rule-formulation stated in the last two sections, we might add that many, though not all, rule-formulations include information about the class of persons whom the rule concerns. Thus a rule may concern actions of householders, or automobile drivers, or aliens, and so on. (A rule-formulation that is supposed to apply to *anybody* who might do the actions specified determines what might be called an unrestricted or "open" rule. When no special class of persons concerned is indicated, it is usually understood that the rule is intended to be unrestricted.) If we count an indication of the class of persons concerned as part of the definition of the class of actions in question, we can think of the rule-formulation as having just *two* aspects: (i) a description of a class of actions, possibly restricted to actions performed by a designated class of persons; and (ii) an indication whether that class of actions is required, forbidden, or allowed.

The general form of a rule-formulation can, accordingly, be presented as follows: *Such-and-such actions in such-and-such circumstances, done by such-and-such persons* (done by anybody), *forbidden* (required, permitted).

[108]

5. FOUR MAIN SENSES OF "RULE"

In order to make further progress, it will prove essential to distinguish different senses of the word "rule." For it will be discovered that the word is used in ways which are markedly different.

(1) There are some uses of "rule" for which "regulation" is an approximate synonym. We can speak indifferently of "traffic rules" and "traffic regulations," of "rules for the conduct of an examination" or "regulations for the conduct of an examination," and even (though admittedly in a rather strained fashion) of "regulations for playing chess." (Other words that can be grouped together with "rule," when used as an approximate synonym for "regulation," are, according to circumstances, "law," "bylaw," and "ordinance," though each of these carries certain special connotations in addition.)

When "rule" is being used in what I shall call a "regulation-sense," it is permissible to speak of the rule in question as being announced, put into effect, enforced (energetically, strictly, laxly, invariably, occasionally), disobeyed, broken, rescinded, changed, revoked, reinstated. And it makes sense also to ask such questions as "When was the rule put into force?" "How long since the rule was reinstated?" "Is this the first time there has been a penalty for breaking this rule?" and other questions involving reference to *times*. It might be said, briefly, that rules (in regulation-senses of that word) have histories—come into effect at certain times, continue unchanged or suffer modification, and eventually cease to be in effect. With respect to this kind of rule, it also makes sense to ask such questions as "Who made this rule?" "Who has the power to waive the rule?" "Who punishes breaches of the rule?" We can say, briefly, that rules (in regulation-senses) have authors.

But these criteria must not be taken too strictly, or they will select a narrower class of rules than is here intended. Cases

[109]

can be produced to which some of the listed criteria apply, while others seem inappropriate (e.g., it seems farfetched to speak of anybody punishing breaches of the rules of chess). Yet this does not make the group of criteria valueless, since we shall see that there are other uses of "rule" that fall well outside the somewhat ill-defined set of senses that the criteria determine.

(2) There are clear cases of the use of "rule" which fail to pass the tests given above for regulation-sense of "rule." Two clear cases of rules are the rules "In solving quartic equations, first eliminate the cubic term" and "Do not plant tomatoes until after the last frost." It is absurd to regard these as regulations for solving equations or planting tomatoes—or to speak of either of these rules as being enforced, rescinded, or reinstated. It is absurd to speak (except metaphorically) of a "penalty" for breaking either of these rules or to inquire about the enforcers of the rule. These rules have neither authors nor histories.

As a positive test for isolating this second set of senses of "rule" we can ask whether it is possible to treat "rule" as an approximate synonym for "instruction" or "direction." When "rule" is being used in what I shall call an "instruction-sense," it is permissible to speak of the rule as effective or ineffective, confirmed or unsupported by experience, tested or untested, practical, hard to follow, and so on. This group of verbs (very different, it will be noticed, from the group cited in connection with regulation-senses) evokes contexts in which some *end* or *purpose* is in view. Indeed, it is always relevant to ask of a rule in an instruction-sense, "What am I supposed to achieve by following this rule—what is it supposed to help me accomplish?" And it is for this reason that appraisals like "useless," "helpful," "misguided," can here be made. (Unfortunately, some such appraisals can also be made of some regulation-rules. And it is not always clear whether a metaphor is involved. The boundaries between the various sets of senses that we are trying to distinguish are neither sharply defined nor immutable.)

[110]

(3) I turn now to a group of uses of "rule" in which the rule cannot plausibly be classified either with regulations or with instructions. Consider, for example, the statement, "It is a sound rule to pay one's debts promptly" and "A good rule is: to put charity ahead of justice." (The first of these might be said to state a prudential rule; the second a moral rule.) Neither of these can be called a regulation or an instruction. In these uses, the word "rule" can be replaced, without serious distortion in meaning resulting, by the words "precept" or "maxim." I shall accordingly speak of "precept-senses" of the word "rule."

That precept-senses are distinct from regulation-senses of "rule" is quickly seen by applying the tests listed above. It is obvious enough that there can be no question of anybody enforcing, rescinding, or reinstating either of the rules stated in the last paragraph; nor could there be any question of their having a history—i.e., of their coming into force at some time, and remaining in force during some period of time. Indeed, to such cases, the phrase "being in force" seems quite inappropriate.

It is not quite so obvious that rules of prudence or of morality cannot be construed as expressing some kind of instruction. I said that the chief mark of an instruction-sense of "rule" was that the rule expressed some alleged means for achieving a purpose. Now it might be urged that rules of prudence and morality are, likewise, the expression of means for achieving certain specifiable purposes. The Golden Rule, it might be said, is a prescription for achieving a good character (as it were, a recipe for "How to Become a Good Man"); the rule of being polite even to one's enemies (and similar prudential rules) a prescription for success in social life (i.e., what sociologists like to call "adjustment").

The contention has some plausibility with respect to prudential rules. If anybody urges me to follow some rule of conduct that is not a moral rule, I can reasonably ask him to explain what end would be achieved by following that rule. And in this type of case, it is correct to use the appraisal words, "effective," "ineffective," which we also saw to be appropriate in the cases of instruction-senses of "rule." (See also popular manuals on "how to be an important executive" or "how to make friends easily" or "how to have a happy old age." In such cases, rules of conduct are no doubt conceived as conveying instructions about techniques for achieving purposes.) These cases are distinguishable from those of instruction-senses proper, because such purposes as "success" or "adjustment" or "happiness" are less circumscribed, less concrete, than the purposes of growing tomatoes, raising poodles, or clearing a clogged drainpipe. (Nor can the vaguer "purposes," if we are to call them such, be achieved except indirectly— they are by-products of more concrete, more definite purposive activities.) But a more important difference is that prudential rules are not offered in the neutral spirit appropriate to the offering of instructions ("If you want to bake a chocolate cake, this is the way to do it"); a man who states a rule of conduct is taking the stance of one who gives advice, and is exerting influence in a way that is not the case in the neutral statement of a rule for doing X. (But technical instruction can be didactic in tone and propagandistic in intent, while practical advice can be relatively neutral and disinterested. Here, as throughout this subject, the differences between the types of cases selected as points of reference can be bridged by intermediate cases.)

If it is fairly plausible to regard prudential rules as instructions, the case alters when we reach rules of morality or religion. A speaker can exempt himself from the application of a rule expressing an instruction by disclaiming interest in the relevant purpose ("I don't want to solve quartic equations," "I have no wish to live to a ripe old age"), but such a defense is not available against the application of a moral rule. The attempted defense, "I don't want to be good" and "I don't want to do the right thing" (both of which may be true) in no way exempt the speaker from the application of a moral rule to his own person. (Moral precepts bind the Laodicean

[112]

no less than the Pharisee; there are no escape clauses in the categorical imperative.)

(4) There remains a class of uses of "rule" that seem at first glance strikingly different from those already considered. A man might offer, as example of rules, the statements, "Cyclones rotate clockwise, anticyclones anticlockwise" or "Years like 1952 that are divisible by 4 are leap years." These are clear cases of "rules," yet their formulations do not seem to satisfy the tests previously elaborated. These formulations do not seem to identify a class of human acts; nor do they seem to indicate that something is to be done, is forbidden, or permitted. (By contrast, all three types of senses already discussed do show just these features in their characteristic formulations.)

In the present type of case, the content of the rule-formulation is an actual (or alleged) *uniformity*. An approximate synonym for "rule" in such uses is "principle" or even "general truth." Accordingly, truth values ("true" and "false") can be ascribed to such rules in ways that are clearly inappropriate for regulations, instructions, or precepts. And by the same token, the use of imperative language or "modal" words ("shall," "must," "may," and the like) is clearly unfitting. The vocabulary is that appropriate to discourse about any truth claims (declarative statements): we can speak of the weight of evidence for or against the rule, and so on. Such talk is out of place when the subject is a regulation, an instruction, or a precept.

One might therefore be tempted to say that "rule" (in the senses previously discussed) and "rule" (in the principle-senses now under examination) are mere homonyms, whose meanings have no more than an accidental connection. But to say so would be to overlook at least the suggestions evoked by calling, say, "Like poles repel, unlike poles attract" a rule, rather than a principle. The use of the word "rule" (and the aphoristic form characteristic of the corresponding formulation) suggests an instruction. It is as if the speaker were to say "If you want

[113]

to remember and distinguish the two kinds of cases that arise in electrostatic phenomena, bear in mind the formula 'Like poles repel, unlike attract.' " So construed, as mnemonic devices, rules in the principle-sense can be brought into not very distant relation with the instruction-senses of "rule" previously considered. It is well to bear in mind, however, that something of the suggestions and associations of *any* of the uses clings to any of the others. To say "rule" is to suggest a flavor of regulation (a "must" or a "must not"), of instruction ("This is the way to do it"), of advice ("Believe me, this is the right way to go about it") and exhortation ("Do so, as every good, reasonable, right-thinking, man should"). A word that is used in *many* linguistic constellations tends to conjure up some of its verbal associates upon every occasion of its use.

On the whole, it seems best to consider the use of "rule" in principle-senses as a "degenerate" case (in the sense in which a pair of lines is said to be a degenerate case of a conic). Such uses *can* be brought into relation with more central (more "typical") uses, as I have just tried to show. Yet so many of the criteria characteristic of these more central uses either lapse, or are applicable only in figurative or strained senses, that the relations of the senses are tenuous. (One has a feeling that the use of the word "rule" in this last case is not important, and that nothing of great moment would be sacrificed if we were to abjure *this* kind of use.)

I shall pause to summarize this section. I have been trying to distinguish four distinct if related groups of senses of "rule" (as one might try to get one's bearing in studying a mountain range by distinguishing within it four subranges, distinct, though linked by ridges and valleys). The method I used was to look for approximate synonyms, different in all four cases, and to consider the sets of words (different *on the whole* in each of the four cases) with which "rule" may be coupled. In this way I was able to identify what I called, respectively, "regulation-," "instruction-," "precept-," and "principle-," senses. I have drawn attention to the different types of appraisals and characterizations of the rules that are appropriate in the various cases. Of course, if there were any good purpose to be served by pressing this kind of investigation further, the choice of *four* systems of reference would soon appear somewhat arbitrary. Each of the sets of senses would under closer inspection prove to be analyzable into other subsenses, and then perhaps the linking similarities between the "four types of case" might prove to be more striking than the differences which, for the sake of exposition, I have been emphasizing. But I have said enough for my present purpose.

6. THE ACTIVITIES IN WHICH REGULATIONS ARE USED

I should like now to plot some of the ways in which rule-formulations are characteristically *used*. In order to do so, I shall begin by considering the special case in which the rule takes the form of a regulation, in the hope that this may throw light on the "regulation-senses" of "rule" and eventually upon the other groups of senses of that word. By regulation I mean something laid down by an authority (a legislature, judge, magistrate, board of directors, university president, parent) as required of certain persons (or, alternatively, forbidden, or permitted). I shall call those who bring the regulation into force its *promulgators* and those to whom it applies (i.e., the persons specified or implied in the regulation formulation as performing the actions in question) its *subjects*.

We are to consider activities, whether on the part of promulgators or subjects, that involve a given regulation. An example would be the activity we commonly call "adopting the regulation R" (where in place of "R," the reader may imagine inserted some regulation-formulation). Other designations of activities associated with regulations are obtainable by replacing the word "adopting" in the specimen formula by any of the following: drafting, recording, announcing, proclaiming, stating, understanding, learning, breaking, rescinding, reaffirming, enforcing, amending, revoking. The list is not complete and could be extended to tiresome length.

[115]

An obvious way of classifying such activities is by considering whether promulgators or subjects engage in the activity in question. (Cases in which both are active, say "helping a committee to draft regulations that are to apply to oneself" seldom occur; the relations between promulgators and subjects are usually one-sided—the subjects normally have some kind of subordinate status.) Thus "promulgators" or "rule-makers" do the following: draft, adopt, announce, enforce, amend, and revoke regulations—and only they can do any of these; while "subjects" learn, understand, heed, obey, break, and follow regulations—and only they can do these things. Let us talk about these two classes as those of "P-activities" ("P" for promulgator) and "S-activities" ("S" for subject).

P-activities and S-activities are connected in manifold ways. Some P-activities are done for the sake of evoking some related S-activities—e.g., there would be no point in making regulations if they were to be invariably misunderstood or ignored. And the converse is true, since some S-activities are done for the sake of inducing related P-activities (e.g., agitation for the repeal of a regulation). Some P-activities cause S-activities, and vice versa (drafting a new regulation because the old one is constantly violated). Finally, some P-activities are definable in terms of (have internal relations to) some S-activities, and conversely (e.g., punishing a breach of a regulation, protesting the proclamation of a regulation). So the relations between the two kinds of activities are at least of the following sorts: (i) as motive to act, (ii) as cause to effect, (iii) as part to whole.

Doubtless many other types of connection could be found. For rule-formulations are used in all sorts of intricate ways involving complex interaction between promulgators and subjects, and this in turn is part of a much wider web of human relationships which makes such relations possible. (The formulation of the regulation might be compared to the ball in a game of tennis, where "what is done to the ball" depends intricately upon the developing pattern of responses between the players, and also upon the background community to which both belong.)

Still, we can impose some order by asking whether some activities (whether of the P or the S sort) are not logically derivate from others. I call an activity logically derivative from another if it would be logically impossible for a case of the first to occur without a correlated case of the second occurring, the converse, however, not being the case. Thus the activity of criticizing a poem is logically derivative from the activity of composing a poem; the activity of answering a question is logically derivative from that of asking the question. For one cannot criticize a poem that has not been composed, nor answer a question that has not been asked; but there is no logical impossibility in an uncriticized poem or an unanswered question.

It seems clear that the simpler S-activities are logically derivative in this sense from P-activities. In order for it to be possible to obey or disobey regulations, to criticize or to approve them, to support them or agitate for their change, it is necessary that the regulations shall have been promulgated.

This being so, we can undertake a further sifting among the P-activities. It seems, indeed, obvious that the examples of P-activities that come immediately to mind are all logically derivative from the activity of promulgating a regulation. The primary activity (upon which all others depend like branches of a trunk) is that *of bringing the regulation into force.* For "considering" a regulation (debating whether to bring it into force), enforcing it, revoking it, and so on, are all "second-order activities" which cannot have instances unless there are instances of the primary activity. The "primary activity" of promulgating a rule may be compared to the primary activity of making a promise or even of making a move in chess. Intricate as are the uses that persons make of promises when they use them as motives and reasons, grounds for praise and blame, premises of inferences and so on, yet the whole system of uses depends in the end upon the primary activity of giving one's word (as in the end there would be no

[117]

game of chess, and so no instruction in the game, no aesthetics of chess and so on, unless moves were made). And so our task narrows itself down to that of having a clear view of what occurs when a regulation is promulgated.

But in simple cases, there is no mystery about this. Consider the case of some elected or appointed officer having the legal authority to make regulations. Such a man (say an inspector of weights and measures) presumably derives his authority from a law specifying the form of the regulations, their scope, and the conditions under which they may be promulgated. For the sake of simplicity we can imagine that there is some official form (described in the enabling law) that is used whenever a regulation is announced. The publication of the regulation in proper form and within the jurisdiction permitted by the relevant law is what brings the regulation into effect. The regulation becomes effective from the moment that the promulgating authority attaches his signature to an official statement of the activities to be controlled (i.e., to be required, forbidden, or permitted).

A regulation published in this way can, of course, be challenged and in many different ways. It can be objected that the promulgator did not have the requisite authority, or that the regulation dealt with matters outside his jurisdiction, or that it was defective in form (failed to meet the prescribed conditions for lawful proclamation), or that it was issued in circumstances that invalidated it (e.g., too late for conformity to be possible), and so on. But if all such objections fail because the requisite conditions have in fact been met, then *the publication of the regulation-formulation brings the regulation into force.*

The promulgation of a regulation has, accordingly, a "performatory" aspect. In signing the original statement of the regulation, as the first step in its publication, the properly constituted authority *brings* the regulation into effect, and is not making some assertion that could be independently verified as true or false. (Of course the assertion *that* he was thereby bringing a regulation into force could be tested by

[118]

examination of the relevant law.) Bringing a regulation into effect is like giving written orders. If the commanding officer, acting within the limits of his lawful jurisdiction, signs a document ordering certain actions by his subordinates, he *thereby* orders them to act in the designated fashion. Similarly, in promulgating a regulation, an authority *thereby* demands (forbids, permits) designated actions on the part of those subject to the regulation.

But it would be a mistake to press the analogy too far, since "order" and "regulation" have different though similar grammars. An order closely resembles a command, as being a relatively direct communication to subordinates. But a regulation is a relatively indirect and as it were impersonal communication (it might be called an oblique order), not addressed to designated individuals, but published for the sake of informing "anybody who may be concerned" of the conditions stipulated for the performance of certain acts. (Hence failure to receive orders is a sufficient defense against a charge of disobedience, but ignorance of the law is no excuse.) An order is like a shot fired at a poacher, a regulation like a fence to keep *anybody* off the grounds.

In the foregoing I have been trying to do no more than remind the reader of what is already familiar to him. Perhaps the reference to "authority" of the promulgator may seem obscure, but we may leave this to the students of jurisprudence to explain.

My central hypothesis is that cases like the foregoing, in which somebody has authority to control behavior in a formal way, constitute the paradigms for uses of "rule" in what I earlier called "regulation-senses." That is to say, that when we think of this kind of a rule, we are, more or less clearly, thinking of cases where somebody has authority to tell us what to do, in the "oblique" way characteristic of regulations. And that other cases are then related to these paradigms by plausible variations in the defining circumstances. Thus we may think of groups (boards, committees) framing the rules, or of different sources of the authority requisite (custom, rather than law), of cases where the enabling conditions are created by consent and not by legislation, and so on. There runs through this fabric of related cases, I suggest, the connecting thread of a notion of an authority, having the right to require conformity when pronouncing his wishes in set form. It is this, if I am not mistaken, that gives the "push" that is expressed by such words as "must" and "must not" when they appear in the statement of rules in regulation-senses. We feel these words as *symbolic substitutes for pressure exerted upon us.*

I want to consider now the primary activities on the part of the "subjects" of the regulations, i.e., those to whom the rule formulations are addressed. It is easy and correct to say that the primary activity in question is that of "understanding" the regulation. For certainly nobody can heed, follow, break, or even consciously ignore a regulation, who does not at least understand it. But the term "understanding" (as elusive as nearly all the words we have to use in this kind of inquiry) may suggest too strongly the kind of understanding that is appropriate in response to an assertion. Roughly speaking, a man may be said to understand an assertion if he responds to a case of "honest assertion" (or what he takes to be such) with corresponding *expectations.* (If I hear a man say "There's a knock at the door" and believe him to be speaking in good faith, not to have made a slip of the tongue, and so on, I am led to expect that there is a man at the door. My responses to cases where the speaker is believed to be lying or to have made a mistake can then be described by modifying the account given for the primary case of "honest assertion.") But it would be a mistake to say that to understand a case of what might be called "honest promulgation" of a regulation is to be led to have certain expectations or beliefs. The mistake would be similar to that committed by anybody who treated the offer of a hand to shake as a communication having truth-value. Just as it would be absurd to call the offer of a handshake either true or false, it would be absurd to call the promulgation of a regulation either true or false. We

[120]

must, rather, suppose that understanding a promulgation consists in recognizing it *as* the sort of act ("performance") that it is, i.e., being led by it to be prepared to make the kinds of moves that occur in the system of activities in which rules are promulgated and heeded. (Compare understanding a move in chess as a check of the king. The chess player treats the preceding move as a *motive* for his own move, the specific ways in which such motivation occurs being determined by the "interpretation" he puts upon that move.)

Before I try to say less figuratively what the "regulation-heeding moves" are, I want to draw attention to a point that seems to me of great importance. Consider for a while the parallel case of understanding a promise. The giving and receiving of promises belong to a complex system of activities that include holding men to account for breaking their promises, citing promises as reasons for passing judgment on human acts, releasing men from promises, and so on. Now in order that a man shall be able to understand a particular promise, he must know how to play this "promise game." I can no more make a promise to a man who does not know how to participate in promise-giving and promise-receiving activities than I can revoke against a man who does not know how to play bridge. In this respect, the position of the man to whom the promise is made is exactly like that of the prom-ise-giver himself. For the mere utterance of the promise for-mula does not constitute the giving of a promise unless the speaker is, as it were, trained to make promises. It does not follow that in order to understand a particular promise the hearer must make a standard use of *that* promise, by count-ing on the speaker to deliver, reproaching him if he defaults, and so on. The hearer can choose to ignore the promise, to "do nothing about it," to treat it as if it had not been given. But if he were to ignore every promise, *never* counted on a man to deliver what he had promised, and if the thought of holding a man to account on the basis of his promises never even entered his head, his conduct would show that he lacked the requisite training for understanding promises. Now much

[121]

the same can be said, I think, in cases of understanding any performatory use of language. And in particular, a man cannot understand a regulation who does not have the corresponding experience and "training" of being confronted with "oblique orders" and feeling the pressure behind them.

I must try, however, to say something more about the specific ways in which the promulgation of a rule evokes an appropriate response from a suitably qualified receiver. My suggestion has been that the rule-formulation in appropriate contexts has the standard function of being used as *a conventional* (symbolic) *incentive to action* (a regulation as a kind of linguistic *prod*). Now it is an important feature of this kind of linguistic instrument (as distinguished from the kind of "prod" that we call a command) that it can be transmitted. A man may say to himself "The king may not castle after having moved. Therefore it is no use my trying to get the rook into the centre immediately." The first sentence he uses is not the expression of an assertion; it is a statement *of* the rule. When he is so using it, I suggest, it is acting as an inhibitor of certain actions he might otherwise perform (so that he is, as it were, handcuffing *himself*). It is this kind of use that seems to me distinctive of rules, as contrasted with commands, requests, orders, and other linguistic instruments having "push." Precisely because a regulation is not published in the form of a direct communication between an authority and his subjects, the regulation formula can be used by *anybody;* and when it is thus cited, it becomes a distinctive kind of motive or incentive for action. To respond to a case of "honest promulgation" of a rule by a man with power to promulgate and enforce is to feel *his* words as a particular kind of pressure and to be prepared to reinstate that pressure at will by reciting the formula. To understand deviant cases (cases where one is indifferent to the pressure or denies its real existence, owing to the violation of the contextual conditions) is to behave in ways sufficiently resembling the modes of response to the case of "honest promulgation."

I wish I could make the foregoing clearer. But I hope to

it is always open to us to define another system of activities which is the system of activities of those who do "recognize" or heed the regulations in question. And this derivative system of activities will, according to the account given above, necessarily be constituted by the relevant regulations. Take as an example, the system of activities consisting of the parking of automobiles. This may be said to be subject to (official) regulations but not constituted by them. Call this system S. Now consider the system of activities defined as the activities of those who are aware of the regulations for parking and also take heed of them (in the sense already explained). Call this system S'. Then S' is, although S is not, constituted by a set of regulations. It is clear that no matter what system S, of activities subject to rules is given, we can always in parallel fashion define an associated system, S', which will necessarily be *constituted* by the same regulations. Hence, there seems to be little point in talking separately about activities constituted by rules. It will be a mere matter of arbitrary definition whether we do or do not refer to the activities in such a way that they will have to be said to be constituted by rules or regulations. (Compare F. P. Ramsey's remark about the "scholasticism" involved in saying that it is impossible to break the rules of bridge—*Foundations of Mathematics*, 269.)

Perhaps the uneasiness that I have expressed can be dispelled as follows. Games of skill are played for the sake of winning *according to the rules* (if all you wanted was a touchdown, why not shoot the opposing team?); whereas the aim of parking is to get one's car off the street in a safe place, the aim of respecting the relevant laws in so doing being subordinate (and, as it were, "external"). Think of the absurdity of somebody arriving in a remote village where there are no parking regulations at all and saying "Too bad—it's logically impossible for me to park here." So behind the ways in which we define systems of activities—sometimes including the heeding of rules as part of the definition, sometimes not—there is the factual consideration as to whether people do have a special interest in observing the rules *as such* (and not

[124]

for the sake of any penalties that may be attached to non-compliance). When there is such an interest, so that the system of activities would not continue to be exemplified if there were no such rules, it is natural to count the existence and observance of the rules as part of the definition of the system in question.

An analogy is the following. Saws are in fact made for the sake of cutting, and pieces of metal of the conventional shape would not continue to be brought into existence unless that purpose was on the whole fulfilled. Thus it is natural, in this case, to count fitness for the purpose as part of the definition of a saw. (The Oxford Dictionary accordingly defines a saw as "A *cutting* tool, etc.") On the other hand, nobody uses hay for stuffing pillows (though perhaps it might be so used). Hence there is no point in our culture in having a special term meaning "hay suitable for use in the stuffing of pillows." For such a word would have no useful application, because instances of its application would hardly ever arise.

8. ARE THERE UNFORMULATED RULES?

I wish now to consider whether it can ever be proper to describe a system of activities as involving unformulated or implicit rules (in regulation-senses of "rule"). In the account I gave of the use of regulation-formulations, I regarded as primary the activity on the part of the regulation promulgator of adopting and publishing the regulation. In this type of case, therefore, it would be very hard to make sense of a notion of "unformulated" or "implicit" regulation. The notion would be as refractory as would be that of an "implicit" essay. It is part of the notion of an essay that it should be composed—and it is certainly part of the central notion of a regulation that it should be formulated and announced. The notion of an unformulated regulation sounds like the notion of a decision that has not been made—or an announcement that has not been made—or a proclamation that has not been proclaimed—that is to say, the notion of nothing at all. (But

[125]

this does not mean that we cannot speak of regulations that have not yet come into force and perhaps never will. The chief difficulty in speaking of implicit regulations is that they are supposed somehow to be already in force, although no promulgating authority has adopted them.)

Nevertheless, it is possible to attach a sense to the notion of "implicit regulation" in the following way. I shall try to show that it is possible and even necessary to speak of *logical relations* between regulations. (Once this is done, there need be no mystery about the notion of a regulation being implied without being formulated or promulgated.)

In the analysis of rule-formulations provided earlier in this discussion, I was led to identify three distinct though connected aspects of such formulations—a class of possible human actions, a class of performers of the actions (i.e., of the persons affected by the regulation), and an indication of whether the actions are required, forbidden, or permitted. I shall call these for short, the A-factor ("A" for action), the S-factor ("S" for subject) and the M-factor ("M" for modality). Thus a convenient symbolism for a rule formulation is "A by S is M"—or, more briefly, "ASM." (When the S-symbol is missing, it is to be understood that the regulation is an "open" one concerning anybody who might perform A.) Here "A" is to be thought of as replacing some designation of a class of possible human actions, "S" as replacing some designation of a class of persons, and "M" as replacing one of the expressions "required," "forbidden," or "permitted" or suitable synonyms.

Consider, now, the case of two regulations that agree in their S- and their M-factors, while having different A-factors, so that their formulation have the forms $A_1S_1M_1$ and $A_2S_1M_1$ respectively. (That is to say, both require, forbid, or permit of the same class of persons different classes of actions.)

Now it may happen that anybody who performed an action belonging to A_1 and also an action belonging to A_2 would necessarily perform an action belonging to a third class A_3. Thus if the regulation required all owners of cars to have

[126]

operating licenses and all those having operating licenses to pay a fee, one joint effect of the two regulations would be to require that all owners of cars should pay a fee, though *this* requirement was not explicitly formulated. Similarly if A_1 and A_2 are both forbidden, and every action that belongs to A_1 and A_2 necessarily belongs also to A_3, the regulations in effect forbid A_3, although their formulations do not explicitly say so.

It is easy to see, now, that just as regulations agreeing in their S- and M-factors can imply (as now shown) regulations that have not been formulated, it is possible for such regulations to be *logically incompatible*. (If one regulation calls for the doing of A_1 and another for the doing of A_2 and it is logically impossible for there to be a case of something being simultaneously A_1 and A_2, there is a logical conflict between the regulations—they are logically incompatible.) Indeed we can find parallels in the case of regulations agreeing in their S- and M-factors for all logical relations between *propositions*.

In the next place, such relations between regulations may also arise from relations between the S-factors. Suppose the regulations have the form $A_1S_1M_1$ *and* $A_2S_2M_1$ respectively; and suppose further that S_2 is a subclass of S_1; and that everything that is a case of both A_1 and A_2 is necessarily a case also of A_3. Then it is obvious that the two regulations jointly have the force of a regulation $A_3S_2M_1$. (If there is a regulation that all drivers have a license and another that all teen-age drivers pay five dollars for a license, the joint effect is that all teen-age drivers are required to pay five dollars.)

Again, there may be logical relations between regulations as a result of connections between their respective M-factors. Thus a regulation that *permits* A is incompatible with one that *forbids* the same class of actions A.

Finally, regulations can be combined with assertions to yield regulations that have not been explicitly formulated. If there is a regulation forbidding the entry of dogs less than six inches long at a dog show; and if as a *matter of fact* the only dogs that are less than six inches long are chihuahuas,

[127]

the effect of the regulation is to prohibit the entry of chihuahuas at that dog show.

This discussion of the logical relations between regulations could be elaborated without difficulty. I hope I have said enough to show that a set of regulations could properly be said to *imply* regulations that have never been formulated. The crucial point is that regulations receivers respond, and are intended to respond, to the implied regulations *as they would if those regulations were explicitly formulated and announced.* Of course, they cannot be expected to *cite* such implied regulations (nor can they raise questions about the authority behind them, or other questions concerning their validity, except indirectly, through reference to the explicit regulations). Nevertheless, in the crucial matter of the response stipulated in the regulations, it is never a defense to say that the course of action in question was not *explicitly* referred to in the regulations. It would be preposterous for a man charged with breaking into a house on Regent Street to plead that the law had nothing explicit to say about houses on that street. Any intelligent person is supposed to understand that any course of action that the laws, taken together, are found jointly to forbid, is intended to be forbidden by the laws. And so, logical conclusions drawn from regulations function as incentives for action (have a "push" or imperative force) no less than the explicit regulations from which they are inferred. And the same can be said of all rules, no matter in which sense the word "rule" is being used.

9. CAN THERE BE UNINFERRED RULES THAT ARE UNFORMULATED?

There remains for consideration a more controversial question. Is it possible that ways of behaving should be properly describable as the heeding of regulations that have not been formulated and cannot be inferred from regulations that have been formulated? (I shall call such regulations "basic regulations.")

[128]

Let us begin by considering a hypothetical case. I imagine some tribe in which everyday conduct is found to be controlled by a strict penal code. The rules of conduct are stated in traditional formulas known verbatim by every member of the community. (We can imagine that the day begins with a formal recitation of the code on the part of each citizen.) Violations are invariably punished by flogging, and such punishment follows immediately a violation is detected, according to a graded schedule incorporated into the ritual statement of the laws. (The tribesmen chant "I must not lay hands upon my brother's wife, on pain of fifty lashes" and so on.)

And now let us suppose a visitor to notice that there is a fenced enclosure near the center of the village; that the tribesmen take great care to avoid coming into contact with the fence, warn their children against doing so, and so on; and that anybody who does brush against the fence is immediately taken to the ritual place of punishment and given a hundred lashes. On the other hand, no prohibition against contact with the fence appears in the official code (the rules that are recited every morning), so that there can be no question of an explicit law against the practice. We can suppose, further, if we want to make the example seem more plausible, that the whole affair is regarded as too holy for discussion, so that the elders of the tribe refuse to talk about it as a matter of policy and the *hoi polloi* shrug it off as "something that has always been ever since man can remember."

In such a case, one would be strongly tempted, and I think with good reason, to suppose that there was in force an unformulated *basic* law—an "unwritten" law—which *we* could formulate as "Nobody shall touch the sacred fence, on pain of receiving a hundred lashes." The reason that would lead us to say this, is the conformity of the behavior of tribesmen with what it would be *if* there were such an explicit law. In respect of avoiding the fence, admonishing one another to take care when in its neighborhood, and in respect of the mode of penalty that follows contact with the sacred object, there is a

[129]

very close analogy with what happens in the case of the explicit laws of the community. The one respect in which there is lack of analogy is that the law that we have formulated is no part of the well-known code of laws, is never recited and, indeed, never formulated.

This imaginary instance has shown that circumstances *are* conceivable in which we might usefully say that a set of persons behaved as if they were responding to a regulation that had, however, not been formulated and was "basic" in the sense of not logically following from the code of explicit regulations. It as an essential feature of this example that there should be a set of explicit laws in force in the community, so that we could compare the behavior which we wished to call observance of implicit law with the behavior that we had already called observance of explicit laws. The attempt to describe a community living under a system of laws, *none* of which were formulated and cited, would have had no prospect of success.

Now if in actual cases, we find a set of persons behaving in such a way that (i) they make use of a system of explicit rules or regulations, and (ii) they also respond in analogous ways in situations which *we* can describe in terms of a rule which *they* have not formulated, I think we shall be justified in saying they are observing an implicit basic rule.

The following might provide an example. There is no official rule of chess that a threat to the queen shall be announced by saying "Queen." This practice is, however, very common among beginners. Suppose, then, that we were able to watch same young chess players who were able to cite at any rate the most important of the official rules of chess—and indeed appealed to them in cases of dispute as to the legality of moves. Suppose, also, that they were in the habit of saying "Queen" when the queen was attacked and that when this was omitted the player who did so was reproached. But that nobody ever used the words "The rule is that the queen must be warned" or any words conveying the same meaning. In that case, we should have an example, of a not unrealistic

[130]

sort, similar to the case of the tribesmen already discussed. We should be justified in saying that the chess players were observing an implicit or unformulated basic rule.

I do not deny that there might be considerable difficulty in distinguishing the case just described from that in which there was a mere habit or custom of saying "Queen." But there is one good way of rendering the difference between the cases of following a custom and observing an implicit rule more distinct. Having tentatively decided that the players were observing the rule described, *we* could then formulate it and offer it to them as an explicit rule. We could say "I see you follow the rule that the attack on a queen must be announced by saying 'Queen.'" If they agreed, we could take that as strong evidence that they had been following an implicit basic rule. If it is objected that they might *now* be adopting a rule which they had previously not been observing, we can incorporate the new test into our notion of an implicit basic rule. We can say that by calling a rule implicit we *mean,* among other things, that if it were formulated and offered for consideration to the persons concerned they *would* accept it as codifying their previous practice, and that after such acceptance their behavior would not be substantially changed. If the chess players agreed with our formulation and continued to play as before (except perhaps that they now sometimes explicitly cited the newly formulated rule) we would, on this view, be shown to have been justified in our judgment that they had been playing previously according to an implicit rule.

My conclusion is that we *can* sometimes speak of there being implicit rules even if those rules are basic, in the sense of not being logically inferrible from explicitly formulated rules.

10. APPLICATION TO VARIOUS TYPES OF RULES

It will have been noticed that although I earlier distinguished four groups of main senses of the word "rule" (the "regulation-senses," the "instruction-senses," the "precept-

senses," and the "principle-senses"), I have in fact been discussing only the first during the last few sections. One reason
for doing this is that the regulation-senses are, in my judgment,
central. Another is that the discussion of what may be called
the "background activity" (the promulgating and understanding of rules together with all related *P*- and *S*-activities)
is hardest to analyze in this case.

In the case of instruction-rules, the activities of announcing
and responding to rules are relatively simple to describe. The
typical case is that of a man *in a position to know,* informing
a suitable hearer how to achieve a certain end. (All that was
said previously about the special authority of the rule-giver
in the case where the rule is a kind of regulation here ceases
to apply.) A question about the justification of the rule is now
answered by reference to its efficacy or, less directly, by reference to the experience or knowledge of the announcer of
the rule. ("The rule is: Do not plant tomatoes before the
first frost." "Why not?" "Well, I have discovered it doesn't
pay." Or: "Experience shows that they usually die if you do
otherwise.") To this family belong the special kinds of instructions known as "recipes," "prescriptions" (in the medical
sense), and "formulas" (for making *X*)—except that these
words tend to carry a suggestion of instructions for a more
specific purpose than is suggested by the use of the word "rule."
On the side of the receiver of the instruction-rule, the primary
activity is that of treating knowledge of the rule as an incentive to follow the means described for achieving the end in
question. (Yet here, as in all cases, we have to make allowance
for the counterbalancing force of other considerations that
may inhibit action according to the rule in question. If I
"know better," I may refuse to follow the instructions for
planting tomatoes; but I must at least consider the proffered
rule as a prima-facie reason for acting in the way it prescribes
and not deviate from it unless I have a stronger opposing
reason. Of course, If I think the man who offers the rules is
an ignoramus, or is trying to mislead me, that is reason enough
for ignoring what he suggests.) Rules in the instruction sense

[132]

can be used as reasons (when they have been accepted by the receiver). Thus we must distinguish here, as we did in the case of regulations, between talk about the rule, and the *citing* of the rule. (When I say "I am not going to plant the tomatoes until next week because tomatoes should not be planted before the last frost," I am citing the rule, not talking about it.)

In the case of rules that can be regarded as precepts, i.e., rules of prudence or of morality, the typical activity on the part of the rule announcer is either *advice* or *exhortation*. When the rule relates to conduct that is not regarded as having strictly moral implications (rules about how to be successful, or to organize one's day) the situations in which rules are announced and heeded approximate to those in which instructions for the achieving of specific ends are in question. (Compare what was said earlier on this point.) If there is a difference, it is a relatively subtle one concerning the imputed status of anybody who puts himself in the position of offering me advice about conduct, as contrasted with that of the man who tells me how to do a specific job. (Compare "How do you know what to do?" with "*Who are you* to tell me what to do?") But I shall say no more about this. When we have to do with moral rules, the "background activity" is notoriously more complicated. I shall leave the matter with the bare reminder that the stating of moral rules is bound up with the various moral activities of assigning blame and praise, deliberating about possible courses of action, formulating guiding maxims for the decision of difficult cases, resolving moral conflicts, and so on. I shall not attempt to show in detail how moral rules (as distinct from other moral statements) function in these many important contexts.

Finally, the remaining "degenerate case" of rules that can be thought of as the expressions of principles (rules of thumb) can be quickly dismissed with the comment that here we have to do with statements that can be treated almost as general assertions about matters of fact. The use of such "rules" is so close to the familiar uses of truth-claiming assertions that it hardly needs special and extended discussion.

[133]

The important thing to stress is that the conclusions reached above with regard to the possibility of logical relations between rules and the existence of "implicit rules" not derivable from other, explicit, ones, apply, with suitable modifications, to all cases of rules. I am inclined to think that even the point previously emphasized about the performatory aspect of the primary activity in which a regulation is announced survives when we pass to the cases of "rule" in some other than a regulation-sense. What, in my view, distinguishes a case of a *rule* being offered (rather than, say, a factual statement about the consequences of certain acts—"The rule is don't put tomatoes in until after the first frost" rather than "Tomatoes planted before the first frost usually die"—or "The rule is: Do unto others as you would be done by" rather than "If you don't treat others as you would like to be treated yourself, you will end by regretting it") is that when a rule is offered an *act* is performed, which cannot be simply identified with the act of asserting something to be the case. *Giving* instructions in the form of a rule is not the same as saying that such and such is an effective way of achieving the desired end; moral exhortation is not the same as confirmable assertion about the consequences of such-and-such acts; even the stating of a rule of thumb differs noticeably from stating such and such to be the case. There is more than a difference of nuance between "Usually eight tricks per hand are found to be won by honor cards" and "The rule is: Eight tricks per hand can usually be counted on as being won by honor cards." The latter carries with it suggestions of advice ("Follow this rule"), of instruction ("This is the way to do it, if you want to win")—even, less strongly, of quasi-moral exhortation ("It would be wrong to act otherwise") or authoritative demand from a superior authority ("I tell you to do this, as one in a position to say how bridge should be played"). It is as if the word "rule" came trailing clouds of suggestion from the many different contexts in which it can play a part. But perhaps in this last case, we are dealing with subtle differences of tone and style; and the difference to conduct made by preferring the rule-formulation to the use of an assertion is minute, and of interest only to a minute philosopher.

11. DOES LANGUAGE HAVE RULES?

I reach at last the question for the sake of which these notes have mainly been written—the question whether a language can be said to have rules—and if so in what sense.

If we glance at our schedule of senses, it will be quickly seen that the group of senses most nearly applicable to the case of language is that in which we talked of a "regulation-sense." If language is subject to rules, those rules must in some sense regulate and control the behavior of the users of the language. But there can hardly be a question of there being regulations in the paradigm senses of "regulation." Except in such isolated cases as the quixotic attempts of the French Academy to control the speech of Frenchmen, there are no discoverable authorities with power to regulate. There are no legal authorities to back linguistic regulations with legal penalties (as there are, on the other hand, magistrates and police to punish the use of obscene language), and misspelling, mispronunciation, and malapropism are not indictable offences. Nor on the other hand is it more than an unplausible fiction to speak, as some writers have done, of "agreements" or "conventions" about the use of language, if such talk is taken literally as implying deliberation and explicit ratification of consent. There are no linguistic treaties between parties competent to negotiate; nor would agreement about the future use of common words be more than a learned farce. It is truistic that language grows as erratically as a jungle and that the attempt to forecast its change or to control it has about as much chance of success as the attempt to cultivate the Sargasso Sea.

Such facts as these have led many students of language (including perhaps a majority of professional linguists) to deny that linguistic rules are in force in natural languages. Language, they say, is a system of social habits, not a rule-

[135]

controlled system of responses. And they are all the more inclined to say this since they have reasons for viewing the notion of language regulation with suspicion or something worse. They are often inclined to hold that the supposed rules of language are at best an attempt on the part of a privileged elite to impose their special habits of speech upon the rest of the speech community. And this advocacy of a special dialect, as they like to say, has no more foundation in the facts of linguistic practice than the prejudice that every man has in favor of habits of speech that he finds familiar and comfortable.

There is some justice in the attitude toward language which I have sketched (no doubt less sympathetically than an advocate might). Yet in its fundamental premises it is, I believe, mistaken. We must allow for the large discretion which a speaker is free to exercise, and are entitled to discount the pedantic claims of those who have tried to turn their own linguistic prejudices into a code binding upon all speakers. It still remains true that in learning a language one also learns the all-important notion of relevant controlling rules of usage (and so "proper" and "improper" ways of talking and writing). Some of these rules are explicitly formulated, and can be checked by anybody who will take the trouble to consult dictionaries, grammar books, and secondary authorities like Fowler. But many more are shown in the behavior of the speakers of the language—in their readiness to correct themselves and others, their willingness to believe that there is a rule even if they do not know what it is, and their endorsement of rules after they have been formulated by an onlooker, as adequately formulating the guiding principles of their previous conduct. No doubt a good deal of linguistic behavior is not subject to rule at all, and perhaps a good deal more is not subject to explicit rules. But if what I have said about implicit rules stands up to critical examination, this is not an insuperable obstacle to the discovery of rules governing the use of language.

[136]

12. SUMMARY

In these notes, I have been exploring the logical grammar of "rule." I began by noting that a rule can be *stated* in a form of words that is not a *designation* (i.e., a name or a description) of the rule. It is impossible, however, to identify the rule with any one of its *formulations*, or with the class of its formulations. The contention that a rule is the meaning of any of its formulations is correct, but not illuminating. To determine the meaning of a rule-formulation we must investigate how such formulations are used. (Similarly to understand the meaning of a command-formulation or a promise-formulation, we must investigate how the corresponding forms are used.)

First, however, I tried to discover what I could from the character of rule-formulations considered in isolation from their distinctive uses in context. If was found that there is no distinctive formula for a rule-formulation (as there is in the cases of commands, promises, and questions) and that there are available a large variety of ways of expressing a rule. All of these, however, were found to agree in certain features of their *content*. It must be possible to read off from each rule-formulation (i) a class of human "actions," (ii) a class of persons who perform those actions, and (iii) an indication of whether those actions are demanded, forbidden, or permitted. (In the case of an "open" rule, intended to apply to "whomever it might concern," the second element might be omitted.)

There followed a rough classification of the various senses of "rule" into four groups. In the first of these, a rough synonym for "rule" is "regulation," while the corresponding alternative synonyms in the remaining cases are "instruction," "precept," and "principle." Other tests for picking out the first sense included the possibility of talking about "enacting," "enforcing," or "rescinding" the rule. The fourth sense

[137]

of "rule" was regarded as "limiting" or "degenerate," in the sense of sharing so little in its pattern of usage with the others that its classification with them seems almost a matter for arbitrary decision.

In investigating the uses of "rule" in the first sense (the "regulation-sense"), I tried to distinguish the role of the promulgator from that of the receiver of the regulation. I picked out as "logically primary" (in a sense I tried to make clear) the activity of the rule-maker, which I called "adopting and announcing" the rule. One of the points I most wished to stress was the "performatory aspect" of this activity—its function as *"bringing* the regulation into effect." I also paid considerable attention to the contextual conditions (such as the established authority of the rule-maker) that had to be satisfied before a rule could be made effective.

On the side of the receiver of a regulation (the consumer, as it were), the most important point was, perhaps, my contention that "understanding" a regulation involved treating knowledge of the regulation as an incentive or motive to behave in the way specified. Correspondingly, I had to emphasize a difference between stating *that* a certain rule is in force and *citing* the rule. It is the latter that occurs when the rule is characteristically used as a *reason* for defending or criticizing courses of action.

I investigated briefly what could be meant by saying that certain systems of activities are "constituted" by rules.

Then, I undertook to determine whether it makes sense to speak of "unformulated" or "implicit" rules. In so doing, I had to explore the logical relations to be found holding between explicit rules. A good sense was found to be attached to the notion of rules being implied by given rules. In this sense, there can certainly be implied rules, viz., those that are so implied. I also came to the conclusion that there can occur cases of implicit or unformulated "basic" rules (i.e., such as cannot be inferred from the explicit rules).

Similar conclusions were found to hold for the sense of

[138]

"rule" other than those grouped together as "regulation-senses."

Finally I considered whether it was proper to speak of rules of language and answered this question in the affirmative.

VII

Possibility

MY OPPONENT has just announced "Check," and now it is my turn to move. There are only two places for the king to go, neither of them inviting, so I take time for reflection. As I sit there, trying to avoid checkmate, what am I thinking *about?* A natural answer would be: I am thinking about two *possible moves.* Another would be: I am trying to choose between the two possible moves.

When the expression, "possible move," is used in this way, the adjective has approximately the same force as "available," or "permissible," or "legal." The rules of chess allow me to make either of two moves in the given position, but forbid me to make any others. Were I to try moving the king to a forbidden square, my opponent would have the right to object, "That move is impossible—you're still in check!" He could challenge the move by appeal to the rule requiring the king to move immediately out of check.

Similar remarks apply to every case in which a chess move is branded as "impossible": the intended meaning is that the rules of the game prohibit the move in that particular situation. Conversely, the possible moves are those not forbidden by the rules—the moves that are permitted. Players also use the word "possible" to mean that some move is worth considering because it seems "good" or tactically appropriate. In that sense, "possible" is opposed to "obviously bad" or "out of the question." I shall ignore this and many other senses of "possible."

It follows from what I have said that whether a given move is "possible" or not in a given situation is something that can be settled by a strict proof. Given a description of a position of the pieces on the board, and the accepted rules of the game, a conclusion about the legality of a given move follows by deductive inference. That a given *chess* move is possible in a given chess position is an analytic proposition.

Consider next a familiar ambiguity in the word "move." At a simultaneous chess exhibition, it may happen that the man sitting on my right has reached the same position as I have and therefore has the same choice to make. If my possible moves are K-Q1 and K-Q2, he will then have the *same* moves, K-Q1 and K-Q2, at his disposal. Indeed the very same move can be played by any number of players on any number of occasions, or by the same player at different times. But a move in this sense need not be played by anybody: indeed it is quite certain that some moves have never been played at all. Whether moves are to count as the same or different is immediately determined by their description in chess notation. Identity statements about moves in this sense, like a host of other statements about them, contain no references, explicit or implicit, to particular players or particular occasions of play. When a great chess master said "All the mistakes are there, waiting to be made," it was this conception of a move that he had in mind. Moves might be compared to numbers, or geometrical lines, or any other so-called "ideal entities."

On the other hand, it is not unusual to count the number of moves in a particular game, and then the word "move" is used in another, though related, sense. Even though I found myself in check in exactly the same position at two junctures in the same game, and moved the king to the same square each time, the record of the game would show me as having made *two* distinct moves. In one sense the moves are the very same, though in another they are different. In the second sense of "move," nobody can make my move except myself, the same player cannot make the same move on two occasions, and there is no such thing as a move that is not played. Words such as "position" and "game," which I have been using, display the same ambiguity. The distinction is reminiscent of the so-called "type-token" distinction, but I shall not pursue this.

Now back to the game, where I am still wondering how to move the king without being checkmated. I am still hesitating between two possible moves. In saying this, have I just used "move" in the first or in the second of the two senses I have indicated?

Well, *both* answers would be right. We have seen that two players might have to choose between exactly the same moves. On the other hand, it is also correct to say that I am perplexed about *my move* (not his)—the move which I alone can make, and must make at a determinate time and on a determinate occasion. A philosopher might even perceive an absurdity in speaking of choosing *the* move K-Q2, in a sense of "move" in which there just *is* that move whether anybody plays chess or not. Such a philosopher would also object to the expression, "choose a number," on the ground that one cannot *do anything* to an "ideal entity."

I have to decide what *I* am going to do, here and now. If I am satisfied that the two moves are possible, my interest then shifts to the particular consequence to be expected of each. As I ponder the move K-Q2, I wonder whether *it* would worry my opponent, deceive him as to my intentions, and so on. It seems now as if my choice is between two particular actions, in a sense of "action" in which an action has necessarily a determinate place, time, and performer.

There is nothing wrong in describing my choice as one between two moves, in a sense of "move" in which you might have the same moves from which to choose. Clearly, this is an ordinary and correct way of speaking. But it is equally correct to say that my choice is *not* the same as yours, since I must consider my opponent's intentions and the probable results of the actions I alone can take. The possible move that I shall inevitably *not* play, since I can at best play one, appears more puzzling on the second conception than on the first.

I have contrasted the two "possible" moves with the host of "impossible" ones forbidden by the rules. Another contrast is with the *actual* move that I eventually play. Suppose

I in fact play K-Q2; then the other move, K-Q1, that I had been considering, remains a move that *was* possible in the position now irrevocably altered. Although it is no longer possible, the truth remains that it *was* possible in the position in which I moved. Consider now the following comparisons between the actual move K-Q2, and the move that was possible (K-Q1).

(1) The two moves are described in the chess notation in exactly similar ways. If I first wrote down the possible moves, I would need only to add a check mark to indicate my actual move. The difference between the formulas for the possible move and the actual move is like the difference between an unasserted and an asserted proposition, or between the painting of an imaginary landscape and of an actual one. It is as if the difference between the formula for the actual and the corresponding formula for the possible resides not in the formula itself but in something extrinsic to it.

(2) The actual move has an indefinite number of properties, in a somewhat broad sense of that word. For instance, it is a move of the king, removes that piece from check, and results in a capture; perhaps it surprises my opponent and is applauded by the spectators. Of these and other true statements that can be made about the actual move, some are necessary truths, following from the rules of the game and the character of the position reached, while others, like those about the responses of the opponent and the spectators, are contingent.

Similar remarks can be made about the alternative move that was not played. It too was a king move, taking the piece out of check and resulting in a capture. It seems, however, that all the true *unconditional* statements concerning the unplayed move follow necessarily from the definition of the move and its setting in the game. An attempt to make statements about the unplayed move that parallel the contingent statements about the actual move results in an important shift in formulation. It is ridiculous to say that the possible move *will* surprise my opponent or delight the spectators:

[143]

so long as the move is under consideration we are forced to say that it *would* surprise the opponent and *would* delight the spectators. The enforced use of the subjunctive strongly suggests that the possible move does not have any contingent properties unless it is actually played. And this, in turn, reinforces a tendency to think of a possible move in what I earlier called the "first sense" of move, in which I compared the move to a number or any other "ideal entity."

Connected with this is what I will call the *schematic* character of the possible move. The eleventh move played by Botwinnik in the third game for the world championship might be reported as having been made confidently, energetically, without hesitation; but it would be absurd to apply any of these epithets to the possible moves that he did not choose to play. Again, somebody might object that the reporter had *misdescribed* the eleventh move, by using the wrong formula; but it would be absurd to speak of misdescribing a possible move. A realistic painting of the Statue of Liberty that showed the goddess brandishing a sword could be criticized as inaccurate, but it would be preposterous to inquire whether the painting of some imaginary statute was a faithful representation. It is as if the description of the actual move referred to something that allowed for endless empirical investigation, while the supposedly parallel description of the possible move completely defined that move in a way that makes "further investigation" an absurdity.

At this point some philosophers might be tempted to say that the description of the actual move has reference, while the description of the possible move has only sense, and does not stand for anything. Yet if "K-Q1" stands for nothing, how can I say that *it,* the move I did not play, *would* have surprised the other player? Is it really a mistake to use the pronoun here?

(3) There is a strong inclination to say that the possible move is something "real" or "objective," whose properties can be "discovered" if enough trouble is taken. When I think

[144]

about the possible moves, I am not spinning fancies or day-dreaming: I have to pay close attention, I may overlook consequences, I can *make mistakes*. The attitude expressed by such remarks seems even more appropriate when the choice is not defined by the arbitrary rules of a game: in choosing whether to have a tooth extracted or merely filled, I feel that I am choosing between *real* alternatives, each invested with genuine properties beyond my power to alter. Of course, the uses of "possible" and "possibility" in such a case differ from those appropriate to the game of chess, but parallel considerations apply. There is an inclination to say that the "possible fact" is just as "hard" as the "real fact" [1] though there is also an inclination to say the opposite.

Moreover, the choice of one alternative does not cancel the considerations favoring or opposing the unchosen alternative, though they may become academic. I do not disown my appraisal of the unplayed move: after the event, I may feel regret at having made the wrong choice, basing that regret on what *would have been* the consequences of the rejected choice. Indeed, retroactive judgments about unrealized possibilities play so indispensable a part in the assignment of responsibility that prohibition of reference to unrealized possibilities would render much discussion about practical affairs impossible. An unrealized possibility seems to be a

[1] Excellent illustrations of this attitude toward possibilities can be found in the writings of J. S. Mill. A characteristic remark is: "We speedily learn to think of Nature as made up solely of these groups of possibilities [he is talking about Matter, regarded as a 'Permanent Possibility of sensation'], and the active force in Nature as manifested in the modification of some of these by others. The sensations, though the original foundation of the whole, come to be looked upon as a sort of accident depending on us, and *the possibilities as much more real than the actual sensations,* nay as the very realities of which these are only the representations, appearances, or effects" (*An Examination of Sir William Hamilton's Philosophy*, 5th ed., London 1878, pp. 230–231—italics supplied). He talks of "the immediate presence of the possibilities" (*ibid.*, p. 237), says they "are not constructed by the mind itself, but merely recognized by it" (*ibid.*, p. 239), and calls the "groups of possibilities" the "fundamental reality in Nature" (*ibid.*, p. 232).

[145]

genuine subject of discourse, however hard it may be to be sure that one is speaking the truth about it.

In the light of the considerations I have been sketching, possibilities can come to look exceedingly mysterious. Imagine the following soliloquy:

The possible moves I must consider *exist* in some sense, here and now. If there was nothing there to be considered, I couldn't even think about the possibilities, let alone compare their properties, probable consequences, and respective merits. But I *can* think about them, talk about them, even visualize them. I can virtually see the king moving out of check! Now what difference is there between the move that I "see" and the move that I play except that the one exists and the other doesn't? The same considerations and questions apply to both—except that it's harder to make sure about the possibilities. The only difference between the actual move and the corresponding possible move is that the one happens and the other doesn't. Now since the merely possible move is real, even though it doesn't happen, a thing can be real without actually existing!

From this standpoint, making the actual move is like selecting *one* card from a pack. There is the pack of possible moves—the impossible ones having been discarded—from which I must draw just one. But this image is still inadequate for the peculiar conception I am evoking. It is as if the cards in the pack were in monochrome, while the one I choose becomes vividly colored as I draw it. As if my choice made the "mere" possibility become fully real. My choice, as it were, brings the sleeping possibility to life, as the prince did when he kissed the sleeping beauty. The realized possibility comes to life while the others slumber on.

At the center of this conception is the idea of a direct *comparison* between two things—the actual move and the possible one—the two conceived as differing only in the presence or absence of some quality or character. I believe Wittgenstein was thinking of the same or a similar conception of possibilities when he said that "the possibility of a movement is . . . supposed to be like a shadow of the movement

[146]

itself" (*Philosophical Investigations,* Oxford, 1953, section 194).

We might also say that the possible move is conceived as being the *ghost* of an actual move. For as a ghost is a man without material substance, so the possible move appears bloodless or unsubstantial, needing only an infusion of reality to become actual. (This is connected in turn with a meta-physical conception of reality or "Being" as an attribute able to be present or absent in varying degrees.) When I "see" the possible move on the unchanged chessboard, I see a partly transparent image, a ghostly emanation of the unmoved piece; when I try to imagine unrealized possibilities, I imagine transparent "facts" superimposed upon what is authentically the case.

The ghostly conception of possibilities is picturesque but incoherent, for, taken seriously, it soon generates contradictions. The possible moves are those that could be played *now,* i.e., they are somehow determined by, or present in, the actual configuration of the pieces. So, if the moves are to be possible, but not yet actual, the pieces *must not move.* (When they do so, a possibility becomes an actuality.) It is of the essence of the possible move, one might say, that the piece concerned shall *not* move. So the movement of the king in the king's possible move is just as unsubstantial as every other feature of that move. (One is even tempted to say that the sense in which the king moves in the possible move is other than that in which it moves in the actual move.) But if nothing moves when the possible move exists, it begins to seem absurd to think of the possible move as a *kind* of move: we might as well speak about a kind of "possible walking" that requires no use of the legs.

Again, it seems of the essence of a merely possible move that it should not be observable in the way that the actual move is. William James says:

Science professes to draw no conclusions but such as are based on matters of fact, things that have actually happened; but how can any amount of assurance that something actually happened give

[147]

us the least grain of information as to whether another thing might or might not have happened in its place? Only facts can be proved by other facts [*The Will to Believe*, New York, 1903, p. 152].

We can photograph the actual move, but it is nonsensical to speak of photographing the possible move. So here we have a ghost that threatens to disappear altogether: ghosts that clank chains and show their wounds are feared because they can be heard and seen; but a wholly unobservable ghost is innocuous—is nothing at all. What happens to the ghostly conception of possibilities when the ghost has to be invisible? It won't do to say that the properties of the ghost-possibility must be *inferred*—for this implies that the possibility *might be* observed without inference.

No wonder, then, that possibilities look to some philosophers like occult entities, talk about which is a sign of superstition. Nelson Goodman includes "experiences that are possible but not actual" among "things inacceptable without explanation" in a list including "electrons, angels, devils, and classes" (*Fact, Fiction and Forecast*, p. 44). He says "Possible occurrences are for us no more admissible as unexplained elements than are occult capacities" (*ibid.*, p. 45) and proposes to expel what he calls the "ghost of the possible" (*ibid.*, p. 57). By "explanation" he means definition in terms of the actual: "My main purpose," he says, "has been to suggest that discourse, even about possibles, need not transgress the boundaries of the actual world" (*ibid.*, p. 56).

The strongest source of philosophical discomfort about possibilities is the absence of verifiability, felt most acutely in the case of so-called "counterfactual possibilities" (the moves I might have made but did not), where any conceivable verification seems excluded. Some of the as yet unrealized possibilities may yet be submitted to verification; but a possibility known to have been unrealized has not even a change of verification and therefore seems exceptionally "occult."

[148]

One escape lies in the contention that talk about possibilities is simply superfluous. If the supposed existence of the possible moves *follows from* the rules of chess and the description of the configuration of the pieces (or, in the case of empirical possibilities, from the laws of nature and the "boundary conditions") could we not manage without talking about "possibilities" at all? Perhaps talk about them is simply an indirect way of talking about the rules and the configuration, both of which can be regarded as "actual"? And perhaps talk about empirical possibilities is merely a roundabout way of talking about facts of observation and the relevant laws of nature? For a determinist, this line of thought can easily seem to entail a denial of "objective possibilities." [2] If all the relevant laws of nature were known, it would then be seen that whatever happens must happen; the unknown laws that obtain in nature leave no room for unrealized possibilities, and our talk about them is no more than an expression of partial ignorance. Only in what might be called a myopic view of the universe is the word "possible" needed.

It is not hard to imagine ways in which the desire to explain the possible in terms of the actual might be partially gratified. Suppose that while thinking about my move, I am allowed to set up the position on a pocket chessboard, on which I may then freely *try out* moves I wish to consider. Then, somebody puzzled about the whereabouts of the "possible moves" in the original game might be shown the actual moves made on the supplementary chessboard. The possible moves in one game would then be the actual moves in another. From this standpoint, what is called "considering" or "thinking about" possible moves is a kind of *rehearsal* for the real thing. We meet the objection that after all we do not have the supplementary chessboard by drawing attention to our images and thoughts. "Seeing" the moves on the board, or thinking about them, we might try saying, is no

2 "Possibilities that fail to get realized are, for determinism, pure illusions; they never were possibilities at all" (James, *op. cit.*, p. 151).

[149]

different in principle from "playing" them on a second chess-board. In all cases, it might be said, there is an *actual* rehearsal or preparatory performance (moving pieces on another board, having images, pronouncing words): there is no need to assume the reality of mysterious "possibilities" over and above what is in principle directly observable. This is similar to the maneuver of the many philosophers who have tried to explain "counterfactual statements" in terms of deductive relations between selected propositions. They say, in effect: "Why bother with mysterious things answering to counterfactual statements? We certainly can write down scientific generalizations and perform actual inferences with their aid. *There* is the place to locate the reference of counterfactuals."

Such attempts to reduce the possible to the actual are bound to fail, because they do violence to the ways in which we use the words "possible," "possibility," and the related modal words, "can," "could," "would," and "might." Consider what would be involved in teaching a child how to say correctly of a mechanism that it *can* move in one way but not another. Certainly the training would call for actually moving the mechanism in the ways in question, and to this extent reference to the actual would be involved. But if the child refused to say in any instance that the mechanism *could* move in a certain specified way until it *had* actually been made to move in that way, the training would have failed. We would be unable to tell whether he took the modal statement as a sheer report on what had actually happened. Language practices in which "can" and "possible" are used differ in sharp ways from those in which room is provided only for indicative or categorical reports.

Attempts to model possibility statements in more or less ingenious ways upon categorical statements commit the initial mistake of accepting the ghostly view. It does not matter in a way whether a philosopher argues that because possibilities would have to be ghosts they cannot exist, or argues that since they do exist reality must be queerer than

[150]

Horatio imagined. In either case, an incorrect conception of the uses of "possible" has been accepted as a starting point. Meinong and Russell have equally succumbed to the lure of the ghostly conception.

If the ghostly view were merely a picture having no consequences, we might regard it as harmless. What does it matter, after all, if I see everything blurred by a mist of possibilities? Although it might interest a psychiatrist, the imagery is irrelevant to a conceptual analysis. The picture becomes philosophically important only when it leads to the drawing of metaphysical consequences and the raising of metaphysical questions.

The metaphysical difficulty is that of finding room in the universe, as it were, for the unrealized possibilities. There seems something absurd in the notion that God might first have created the observable universe in its entirety, and then paused to consider whether or not to add the unrealized possibilities. We are thus impelled to regard talk about "possibilities" as fictitious or redundant.

On the other hand, there are powerful motives, as I have tried to show, for saying that possibilities are not fictitious but in some sense "real" or "objective." But then we want to know *where* they can be—we are embarrassed to find a place for them.

The basic mistake underlying both metaphysical conceptions is that of treating an expression such as "possible move" as *referring* to something, the mistake of assuming that the expression "possible X" has an objective counterpart—or else no proper meaning at all. Closely related is the mistake of treating "possible X" and "actual X" as co-ordinate species of a single genus. These are mistakes about the "logical grammar" of the word "possible," traceable to an oversimplified and faulty conception of the ways in which we use that word and its cognates, and the ways in which they differ from the uses of adjectives such as "thin" and "bloodless" that apply to material objects. One way to overcome the conceptual confusion that underlies metaphysical argument

[151]

about possibilities would therefore be to undertake a detailed survey of how we do in fact use the words "possible," "possibility," and their cognates. But that still remains to be done.

VIII

Making Something Happen

YOU ARE thirsty, but there is a glass of beer within easy reach: you stretch out your hand, bring the glass to your lips, and drink. Here is what I call a *perfectly clear case* of making something happen. When you brought the glass nearer, that was a perfect instance of what all of us *call* "making something happen." [1] But of course many other simple actions would serve just as well: closing a window, opening a drawer, turning a door knob, sharpening a pencil. Any number of perfectly clear cases can be found of *making something happen.*

The following is not a clear case of making something happen. On hearing the opening of this paper, a member of the audience leaves the room, to be found later in the nearest saloon. To establish that my remarks *made* him leave the room would require a specific investigation. Evidence could be obtained for or against the view that talk about drinking had *made* the hearer leave: until such evidence had been provided, the final verdict would remain in doubt.

In the case of the thirsty man reaching for the glass, an investigation to determine whether or not he really did move the glass would be out of place. There would be an

---

[1] Or, rather, a clear case of "moving a glass." The expression "making something happen" is introduced for brevity in referring to similar cases. The first part of the paper investigates a class of transitive verbs, like "moving," "breaking," "opening," "upsetting," etc., indicated by the blanket expression "making something happen." When the expression "making something happen" occurs, the reader may usually imagine the more specific expression "moving a glass" substituted—with the understanding, however, that the discussion is intended to apply indifferently to an entire class of similar expressions.

absurdity in saying that evidence could be provided for or against the view that he had moved the glass, or in saying that whether he had made anything happen was an hypothesis. It would be absurd to say that there was a question whether he had moved the glass, whose answer would be undecided until further evidence had been weighed.

For what could be the goal of the supposed investigation? If anybody is not already satisfied that the familiar episode *is* a case of what we ordinarily call "making something happen," it is inconceivable that further empirical evidence would satisfy him. The supposed investigation would have no terminus; criteria would be lacking by which to judge the relevance and strength of testimony.

I am trying to affirm something noncontroversial and hence acceptable in advance of any philosophical analysis or commitment. I am contending that we do all treat simple episodes like the one described as perfectly clear cases of making something happen.

We do in fact recognize the absurdity of a supposed attempt to *find out* whether the drinker had made the glass move. Suppose I were to say to somebody "You saw that man reach out for that glass of beer just now—well, *find out* whether he moved the glass." I have no doubt that a layman would be dumbfounded and quite at a loss to know what could be meant. A sufficient reply would be: "Surely, we *saw* him move the glass." If I insisted that I wanted *evidence* that the drinker had moved the glass, my interlocutor might begin to suspect the situation was abnormal—for this would be one way of making sense of my demand. Suppose we were suddenly to see the glass of beer levitate, and fly like a homing pigeon straight to the drinker's mouth! Then we might rub our eyes and begin to wonder whether the man in the armchair had really moved the glass the first time. We might then plausibly suspect ourselves to be in some magician's establishment, well stocked with trick devices for making objects move in extraordinary ways. This would be a fantastically abnormal situation: in describing the case of the thirsty drinker, I wished to present a situation that was *normal*, one whose description was intended to exclude monstrosities and miracles.

I was therefore taking for granted that the person concerned was neither hypnotized nor walking in his sleep nor obeying a neurotic compulsion to reach for the glass nor acting in response to threats. And I was assuming that the glass of beer was an ordinary vessel, having no concealed magnet or other special devices and subject to no remote physical or mental controls. In short, I was taking for granted that the exemplary situation was a perfectly familiar, ordinary, case. If a situation were not of this familiar sort, it might then very well be necessary to investigate and find out whether the man concerned really had made something happen.

So far, I have been contrasting a perfectly clear case of making something happen with cases in which an investigation would be in order. The latter we might call *problematic cases*. A second kind of contrast is between a perfectly clear case and a *borderline case*.

Suppose you jogged my hand, so that my elbow caught the glass and spilled its contents. Did *I* spill the glass, or did *you* really do it? Both answers are plausible. We are inclined to say something like "I spilled the beer all right, but you made me do it, so really *you* spilled it." Here, the presence of the qualification "really" in "really you spilled it" is a sign that criteria for the use of the expression "making something happen" are no longer precise and determinate. We would not teach a child what "making something happen" means by citing *this* kind of case, nor a case in which somebody's involuntary gesture displaced an object. Similarly, we would not teach somebody the meaning of "orange" by showing color patches that most of us would hesitate whether to label orange or yellow.

The uncertainty here is not due to lack of information, and could not be removed by any empirical investigation. Uncertainty of application is a feature of our uses of "orange"

[155]

and can be removed only by *stipulation*. Our uses of the expression "making something happen" is infected by similar uncertainty. Only I would wish to deny that any such uncertainty of application is to be found in the clear case that I began by describing.

Indeed, if anybody were to show genuine hesitation about using the expression "making something happen" in the situation described, that would be evidence that he did not really *understand* that expression. If I were teaching a foreigner how to use that English expression, a test of my success would be his unhesitating identification of the exemplary situation as a case of making something happen. (Of course, he must also hesitate in borderline cases.) Should the pupil waver in the clear case, we might try to find out whether he suspected some hidden mechanism or trick device, i.e., whether he mistakenly took the situation to be abnormal. But if he convinced us that he fully understood our description of the familiar case, yet still did not know whether to say that something had been made to happen, we could be sure that efforts to teach him the uses of the English expression had not yet succeeded.

I have said that the case of the thirsty drinker is a perfectly clear case of making something happen, leaving no room for further empirical investigation—a case neither "problematic" nor "borderline." I want now to add that the episode is also a *paradigm* for application of the phrase "making something happen."

That it is a paradigm is closely connected with its being a perfectly clear case, yet to call it a "paradigm" is to say something new.

Suppose we are faced with something that is *not* a clear case of making something happen and wish to decide whether or not to apply the expression. A natural recourse is to compare the doubtful case with some perfectly clear case with a view to finding sufficient similarity or dissimilarity to yield a correct decision. By treating the clear case as a *standard*, we can base our decision to use or withhold the expression upon *reasons:* we appeal *to* the clear case to resolve doubt. It follows, therefore, that no such reasons can be given why the clear case itself should bear the identifying label in question. There is nothing else to which the clear case can be compared—nothing more to serve as a standard. The absurdity of asking for reasons for the application to the clear case would be just like the absurdity of trying to give reasons why the standard meter rod is counted as being one meter in length, or a standard color sample is counted as being "red." Should someone demand reasons in defense of calling my exemplary instance a case of making something happen, the best I could do by way of reply would be to say "That's what I *call* 'making something happen.'" Now here I am not offering a genuine reason, but repudiating the demand for one. The retort "That's what I *call* 'making something happen'" is a way of *showing how* I use the expression. In making that retort, I show that I treat the instance as a paradigm. But showing is not arguing, and brandishing a paradigm is not offering a reason.

The case of the thirsty drinker differs from that of the meter rod in one important respect. The meaning of "one meter long" is formally defined in terms of a standard measure, so that those who understand how the expression is used know that a dispute about the correctness of any attribution of metric length would ultimately have to be resolved by appeal to a known and identifiable standard of comparison. But there is no formal definition of "making something happen," and of course no permanent and identifiable situations to serve as standards of comparison. We have a wide range of choice in exhibiting "perfectly clear cases," and they are not preserved in official bureaus of standards. Nevertheless, we *do* appeal to them in case of doubt, our choice of just *these* situations as acceptable standards being a feature of our use of the expression in question. Instead of the unique arbiter, we have, as it were, a reserve of available judges, *any* of which can serve indifferently to remind us of our linguistic conventions. Pressed to give reasons, we even-

[157]

tually stop at situations of which we can say no more than "That's what I *call* such and such." Our choice of halting places shows *which* instances we in fact treat as paradigms.

In calling my exemplary situation a *paradigm* for the use of the expression "making something happen," I am therefore claiming that it is used as a standard for the correctness of application of the expression in question.

Paradigm cases also serve as standards of reference when we pass from primitive uses of an expression to other uses, derived by resemblance, analogy, and metaphorical extension. Uses of "making something happen" and cognate expressions are strikingly various: yet the paradigm helps to illuminate *all* such uses. The exemplary instance, or a sufficiently similar alternative, functions as a *prototype* for the derivative uses of "making something happen." We refer to it in testing the plausibility of analogy and metaphor.

As we pass from the homespun language of "making something happen" to the more sophisticated language of "cause" and "effect," the influence of the paradigm remains powerful. We continue to model descriptions of cases remote from the prototypes upon the simpler primitive cases, often by using metaphors literally applicable only to these clear cases. In order to understand clearly what we mean by "cause" and "effect" we must labor to understand what we mean by the precausal language in which the more sophisticated vocabulary is embedded.

If my exemplary situation is a clear case (a paradigm, a prototype) of making something happen, it follows that it would be nonsensical to speak of there being any possible *doubt* that something was there made to happen. This remains true, no matter how much the original description of the situation might be augmented or elaborated by scientific explanation, provided only that the additional information did not conflict with the original assumption of "normality." A scientist might explain why the pressure of the fingers required the glass to change position without slipping through the hand; another scientist might offer elaborate explanations of the physiology of thirst; a third might connect your present thirst with childhood deprivation. But such accounts, informative as they might be, would have no tendency to discredit the correctness of the use of the expression "making something happen." They could not do so, because the description of the paradigm case is complete. If the description left gaps to be filled by scientific data as yet unknown, none of us would be able to use the expression "making something happen," correctly. The expression would be a blank check drawn upon an uncertain future.

My chief contention, so far, is the commonplace one that it is perfectly certain that persons do sometimes make something happen. It might be unnecessary to insist on anything so obvious, had not philosophers sometimes claimed to have arguments to show that it is logically impossible for anything to be a cause, since the notion of a cause is self-contradictory. Now to make something happen is to cause something to happen. It is certain therefore that the notion of a cause is not self-contradictory.

2

Once we are satisfied that we have identified and sufficiently described a paradigm for the use of a given expression, we can proceed to look for *features* and *criteria of application*. That is to say, we can ask *"What is it about* this clear case that we treat as relevant in using it as a standard of comparison?"

Sometimes the search for criteria leads nowhere: there is no answer to the question "What is it about this clear case of red that makes us call it 'red'?" But sometimes a demand for criteria can be met. Raised about our paradigm case of making something happen, it can elicit a set of relevant features, some trite and uninteresting, but others surprisingly at variance with accepted analyses of causation.

I shall list some of these features and comment upon a few of them. In order to save time, I will refer to the person who moved the glass as *"P."* I will call the object moved, *"O,"* its motion *"M,"* and the action performed by the agent, *"A."* The following assertions about the episode seem to me to be plainly true:

1. What happened was made to happen by *P*.
2. What he made happen was a *motion* of *O* (i.e., *M*).
3. *P* made this happen by *doing* something (moved his hand to *O*, clasped it, and brought it back to him).
4. In doing *A*, *O* was acting *freely* (was not in any way being forced or constrained to do *A*).
5. *A* occurred throughout the time that *M* was occurring.
6. *M* (the motion of *O*) would not have occurred unless *A* had occurred.
7. When *A* occurred, *M* had to occur.

If we used the accepted terminology of discussions of causation, we could roughly summarize the foregoing seven points by saying that the cause was a *free act* of a person, the effect a *motion* of an inanimate object, the cause and effect were *co-temporal* (operative throughout the same time interval), and the effect was a *necessary consequence*. (We might add that the cause and the effect were spatially contiguous, in a way too obvious to detail.)

I shall now comment on some of these points.

The agent acted freely. The contrast to be made here is with forced or constrained action and, again, with action as an intermediary. If *P* had been compelled by physical coercion or by threats, we would confidently say he had not acted freely; there might be more hesitation about saying the same when he acted because asked to do so, or when he expected to receive some reward, or had some other ulterior motive. But neither coercion nor inducement were present in our paradigm case: *P* took the glass because he "just wanted to." If he had any motive at all, it may have been that he was thirsty, but he might equally well have had no antecedent and separable thirst. There would be no harm in saying the act was unmotivated— which is not to say it was irrational or unintelligible. On the other hand, the presence in other cases of a distinct and sepa-

[160]

rable motive prior to the act would not disqualify an episode as a clear case of making something happen. Neither presence nor absence of a separable motive functions as a clear-cut criterion.

It may provoke surprise and an accusation of anthropomorphism to find the presence of a person insisted upon as a feature of the paradigm. But the insistence is necessary. A candid examination of causal language will show that our prototypes involve persons. Certainly, the word "make" strongly suggests a maker; and we find it not at all unnatural to substitute "make" for "cause." If this be anthropomorphism, we must make the best of it.

To return to our illustration. Not only is it true that the agent acted freely; we are entitled, I think, to add that the very same situation is a clear case and a paradigm for acting freely. This means, as I previously explained, that it would be logically absurd to demand an investigation as to whether the agent acted freely—and also that there could be no doubt that he had acted freely, nor any further reason to show that he had so acted.

Now if this is so, it follows that so far from there being a radical conflict between the notion of causation and freedom, as many philosophers have insisted, the two notions, or their informal progenitors, are logically inseparable. Our paradigmatic conception of causing something to happen is a conception of somebody *freely* making something happen. So, anything having a tendency to show that the agent was not acting freely, but responding to constraint, duress, or ulterior inducement, would immediately have a tendency to show that he was not *the* cause, but merely an instrument, or an intermediary between the true cause and its effects.

It also follows that no scientific elaboration of the antecedents of the paradigmatic episodes could destroy their characters as paradigms of acting freely, and so of causing something to happen. No physiological or psychoanalytical explanation of the unconscious cause, if any, of P's moving O can have the least tendency to discredit our calling his act a case of freely

[161]

making something happen. Of course, the case would be altered if such scientific elaboration led us to view his act as pathological—but this outcome was excluded by our description of the paradigm.

The effective action lasted throughout the motion it produced. It has been a truism for writers on causation that the cause must *precede* the effect. And certainly there would be a logical absurdity in supposing that the cause might succeed its effect. But our paradigm has cause and effect occurring together. It might be objected that the initiating action, *A,* began before the motion, *M,* it produced. But it would be easy to define the action as lasting exactly the same period of time as the motion generated; we must therefore allow that sometimes cause and effect can be simultaneous or cotemporal. This will not render the causal relation symmetrical, as might be feared; the desired asymmetry is here ensured by the cause being a *free action,* while the effect is not an action at all, but the motion of an inanimate body. And when one person acts upon another, so that one action is contiguous and cotemporal with another *action,* we can still immediately identify the cause as that action of the two that was *free.* If John pushes James, John acts freely, but James does not; and conversely, if James was moving of his own free will, John did not push him.

Now cotemporality of cause and effect is not a mere peculiarity of "prescientific" thinking; it is a commonplace of causal description at scientific levels, as philosophers have occasionally noticed. The moon's gravitational pull lasts as long as the tide it produces; difference of temperature operates throughout the period that thermometric expansion occurs; a catalyst continues to act during the chemical reaction it is influencing; and so on, for any number of similar cases. There is some reason to regard the principle of strict priority of the cause as a metaphysical prejudice. And, like other metaphysical prejudices, it can be opposed by equally powerful metaphysical prejudices of opposite tendency.

The induced motion would not have occurred but for the

[162]

action that produced it. As it stands, this formula is incorrect. It is untrue to say the glass would not have moved as it did unless *P* had made it do so—for if *P* had not moved it, some other person might have done so. What we mean, of course, is that the glass would not have moved *by itself,* i.e., that if *P* had not performed action *A,* or some other action resulting in *O*'s moving, the glass would have remained stationary. In short, the glass would not have moved, had *A* not occurred, while all other features of the setting remained unchanged. One might perhaps say that *A* is *conditionally necessary* for the occurrence of *M.* Or again: the occurrence of *A* included *part* of the necessary conditions for *M* to occur.

In speaking of this feature of the paradigm, I have used a "counterfactual." I said that, in the presence of certain contextual factors, *M would not* have occurred but for *A*'s occurrence. Alternatively: if *A* had not occurred (other things remaining unchanged), *M* would not have occurred. Now such a statement is a so-called "counterfactual." Some contemporary philosophers have found this notion troublesome—possibly because they have failed to satisfy themselves how a counterfactual conditional could be verified. Yet the notion of *would not have happened unless* is as primitive and unproblematic as the notion of *making something happen.* Both are applicable in the same circumstances, long before any question of scientific terminology arises. There are, accordingly, relatively direct and unsophisticated ways of establishing such a claim as: The glass would not have moved unless somebody had moved it. In making such an assertion we do, in fact, simply rely upon our commonplace knowledge that when nobody is "doing anything" the glass stays put, and that when somebody does "do something" of a certain sort the glass moves. It would, however, be a mistake to say that the statement "The glass would not have moved by itself" has the same meaning as "Glasses do not move when left alone"; for the two statements are made in different contexts and have different uses, even though their verification procedures may sometimes be identical.

[163]

When pushed, the glass HAD to move. Certainly it is natural to say this, and there must be some sense in which it is true. No doubt mythology plays a part: there is a discernible inclination to think of the moving object as animate—a manikin, helpless in our grasp, "having no choice" but to move. But good sense remains when the mythology has been discarded. We need only to remind ourselves of the circumstances in which we say that an object acted on by an external force does *not* have to move. We say so when the given force is insufficient to produce the desired motion. If I push my cat gently, Hodge may or may not move, though if he does I shall say he did *because* I pushed him; but if I push hard enough, Hodge *has* to move. Again, a penny tossed into the air *has* to come down again, but it does not *have* to come down tails. Here and elsewhere, the relevant contrast is between what sometimes happens and what invariably happens. To generalize: We say that *M had* to happen when *A* happened, only if *M* would always ensue, given an unchanged setting and the same concomitant. Using a phrase parallel to one introduced earlier, we might call *A conditionally sufficient* for *M*. Alternatively, we might say that *A* is a part of a certain sufficient condition for the occurrence of *M*.

In this cursory examination of some features of a paradigm of making something happen, I have had little occasion to refer to any "constant conjunction" between producing action and induced motion. The omission has been deliberate. The assertion *"P* made *M* happen by doing *A"* does not mean the same as "If *P* were to repeat actions sufficiently like *A,* then, other things being equal, motions sufficiently like *M* would invariably ensue." If the analysis were correct, the original causal statement would include as part of its meaning a generalization, whose verification would need repeated observation and an induction upon an indefinite number of situations resembling the original situation. Far from the original statement ("*P* made something happen etc.") being verifiable by inspection, a lengthy inquiry would be needed to establish its truth. (It is as if we had to perform a long inductive inquiry into the behavior of meter rods before we could use a given meter rod to measure a given object.) But I think the truth of the matter is much simpler: In order to be sure that P and O move, *we need only look*. The verifying situation is right before our eyes. To establish conclusively that P did make O move, we need only be sure that P did do such and such, and that O was moving thus and thus meanwhile.

I do not say we would be right in saying that A made M happen whenever an action and a cotemporal motion are contiguous. In using the language of "making something happen," we take for granted that the episode in view has a special and appropriate character. Should we be challenged to specify the requisite conditions in analytical detail, we would eventually need to talk about constant conjunctions; and in deciding in unusual, unfamiliar, or abnormal settings, whether the use of causal language is appropriate, prolonged inductive investigations might be needed. But such investigation would establish the *presuppositions* for the proper use of causal language, not the meaning of the assertions made by means of such language.

Consider the following analogy: If I say, "Jones just made the move, 'pawn to king four,'" a full and sufficient verification of my claim is that Jones shifted a characteristically shaped piece of wood from a certain place on a chessboard to a certain other place. Yet, this is only part of the story. I would not say that Jones had made the move, should he know nothing of the game, and were merely moving the piece at random; nor would I say so if he knew how to play chess but were amusing himself by replaying some master's game or were composing a chess problem. In using the language of chess, I take for granted the institution of chess playing and a host of related facts. Before I can teach anybody how to use the language of chess, I must acquaint him with this background of presuppositions. But once the background has been established, I do not *refer* to it each time I announce somebody's move.

There is a general background also to talk about "making

things happen." Such words could not properly be used by anybody ignorant of a host of familiar facts about motions of human bodies, obstructions and resistances offered by other bodies, the dependable behavior of relatively permanent solid objects, and so on. But when we say, "Jones moved the glass," we do not *refer* to these uniformities, or to the remainder of the background of presuppositions. When we say "Jones moved the glass" we draw a line around an episode, whose relevant features are directly observable. An informal causal statement is a straightforward report. Stripped of its background of presuppositions, it would have the simple form "While P did *this, that* happened."

There is a sense, therefore, in which *"P* made M happen by doing A" can be said to mean the same as "While P did A, M happened"—the sense in which both statements would be verified by the same state of affairs. But there is also an important sense in which the two are strikingly different—because they imply different presuppositions and are connected with diverse linguistic practices.

A full account of the linguistic practices connected with the vocabulary of "making something happen" would be lengthy and complicated. One obvious connection is with the language of imperatives. When we order somebody to do something, we envisage his making something happen. If our language contained no provision for isolating causal episodes, we could issue no orders, give no commands. And the same could be said for recipes, plans of operations, and other features of linguistic transactions. All that part of our life concerned with getting things done, or with anticipating and controlling the consequences of our actions, uses the language of making things happen, and is inconceivable without it.

Another connection is with moral language. To say that somebody made M happen is to hold him responsible for it; it can be a prelude to the assignment of praise or blame, punishment or reward. And the further connections with ethical practices are equally obvious. To state the point negatively: A language containing no provision for linking persons with events for whose occurrence they were held responsible would be one in which moral judgments as we now know them would be impossible.

3

So far, I have been considering primitive cases of making something happen. But we also talk about "making something happen" in an enormous variety of derivative situations. Some of the ways in which these related uses are connected with the paradigm are fairly obvious. I have been confining myself to cases where some person causes a *motion*. But it is very natural to extend the language to cases where the agent produces a cessation of motion, i.e., where the motion would not have ceased but for the person's intervention. Or again it is equally natural to talk of making something happen when what is produced is a *qualitative* change, and so we pass, by easy transitions, from the material realm to that of the affections and sentiments. We talk of making somebody laugh, of making somebody reconsider, or making somebody happy— without always realizing how far we have strayed from the prototypes.

Criteria for the use of causal language can also shift in other ways. For instance, we commonly speak of intermediaries as causes. If I make a billiard ball move in such a way as to set another in motion, I can think of the impinging billiard ball as the causal agent. Here we discard the criterion of the human agent, allowing the motion of an inanimate object to count as what "makes something happen." It is easiest to make this type of transition when the new field of application most plainly resembles the original paradigm. We freely attribute causal efficacy when some motion can be made to look like the motion of a human body. So we find no difficulty in conceiving of "forces" that push or pull, bend or squeeze—but extreme discomfort in trying to imagine "action at a distance." The idea of a body "impressing" an external force is altogether natural, but we cannot understand how one body can "attract" another without being joined to it by an unbroken chain of physical intermediaries.

Anybody with a logician's desire for clear-cut distinctions may well be exasperated by the lack of systematic principle in these patterns of analogical and metaphorical extensions of causal language. A search for a common denominator in this kaleidoscope of applications leads at best to "universal conjunction" or the even vaguer notion of "predictability." But such abstract and simplified formulas fail to do justice to the actual uses of "cause" and its cognates. It would be more to the point to ask what role the language of causation plays—to inquire into the purposes served by passing from the homespun language of "making things happen" to the more abstract language of causation.

A partial answer might be that the language of causation seems most fitting when we are concerned with the effective production, prevention, or modification of events. Roughly speaking, an event X is most plainly eligible as a possible cause of another event, Y, if we can manipulate X in such a way as to modify Y. A cause is something that we can or might be able to control. But we invoke causes also when our interest is in explaining something rather than controlling it. And as our accepted patterns of explanation become more complex, our notion of a cause becomes correspondingly more elusive, until it threatens to vanish altogether into the abstract conception of a law, a parameter, a boundary condition, or some combination of all of these. As scientific modes of investigation develop, the language of cause tends to its own supersession.

But this is not a special quirk or weakness of the language of causation. It happens regularly and characteristically in the transition from ordinary language to scientific terminology. Dominating my discussion throughout has been the notion that the vocabulary of "cause" and its informal progenitors is indigenous to ordinary language—the language of practical affairs and common-sense observation or understanding. The vocabulary of causation can be adapted to a scientific context, but the sophistication it suffers proves ultimately fatal. Scien-

[168]

tific insight is the death of causal conceptions. But this does not mean there is anything amiss with the language of causation, when employed in its proper settings. To say the opposite would be as unplausible as to hold that the supersession of words like "hot" and "cold" in favor of the scientific terminology of thermometry shows that there is something wrong, or in need of correction, in the prescientific uses of thermal words.

4

I have been arguing that "cause" is an essentially schematic word, tied to certain more or less stable criteria of application, but permitting wide variation of specific determination according to context and the purposes of investigation. Now if this is so, any attempt to state a "universal law of causation" must prove futile. To anybody who insists that "nothing happens without a sufficient cause" we are entitled to retort with the question "What do you *mean* by 'cause'?" It is safe to predict that the only answer forthcoming will contain such schematic words as "event," "law," and "prediction." These too are words capable of indefinite further determination according to circumstances—and are none the worse for that. But universal statements containing schematic words have no place in rational argument. The fatal defect of determinism is its protean capacity to elude refutation—and by the same token, its informative content is negligible. Whatever virtues it may have in encouraging scientists to search for comprehensive laws and theories, there can be no rational dispute about its truth value. Many of the traditional problems of causation disappear when we become sufficiently clear about what we mean by "cause" and remind ourselves once more of what a peculiar, unsystematic, and erratic notion it is.

IX

Can the Effect Precede the Cause?

SUPPOSE a child were to ask "Why must Monday always come before Tuesday, instead of the other way round? Why can't Tuesday sometimes be the day before Monday for a change?" Such an extraordinary question would be most difficult to answer in a sensible way. But once we had recovered from our initial stupefaction, we might make a first attempt as follows: "There is no 'must' about it at all. The first day of the week is simply *called* 'Monday' and the second day 'Tuesday.' In just the same way one child is called 'Jack' and another 'Mary.' That is how the names are used. But if you wanted a change, you *could* call the first day 'Tuesday' and the second day 'Monday.' And then Tuesday *would* come before Monday. Of course, if you did make this change, other people would probably not know what day of the week you were talking about. So perhaps you had better do as they do, after all!"

This answer treats the original question "Why must Monday always come before Tuesday?" as meaning "What reason is there for using the *words* 'Monday' and 'Tuesday' in such a way that the earlier, not the later, day is always called 'Monday'?" The questioner is taken to be puzzled about one feature of the use of certain *words;* and so the answer is about words, too. This interpretation of the original question precludes a straightforward answer to that question. We have *rejected* the sentence, "Monday *must* come before Tuesday." And instead of giving a reason for the present use of the words "Monday" and "Tuesday," we have said that there is *no* reason for their use.

Sometimes, reasons can be given for particular features in the use of certain words. For instance, if somebody were to ask "Why must a final examination always be given at the end of a course, rather than at the beginning?" we could take this, also, to be a question about the use of the words "final examination." This time, however, we *can* give an explanation. A plausible answer might be: "What we call a 'final examination' is intended to be a test of what the student has learned as a result of taking a course. To give the examination at the beginning of a course would defeat this purpose. And *that* is why a final examination comes at the end." It might be supposed that in this type of explanation we are treating the statement "A final examination is a test of what the student has learned as a result of taking a course" as a necessary statement. But I think this is not correct. So far as I can see, there is no self-contradiction in saying "This final examination was not intended to test what the students had learned, and in fact did not test what they had learned." But on the other hand, the examination does have a purpose. This purpose explains the use of the label "final examination" to stand for a performance at the end, rather than at the beginning, of a course.

To return now to the question about Monday and Tuesday, we imagined ourselves giving a sensible interpretation to the question, and perhaps a sensible child ought to be satisfied with the answer he received. But might it not happen that he remained dissatisfied? Suppose he were to retort as follows: "I know you could change the *names*—I know you could call Monday 'Tuesday' and Tuesday 'Monday.' But that wouldn't make Monday itself come after Tuesday. You could call me 'Mary' but that wouldn't make me a girl. I *still* want to know why Monday always comes before Tuesday."

Such persistence suggests either imbecility or a precocious talent for metaphysics. Hoping that the second alternative is correct, we try once again: "Well, Monday is the first day of the week, isn't it. And Tuesday is the second. The first day of the week comes before the second. So that is why Monday comes before Tuesday." This time we are trying to prove the necessary statement. The proof is valid, and yet I doubt that it would satisfy a serious questioner. For it does not go to the roots of his perplexity.

When somebody seriously asks a question that begins with

[171]

"Why . . . ," he shows that he feels some discrepancy, or else lack of connection, between two things he supposes to be the case. "Why doesn't a pound of feathers weigh less than a pound of lead?" Here the supposed discrepancy is between two things, both of which seem to be true to the man who says "Why?"—that feathers are lighter than lead, and that a pound is always the same weight, no matter whether it is a pound of feathers or a pound of anything else. To understand the question fully, we must bring to light the considerations that make it appear sensible to the speaker. And this may be enough, as in the case of the question about the feathers, to show that it is *not* a sensible question, after all.

What are the considerations that make the question "Why must Monday always come before Tuesday?" seem sensible to the questioner? What is the supposed discrepancy that gives rise to the question? I suggest that the regular order in which the two days come is being thought of as an unexplained and remarkable *fact*. Lightning precedes thunder as a *matter of fact*, for which an explanation might reasonably be demanded. And so, perhaps, the child thinks it is a peculiar matter of fact that Monday always precedes Tuesday, and wants to know why.

So long as no explanation is forthcoming, the regular order of the two days appears *arbitrary*, as if there ought to be some hidden factor which, being brought to light, will render the uniformity intelligible. But this demand (if indeed it does underlie the question) it is impossible to satisfy. It would be absurd, for example, to say "Monday comes first because that is the day on which people start the week's work"; but it also seems to me that *every* answer of the form "Monday comes first because X" would be absurd. It makes no sense to try to give this kind of reason; for it makes no sense to treat a necessary statement as if it were the expression of an empirical regularity.

I cannot call to mind any philosopher asking why Monday always comes before Tuesday. But many philosophers have asked, "Why must there be just *three* dimensions of Space?" and "Why cannot thought be extended?" and "Why is it impossible to remember the *future?"* and "Why cannot an effect precede its cause?"

All of these questions can be treated in the same way as the Monday-and-Tuesday question. Construed as questions about the use of *words,* having the form "Why are such and such words used in such and such ways?" they look trivial and give rise to equally trivial answers. Again, the necessary truth in question may sometimes be logically inferred from other necessary truths (as we did when we offered a kind of proof that Monday precedes Tuesday); but this, too, will probably not satisfy those who ask such "deep" questions. Philosophers who are puzzled by the apparently arbitrary character of some necessary truth wish to know what it is in *the world* that underlies the necessary truth. But this wish cannot be fulfilled. There is no mystery to be unraveled—or, rather, it is absurd to talk of there being a mystery.

A man who asks "Why cannot an effect precede its cause?" has more excuse for perplexity than a man who might ask why Monday comes before Tuesday. The ways in which we use causal words are so complex and flexible that we cannot answer all questions about their uses without hesitation and reflection. It is therefore not unreasonable for a man to wonder whether in exceptional circumstances the labeling of an earlier event as an effect of a later one would necessarily constitute a violation of the current rules for the use of causal words. It has been seriously suggested that such curious phenomena as those nowadays called cases of "precognition" provide just this kind of exception to the general rule about the temporal order of cause and effect.

Let us find out. Since we are to examine a *necessary* statement ("An effect cannot precede its cause"), it is of no importance whether the alleged "parapsychological phenomena" do actually occur or not. We have only to investigate whether, *if* they should occur, they would properly be described as cases of an effect preceding its cause.

Imagine the following remarkable state of affairs. First, we hypnotize a certain man—Houdini, say—ask him the question

[173]

"How will the penny fall?" receive one of the two answers "Heads" or "Tails," and then proceed to toss a penny exactly one minute later. Repeated trials then establish that Houdini's answer, in the circumstances related, always agrees with the outcome of the subsequent trial. Under hypnosis he can always foretell how the penny will fall.

Such a state of affairs would be more remarkable than any so-called "precognitive" phenomena already reported in the literature of psychical research. Yet it is logically possible that we should discover such a uniform correlation between answers given under hypnosis and the results of subsequent trials with coins. And we can properly ask, here and now, how such a state of affairs ought to be described.

Let us call the event consisting in the hypnotized subject's reply, A (for "answer") and the event consisting in the toss of the coin exactly one minute later T (for "toss"). The question before us is "In the circumstances described, would it be proper to say that the later event, T, caused, or partially caused, the earlier event, A?"

Before taking the drastic step of answering this question in the affirmative, there would be several alternatives to be considered. Surely our natural response in the circumstances imagined would be to suspect some concealed trickery. Our first thought would be that a confederate of Houdini was *arranging* for the penny to fall as predicted. If so, the answer, A, would be a partial cause of T; and we would then have a case of a cause *preceding* its effect as we normally expect. If we are to say otherwise, it must, therefore, be further stipulated that A is not a partial cause of T. This stipulation eliminates not only the possibility of human trickery, but also the possibility of any sort of hidden causal mechanism in virtue of which T occurs *because A* occurred.

To say that A is not a partial cause of T is to imply that T would have occurred in the absence of A. Unless we are to hold that T has no sufficient cause anterior to it, this will mean that T is caused by factors that can operate in the absence of A. Now, in the particular case imagined, this condition is fulfilled.

[174]

For we know, or think we know, that the outcome of the toss of a penny is determined by its initial momentum and spin, the distribution of air currents in the room and such other physical factors. And we know, or think we know, that such physical factors operate quite independently of the occurrence of events consisting of answers being given under hypnosis. I take it for granted, then, that we do have good reason to maintain that T *would have occurred in the same way as it did* (i.e., with the same outcome) *whether A had occurred or not*. So we need not fear trickery or a hidden causal mechanism.

Another natural way of explaining the correlation between A and T, without reversing the order of cause and effect, would be to suppose both of them to be effects of some common earlier cause. This would mean that there was some prior event, X, say, such that whenever X occurred both A and T would always follow. But we have supposed that we have a causal explanation for T that permits T to occur in the absence of A. Thus T must have a sufficient cause, which is *not* a sufficient cause for A. And so this second natural way of explaining the correlation is blocked.

But we are not yet required to say that T causes A. For one thing, we have not yet discussed whether or not the earlier event A is caused by some still earlier event. If it is, the situation is that T is caused by some event Y (earlier than T) and A by some event X (earlier than A), while X and Y are causally independent of one another. But then it would be absurd to say that T causes A. We already have a satisfactory conventional explanation of A, viz., the occurrence of the earlier event X; and we know that T is caused by another event Y not causally connected with X; and so it follows that T and A are causally independent of each other. Of course, the correlation between T and A would then appear as a remarkable coincidence; but we certainly would not have to say we had a case of an effect preceding its cause.

So if our hypothetical example is to serve the purpose for which it was constructed, we must add one last stipulation— that the event A (Houdini's answer) is not caused by any prior

[175]

event. (For we have already ruled out the possibility that it had the same cause as T and also the possibility that it had a cause independent of T's causes.)

The final description of the hypothetical case is, accordingly, as follows: When Houdini is asked under hypnosis the question "How will the penny fall?" there is no earlier cause for his saying heads rather than tails. When the penny is tossed a minute later and agrees with Houdini's answer, there *is* a sufficient cause for that outcome of the toss, the cause in question being causally independent of the previous answer. Supposing all this to be the case, the question is "Is A (the earlier event) properly described as caused by T (the later event)?"

There is at least one good reason for saying "No." In the circumstances described, we can wait until A has happened and then *prevent* T. For we assumed that the causes of T (the way the penny was thrown, the air currents in the room, and so on) were causally independent of A. So, A having occurred, it is within our power to prevent T's occurring—by simply not tossing a coin.

This being so, a man who insists upon describing the circumstances as a case of effect preceding cause must qualify his assertion that the character of T causes A by adding that this is so only *when* T occurs. In other words: T causes A *if* T occurs, yet A may occur without T occuring at all. So A may sometimes occur without being caused either by an earlier or a later event, and yet on other occasions, a precisely similar A, though again not caused by an earlier event, is now held to be caused by a later one. This would be hard, if not impossible, to reconcile with our present uses of causal terminology.

But there is a still better reason for refusing to call T a cause of A. If T's causal antecedents are independent of A, as we found ourselves required to stipulate, we can arrange for T to *disagree* with A. Thus, it would be theoretically possible to learn to toss the coin so that it came down heads or tails as we pleased; all we need to do is to wait for Houdini's answer, and then arrange for the coin to fall contrary to his prediction. If we *can* do this, the stipulations for the supposed precogni-

[176]

tion are logically impossible of fulfillment, because Houdini's answer will *not* always agree with the subsequent trial. On the other hand, if we find that once Houdini has answered we cannot arrange for the penny to come down as we please, we shall be compelled to say that the causal antecedents of T are not independent of A. We shall have to say that Houdini's answer exerts a causal influence of an esoteric sort upon the subsequent toss of the coin. This would be extraordinary enough, to be sure. Yet it would not be preposterous, as would be the logical absurdity of saying that an effect precedes its cause.

I have been trying to show that a full description of the supposed case of "precognition" involves self-contradiction. Anybody who says that a later event is a sufficient condition for the occurrence of an earlier one, while also saying that the later event has anterior causes that are causally independent of the earlier event is contradicting himself. But unless such self-contradictory stipulations are made, there is no temptation to speak of an effect preceding its cause.

If I am not mistaken, a similar analysis will apply to all cases of so-called "teleological causation." Suppose a man says that the nest-building behavior of a bird is *caused* by the impending arrival of offspring. He is then committed to saying (i) that there is no *prior* reason for the nest-building, no earlier causal factors that would explain it. (For otherwise it would be redundant to invoke a further cause.) He is committed to saying (ii) that if the fledglings are hatched the nest must have been built (for otherwise the arrival of offspring would not be a sufficient condition for the nest-building). But in that case, the natural and proper way of describing the situation is to say that the nest-building is a partial cause of the arrival of the fledglings, and not vice versa.

I have been arguing that our established uses of the words "cause" and "effect" leave no possibility open for applying them in such a way as to describe an earlier event as an effect of a later one. If I am right, to speak of an effect preceding its cause is as absurd as to speak of Tuesday preceding Monday. To see the absurdity we have only to remind ourselves of some

[177]

of the features of our uses of causal language. And this is what I have tried to do.

In a recent discussion of the same subject (*Aristotelian Society Supplementary Volume* 28, 1954, pages 27–44), Mr. M. A. E. Dummett agrees after some discussion that an effect cannot precede its cause (p. 31), but goes on to say that this conclusion does not end the matter. Dummett suggests that in certain situations we might still want to say that a later event stood to an earlier, not, to be sure, in the relation of causation, but in what Dummett wishes to call "quasi-causation."

Dummett says:

We may observe that the occurrence of an event of a certain kind is a sufficient condition for the previous occurrence of an event of another kind; and having observed this, we might, under certain conditions, offer the occurrence of the later event, not indeed as a causal, but as a quasi-causal explanation of the occurrence of the earlier. There are three such conditions which would have to be fulfilled if it were to be reasonable to offer such a quasi-causal explanation. First, the occurrence of the earlier event, which was to be explained by reference to that of the later event, would have to be incapable, so far as we could judge, of being (causally) explained by reference to simultaneous or preceding events; there must be no discoverable explanation of the earlier event which did not refer to the later. Secondly, there would have to be reason for thinking that the two events were not causally connected; i.e., there must be no discoverable way of representing the earlier event as a causal antecedent (a remote cause) of the later. Thirdly, we should have to be able to give a satisfactory (causal) account of the occurrence of the later event which contained no reference to the occurrence of the earlier. If these three conditions were fulfilled, and there really was good evidence of the repeated concomitance of the two events, then the quasi-causal connection between them would be a fact of nature which we could do no more than observe and record [pp. 31–32].

It will have been noticed that Dummett has been laying down four conditions for the possibility of a quasi-causal explanation—conditions precisely parallel to those that emerged in our discussion of the Houdini example. And it should be clear by now why Dummett's search for a quasi-causal connection holding between a later event and an earlier one led him to formulate just these conditions and no others.

I have claimed that the four conditions are mutually inconsistent. But if Dummett had thought so, he would certainly not have asserted that cases of "quasi-causation" might occur. In fact, he provides ingenious descriptions of cases that he thinks would be examples of quasi-causation; these descriptions will provide convenient checks of the accuracy of my own analysis.

Dummett says that all of his conditions would be satisfied in the following case:

A man is observed regularly to wake up three minutes before his alarm-clock goes off. He often does not know when he goes to sleep whether or not the alarm has been wound, nor for what time it has been set. Whenever the alarm has been set and wound, but fails to go off because of some mechanical accident, which is later discovered, he always sleeps very late. One morning he woke up early, when the alarm-clock had not been wound, but an acquaintance, who knew nothing about this queer phenomenon, came in and, for some quite irrelevant reason, set off the alarm-clock just three minutes after the man had woken up.

"In such a case," adds Dummett, "it would be reasonable to overcome our prejudice against the possibility of giving a quasi-causal account of some happening, and say that the man wakes up because the alarm-clock is going to go off, rather than to dismiss the whole thing as a coincidence" (p. 32).

There is no trouble in applying our earlier analysis to this case. In order to count as a case of quasi-causal explanation, in Dummett's sense, there must be a satisfactory causal explanation of the ringing of the alarm-clock, containing "no reference to the earlier event," i.e., to the man's waking. We know what this explanation would be like—it would involve reference to the mechanism of the clock work, the position of the lever that sets the time, and so on. But this means that whether the sleeper has wakened or not, we can still *make* the alarm-clock ring or *prevent* it from ringing. We need only

[179]

wait for the man to fall asleep, leave him undisturbed for three minutes, and then make the alarm-clock go off. If we can do this, the ringing of the alarm-clock is proved to be not a sufficient condition for the man's waking, and one of Dummett's conditions for quasi-causal connection has been violated. Or again, we can wait for the man to wake, and immediately destroy the alarm-clock. Then *that* waking could not be caused by the subsequent ringing of the alarm-clock, since there will be no alarm-clock to do the ringing. But if we find it impossible to make the clock ring, or to prevent it from ringing, in the circumstances described, we shall have to revise our assumption that we had a correct, mechanical, explanation of the clock's ringing. We shall have to admit, in fact, that the sleeper's waking exerts a causal influence, of a very surprising sort, upon the subsequent behavior of the clock.

I am not denying that an event can be a *sufficient condition* for the occurrence of an earlier one (as when the ringing of the clock is a sufficient condition for its having been wound). So perhaps by relaxing some of his other stipulations, Dummett might be able to purge his account of "quasi-causality" of self-contradiction. But why use the word "cause" in such cases, qualified though it is by the apologetic prefix "quasi-"? If the word "quasi-cause" is to be preferred to "symptom" or "indication," say, some close analogy must be presumed with the case of causation proper. What this analogy is supposed to be is made clear by another example discussed by Dummett. He says:

Imagine that I find that if I utter the word "Click!" before opening an envelope, that envelope never turns out to contain a bill; having made this discovery, I keep up the practice for several months, and upon investigation can unearth no ordinary reason for my having received no bill during that period. It would then not be irrational for me to utter the word "Click!" before opening an envelope in order that the letter should not be a bill; it would be superstitious in no stronger sense than that in which belief in causal laws is superstitious [pp. 43–44].

[180]

So the analogy is supposed to be this, that it is not irrational to produce a later event in order to ensure the occurrence of an earlier event of whose occurrence the later event is a sufficient condition. Now, certainly, if it made sense to talk of producing the later event in order to *make* the earlier event happen, it would be tempting to say that the later event *caused* the earlier one. For a most important use of causal language is to spotlight events or states of affairs that we can *control:* the search for causes is very commonly a search for means by which to produce desired consequences or to prevent undesired consequences.

But when the envelope reaches me, the bill has *already* been inserted into it, or not, as the case may be. To suppose that it is rational to pronounce the word "Click!" in Dummett's way is to suppose that what I do now can make a difference to the past. And this is not superstition, but a symptom of logical confusion. If my saying "Click" is a sufficient condition for no bill to be in the envelope, I cannot say that word unless there is no bill there. So, if I want to try to say the word, no harm will be done. But to suppose that what I say makes any difference is absurd. It would be as reasonable to suppose that the man who eats the omelette makes the hen lay the eggs; for certainly I cannot eat the omelette unless the eggs have been laid. Now even the most daring thinker would hardly recommend the consumption of omelettes as a way of inducing hens to *have laid* their eggs. Indeed, in this form of words, the absurdity of postdating causes is flagrant.

X

The "Direction" of Time

TIME is often said to have a "direction." Recent articles contain such expressions as "the privileged direction of time," [1] the "unidirectionality of time," [2] and "everyone's recognition that time goes in only one direction." [3] Bridgman says that "time is unsymmetrical and flows only forward," [4] and Reichenbach's last book has the title "The Direction of Time."

Instead of saying that time has a "direction," writers will sometimes say that time is "asymmetrical" or "irreversible," or that the passing of time is "irrevocable." Although these alternative expressions are not exact synonyms, they are closely connected in meaning and may well be considered together. Meyerson speaks of "the absolute feeling that nature follows an immutable course in time" (*Identity and Reality*, London, 1930, 216) and also says: "We know that today is not like yesterday, that between the two something irreparable has happened: *fugit irreparable tempus*. We feel ourselves growing old. We cannot invert the course of time" (*ibid.*).

I find it very hard to attach any clear sense to talk about the "direction" of time and equally hard to understand what is meant by the "asymmetry," or the supposed "irreversibility," of time. Writers who use such expressions seem to suppose that their meaning is sufficiently clear in the absence of further explanation. But this is not so.

For one thing, talk about the "directionality" or "asymmetry" or "irreversibility" of time usually occurs in a context in which time is said to be a "stream" or a "flux" or a "flow"— at any rate, something that *moves* in a certain "direction."

[1] A. Grünbaum, *American Scientist*, 43 (1955): 550.　　[2] *Ibid.*

[3] H. F. Blum, *American Scientist* 43 (1955): 595.

[4] *Reflections of a Physicist*, New York, 1950, 162.

[182]

And, indeed, it is very natural to associate talk about "directions" with talk about actual or possible *motions*.

However, some literal uses of "direction" are not directly tied to the use of words referring to motions. If we consider standard uses of "direction" in ordinary language, we can, indeed, distinguish cases involving explicit reference to a motion from those that do not.

Examples of the former are the sentences, "He walked *in the direction of King's College*," "The wind is blowing *in the direction N.N.E.*," and "We are both driving *in the same direction.*" Examples of uses in which there is no explicit reference to motions are "He is facing in the direction of North," "The signpost is pointing in the direction of Cambridge," and "The road runs in the direction East-and-West."

The basic expression, in terms of which it is plausible to suppose all the others might be defined, is "in the direction of." We may notice that this has much the same uses as the pair of expressions, "toward" and "away from" (or the variants, "to" and "from"). Instead of saying "He walked in the direction of King's College," we can simply say "He walked toward King's College"; instead of "The road runs in the direction East-to-West," we can say "The road runs from East to West"; and similarly in the other cases. It seems then that we shall sufficiently understand the uses of "direction" in ordinary language if we are clear about the uses of the pair of expressions, "toward" and "away from."

In cases where the word "direction" occurs in connection with explicit reference to a motion, the situation seems to be as follows: The motion in question is partially described, either by giving two points on the path ("here" and "King's College") or by identifying the path in some other way (e.g., "the same road you took yesterday"). This leaves *two* possible motions, which are then distinguished by using the expressions "toward" and "away from" (or the equivalent expression, "in the direction of") according to a familiar convention. Thus "the trip from London to Cambridge" means something different from "the trip from Cambridge to London," and

[183]

anybody who understands the one expression understands the other, and understands the relation between the two. Since we can make the corresponding discrimination between *any* motion and its opposite, we are entitled to say that every motion has a direction.

In cases like "He is facing in the direction of North," where there is no explicit reference to a motion, we can think of the expression "in the direction of" as selecting one possible position of the object in question, relative to other objects. The man mentioned might have been facing *this* way or *that* way: if we know "where North is," we know *how* he was facing. One might be tempted to try reducing this static sense of "direction" to the earlier sense associated with motion, by explaining that the direction the man faces is that in which he *would* walk if he went straight ahead; but I think this is unnecessary and somewhat artificial. For every sufficiently asymmetrical object, it is possible to define a "direction" in which it "faces" or "points."

The only other uses of "direction" that come to mind are connected with references to *changes*. We do say, for instance, "The British legal system is changing in the direction of greater leniency." This already sounds metaphorical and somewhat strained; but the use is readily intelligible. If we were told only that the degree of leniency of the legal system was changing, we would not yet know whether the laws were becoming more lenient or less lenient; the force of the phrase *"in the direction of* greater leniency," in the context cited, is that it selects one of these alternatives. There is here an obvious analogy with the use of the phrase to select one of two possible motions. Since the corresponding discrimination can be made in connection with *any* change, we can agree that not only every motion, but also any change whatsoever, has a "direction," in the sense explained.

To sum up, we can talk intelligibly of the "direction" of any motion or change, with the understanding that we are referring to ways of distinguishing such motions or changes from

[184]

their opposites; and we can speak intelligibly of the "directions" in which a body faces or points, with the understanding that we are referring to ways of identifying the possible positions of the body relative to other bodies. I can think of no other literal uses of "direction."

Now, can time be said to have a "direction"? We can reject offhand any suggestion that time "faces" toward, or "points" to, anything: the analogy with a signpost or an index finger is too farfetched to be worth considering. There remain possible analogies with motion or change.

I am quite sure that writers who do ascribe a "direction" to time are thinking of time as something that moves or flows. Their thought seems to be about as follows: "Time is *always* passing, and cannot be arrested. Future events become present, and then move back into the past. And once past, they remain forever past and unchangeable. You cannot revisit the past. Time always flows the same way, from the future, through the present, to the past." Any number of proverbial sayings show how natural it is to talk in this way.

Yet such ways of talking, natural though they may be, involve the use of metaphors that will not survive critical examination. To take but a single point, if the claim that time always flows had a literal sense, we ought to be entitled to ask how fast time is flowing. And if so, there would have to be a supertime for measuring the rate of flow of ordinary time. With regard to that supertime, a similar question would immediately arise, viz., how fast *it* was flowing; and this would imply still another time for its answer. And so on without end. Some writers have not boggled at the prospect of an infinity of times, each flowing with respect to the next—yet surely this is to heap paradox upon confusion. I cannot see that any sense attaches to the question "How fast is time flowing?" nor can I conceive of any circumstances that would either support or weaken the claim that time had ceased to flow. Equally, it seems to me, no sense attaches to the contention that time is changing. And hence, I am unable to discover any literal sense

[185]

in talk about the "direction" of time. If it is absurd, as I think it is, to say that time is moving or changing, it is absurd to refer to the "direction" in which time is flowing or changing.

I am reluctant, however, to conclude that the men I have cited were merely talking nonsense (and philosophically uninteresting nonsense, at that). And so I shall make a fresh start.

I propose to contrast certain logical properties of space, with certain logical properties of time. Those who say that time has a "direction" will often say, by way of contrast, that space has no "direction"—or that space is "symmetrical," or "isotropic." Or they will say that events are reversible with respect to their spatial locations, but *not* with respect to their temporal locations. I shall try to explain the sense in which space may be called "isotropic."

Consider any three physical objects arranged in a line—say, a coin, a watch, and an ash tray. I have chosen to arrange them so that from where I sit the coin is to the left of the watch, and the watch to the left of the ash tray. The ordering relation *being to the left of* is asymmetric and transitive. This means that if X is to the left of Y, Y cannot be to the left of X; and if X is to the left of Y, and Y to the left of Z, then X must always be to the left of Z. Such a relation determines a unique order along the line.

Notice that to say that the relation *being to the left of* is asymmetric implies that the relation is different from its converse, *being to the right of*. So, if I now wanted the coin to stand on the right of the watch, I would be demanding a change in the arrangement of the three bodies I placed on the table. And if you imagine any number of bodies placed along the same line, a demand that each one of them should now stand in the converse relation to the others, i.e., to the right of all those on whose left it had previously stood, would be a demand for a change in the arrangement of the entire series. Suppose the whole series changed in this way, by a reflection, as it were: I propose to say that the *order* is unchanged, but that the bodies are in two different *arrangements* in the two

[186]

cases. (People sometimes say that the two series of objects have different "senses.")

Suppose, now, that I inspect a series of bodies arranged along a straight line. In order to discover what the order is, I need attend only to that series, and to nothing else. I observe, for example, that Tom stands *between* Dick and Harry, that Harry stands between Tom and Michael, and so on. Repeated observations of this sort will completely determine what I have called the "order" of the men. But the case is quite different when I try to determine which of the possible arrangements, both compatible with the order now established, actually obtains. It would suffice to decide with respect to a single pair of men whether, for instance, Tom was standing to the left or to the right of Dick. But this question has no determinate meaning until I specify whether "left" is to mean left from my standpoint, or from that of somebody facing me. The question about the arrangement, as distinct from the question about the order, requires the choice of a "point of view" and without such a choice remains indeterminate and therefore impossible to answer.

We might say that the relation *being to the left of* only seems to be a genuine two-termed relation, because its full expression would require reference to at least one other object besides those that seem to be related. The question "Is *A* to the left of *B*?" must be amplified to read "Is *A* to the left of *B* when viewed from the standpoint of C? Without such amplification, explicit or implied, it no more admits of an answer than do the questions, "Is *A* nearer to *B*?" or "Is *A* preferred to *B*?" or "Is *A* better than *B*?" Natural retorts to such questions are "Nearer than *what*?" and "Preferred by *whom*?" and "Better in *which* respect?" We might perhaps say that the expression "*A* is to the left of *B*" is more like a propositional form, containing gaps to be filled, than it is like a proposition having a determinate truth value. I propose to say that the relation *being to the left of* is an "*incomplete relation.*"

The chief point I now want to make is this: If you want to

[187]

identify the arrangement of a given spatial series of objects, you must use an incomplete relation. There is no conceivable way in which you could know that A, B, and C stood in the arrangement with A on the extreme left (rather than with A on the extreme right) except by reference to your own body, or some other body different from A, B, and C. (And does not this now suggest a puzzle as to why reference to any further bodies should help?) Suppose A, B, and C were three men who could observe one another but nothing else. They could then easily determine their order—easily determine who stood *between* whom—but it would be hopeless for them to determine in which arrangement they were standing. This incapacity would not be due to lack of intelligence or lack of information —the obstacle would be a logical one. The reason why the three men could not determine which of the two possible arrangements actually occurred is that the task of finding out which stands on the left is a logical absurdity.

It will not help in the least to search for other ordering relations. If we reflect upon how we arrived at the idea that there must be two different arrangements having the same order, we shall see that the notion of *being to the left of* entered into our definition of "arrangement." We explained what we meant by "being a different arrangement" by saying that in one arrangement A stood to the left of B, while in the other it stood to its right. So any criterion for a series being in one arrangement rather than its opposite will have to use the relation *being to the left of* or some logical equivalent. That is to say, it will have to rely upon what I have called an "incomplete" relation.

In the light of the foregoing consideration, it becomes easier to understand why no references to "sense," i.e., what distinguishes one possible arrangement of bodies from another having the same order, enters into the formulation of the laws of nature. If I am right, an indication of sense would require the use of an "incomplete" relation, i.e., one defined by reference to some contingently existing body or bodies. Such reference is commonplace in history (as for instance in a chronicle of Napoleon's influence—where Napoleon is an individual that has to be identified ostensively), but it is repugnant to theoretical science.

It is a fact, that might have been otherwise, that the sun rises on the right hand of an observer facing toward the North. But in order to state this fact, I have to use the relation *being to the right of,* which, as we have seen, has to be defined by the arbitrary choice of certain bodies. A scientist will never be content with this kind of formulation, whose character varies with the choice of an arbitrary body of reference; he searches for laws that can be formulated without such arbitrary choices. It is a striking fact that in theoretical physics this demand has everywhere been met. This means that nothing in theoretical physics refers to the actual arrangement of bodies in the universe, and consequently nothing would need to be changed in the structure of theoretical physics if that arrangement were supposed reversed. Indeed, for this reason among others, adherents to a principle of verifiability would very likely deny any meaning to the supposition that the arrangement of *everything* in the universe might have been reversed.

It is perhaps instructive to think of the matter in the following way. Suppose we were to discover that the arrangement of the three objects I placed on the table (the coin, the watch, and the ash tray) had apparently been instantaneously reversed. It would then be natural for us to say that these three bodies had been switched around. But if some paradoxmonger were to insist, on the contrary, that it was not these three bodies that had been switched around, but rather everything else had been reversed—why, then, there would be nothing to choose between his view and our own. No conceivable observation could show either of us to be right, and the appearance of a dispute between us would be no more than an illusion. In short, arrangement is a relative notion; but *difference of arrangement* is not. So far as theoretical physics goes, it is only differences of arrangement that need be or can be observed.

These considerations become somewhat more striking when applied to what is sometimes called the *spatial orienta-*

[189]

tion of solid bodies. It is a fact with which all of us are familiar that two bodies can be exactly alike in all respects, and yet be unable to fit into the same space. A left hand might exactly resemble a right hand, in size, shape, and the makeup of its parts, and yet it would not fit the same glove; two sugar crystals can be exactly alike in all physical and chemical respects, except that the arrangement of the molecules in the one is the mirror image of the arrangement in the other; and even two simple bodies, each composed of three bars at right angles, may be "incongruent counterparts," to use Kant's phrase. Let us say that a body and its mirror-image counterpart differ in *"orientation."* Then we can see that for every three-dimensional body having no plane of symmetry, there can exist a mirror-image counterpart differing from it only in orientation.

Now what I have said about the relativity of arrangement applies, with suitable modifications, to the case of orientation. Theoretical physics takes no account of absolute orientation (is inclined, indeed, to attach no sense to such a notion), and so nothing but difference of orientation enters into the formulation of natural laws. If it were suddenly discovered that the orientation of a man's internal organs had been reversed (as in "The Plattner Story" of H. G. Wells), so that his heart was on the right side of his body, his left hand had become his right hand, and so on, there would be nothing to choose between the hypothesis that *he* had changed his orientation and the hypothesis that everything else had changed in orientation.

I have been trying to elaborate some of the considerations that writers have in mind when they say that space is isotropic, or "has no privileged direction." Perhaps we are sufficiently familiar with notions of the uniformity and homogeneity of space not to find such assertions as startling as they would have been to Aristotle. But it *is* startling to realize that, in theoretical physics, time also is treated as if it were "isotropic."

I shall confine myself to a few brief remarks. Consider a simple law, such as that of the free fall of a body in a vacuum. The equation connecting the distance with the time elapsed is the familiar "$s = \frac{1}{2}gt^2$." This represents a body falling from

[190]

rest, say, for a period of 4 seconds, and ending with a velocity of approximately 128 feet per second vertically downward. Now the surprising thing is that exactly the same equation would fit a motion of a body that *started* from the lowest point with a velocity of 128 feet per second vertically upward, and rose under gravity until it *ended* at rest at the highest point. (In this case, however, "*s*" would have to measure the distance still *to be* traversed, and "*t*" the time still to elapse before the motion was completed.) If we call the one motion the *reverse* of the other motion, then there is nothing in the law of free fall to show whether the actual motion or its reverse really occurred.

This conclusion immediately generalizes to all the laws of physics. All of them fail to discriminate between the two possible *temporal* arrangements, or "senses," of events. All of them would need no adjustment if the entire universe were "running backwards," so that everything that now comes earlier came later, and vice versa. (It is commonly held that the Second Law of Thermodynamics is a unique and important exception, but, for reasons that I cannot discuss here, I hold this view to be quite mistaken.)

Should it be held to follow from this that "science shows" time to be "isotropic," our previous discussion would require us to admit the following consequences.

1. We would have to say that the relation *occurring earlier than* was "incomplete," in the sense previously explained. That is to say, whether event *A* was earlier than event *B* would not depend upon those two events alone, but would require reference, explicit or implied, to other events as well. So that the question "Did the Battle of Hastings happen before the Battle of Waterloo?" would not really admit of a straightforward and unqualified answer, as we suppose. It would, strictly speaking, have to be met with the retort "It all depends upon your point of view. If you mean 'Did it occur between say the Fall of Jerusalem and the Battle of Waterloo?' the answer must be 'Yes.' But if you mean 'Did it occur between the Versailles Treaty and the Battle of Waterloo?'

then the answer is 'No.' " On the view that time is "isotropic," there is nothing in the Universe that *could* distinguish the one answer from the other. It is, as it were, an arbitrary choice on our part to be interested in *one* temporal arrangement rather than the other—as right-handed men might be more interested in right-handed crystals than in their mirror-image counterparts.

2. We would have to say that the very same series of events, *A, B, C,* might properly be described by one observer as being in the temporal arrangement in which *A* occurred first, while that very same series of events would properly be described by some other observer as being in the opposite temporal arrangement in which *A* occurred last. (This leads on to the fantasy of time "flowing in opposite directions"—in different parts of the universe, or according to the different motions of the observer.)

3. We would have to entertain seriously, as many writers have done, the notion that any given temporal arrangement might be reversed. If we traveled to a distant galaxy and found people walking backward, oaks gradually turning into acorns, and fragments of omelettes emerging from people's mouths to assemble into unbroken eggs—in short, if we found things looking and sounding as they do when a film is run backward—we would have to be prepared to entertain the notion that for the inhabitants of such a bizarre region time was, as some people like to say, "running in reverse."

Conversely, the contention that time is not "isotropic," in the way that we have seen space to be, commits us to rejecting these consequences. It does indeed seem that the meaning of the claim that *A* happened earlier than *B* does not depend upon the speaker's position or point of view—or on the point of view of anybody or anything else. If somebody says, "It is only true from where you stand that the prisoner first ate a hearty breakfast, and was *then* hanged. From another point of view, equally legitimate, it would be true to say that he was first hanged, and then ate a hearty breakfast," one can only hope that this reflection is a consolation to the corpse.

[192]

It seems to me nonsensical to suggest that if A is earlier than B, it might after all still be the case that B is earlier than A. It is part of our use of temporal words that the expression "A is earlier than B" shall conflict with and be incompatible with "B is earlier than A"—and not merely in the way in which "to the left of" conflicts with "to the right of." And similarly it seems to be part of our use of temporal words that the relation *being earlier than* is not an incomplete relation. If anybody uses such a phrase as "earlier than B from the standpoint of so and so," we are entitled to conclude that the speaker is using the temporal expressions in some unusual and bizarre sense.

It therefore seems to me just as certain as anything can be that time does have a "direction," if that expression is taken to mean that time is not "isotropic" in the sense I have tried to make clear. But to say that time has a "direction" in this sense is perhaps only to refer in a misleadingly pretentious way to a familiar feature of our use of the word "earlier" and related temporal expressions. I would prefer to say, instead, that in order to determine which of two events is the earlier, it can be sufficient to refer to those two events alone, and to nothing else at all. Somebody might then think it important to ask "*How* do we determine that the one event is earlier, given that the two events might be exactly alike in all respects except their temporal position?" This is a question which I have not tried to answer in this paper.

XI

Can Induction Be Vindicated?

PHILOSOPHERS who advocate a "pragmatic justification" [1] or "vindication" [2] of induction are thoroughly skeptical about empirical knowledge. They maintain, as Reichenbach did, that "the aim of knowing the future is unattainable." [3] Statements about the unobserved, they say, cannot be known to be true when asserted—or even *probably* true (more likely than not to be true) in any sense of "probably true" that has implications for subsequent observation. [4] "Practicalists," as it is convenient to call them, [5] are also convinced of the worthlessness of any direct proofs of inductive principles. Orthodox arguments in support of inductive principles are held to beg the question: if deductive in form, they use premises more powerful, less likely to be true, than their problematic conclusion; while inductive arguments in support of induction are rejected as patently circular. [6]

---

[1] Hans Reichenbach, *The Theory of Probability* (Berkeley, 1949), p. 481.

[2] Herbert Feigl, "De Principiis Non Disputandum," in *Philosophical Analysis*, ed. M. Black (Ithaca, N.Y., 1950), p. 22.

[3] Reichenbach, *op. cit.*, p. 480.

[4] A sense of "probably true" in which a prediction about the unobserved strictly follows from observation statements is irrelevant to the present discussion.

[5] I used this label in *Problems of Analysis* (Ithaca, N.Y., 1954). By a "practicalist" I mean anybody who accepts a "pragmatic justification" of induction, whether or not he is also skeptical about the possibility of empirical knowledge.

[6] "The various attempts (by Keynes, Broad, Nicod, Russell, and others) to deduce or render probable the principle of induction on the basis of some very general assumptions concerning the structure of the world seem to me, if not metaphysical and hence irrelevant, merely to beg the question at issue" (Feigl, *op. cit.*, p. 135).

[194]

This skeptical background ensures a more favorable hearing for "pragmatic justification" than it might otherwise receive. For the proposed "vindication" is admittedly modest in its pretensions: its strongest claims are that "we have everything to gain and nothing to lose" [7] by practicing induction and that if induction does not work no method will.[8] Professor Feigl concedes that the resulting view "may seem only infinitesimally removed from Hume's skepticism" but complains that philosophers do not seem grateful for small mercies.[9] Perhaps an infinitesimal mercy merits no more than infinitesimal gratitude.

THE AIMS OF THIS PAPER

Elsewhere, I have tried to show why a "pragmatic justification" of induction is helpless against skepticism.[10] Professor Wesley C. Salmon's spirited rejoinder [11] has failed to change my mind.

Salmon's paper consists largely of objections to objections against pragmatic justification. Tempting as it is to counter his second-order objections by third-order objections, I think it will be more profitable to restate the case against the alleged vindication of induction. In so doing, I hope to make clear the grounds on which the final verdict should rest.

[7] Wesley C. Salmon, "The Short Run," *Philosophy of Science,* 22: 214–221 (1955), p. 220.

[8] "The practicalist does not hold that induction must work. He holds that if any method works, induction does" (Wesley C. Salmon, "Should We Attempt to Justify Induction?" *Philosophical Studies,* 8: 33–48 [1957], p. 35. I think the contrapositive "If induction does not work, no method does" is less misleading than Salmon's formula, since it does less to suggest that *some* method will work.

[9] *Op. cit.,* p. 138.

[10] " 'Pragmatic' Justifications of Induction," in *Problems of Analysis* (Ithaca, N.Y., 1954), pp. 157–190.

[11] "Should We Attempt. . . ."

TWO ASPECTS OF A "PRAGMATIC JUSTIFICATION"

It has been insufficiently emphasized in past discussion that a "pragmatic justification" consists of *two* steps that have sharply contrasting features. The first, which I will call the *formal* step, offers a strict proof that a specified procedure, P, will lead to the successful performance of a given task, T, if the task *can* be performed. The formal step leaves open the question whether the task in question can be performed. Let us say that the formal step consists of a demonstration that P is a *conditional performance procedure* for T.[12]

The second step, which I will call the *directive step*, consists in providing supplementary considerations for treating the proof supplied in the first step as a sufficient reason for undertaking T. Practicalists usually overlook the importance of this second step, mistakenly supposing that successful completion of the formal step is sufficient to justify commitment to an inductive task.

REMARKS ABOUT THE "FORMAL STEP"

Why is it necessary to provide a strict proof that P is a conditional performance procedure for T? The practicalist tries to model his argument upon "practical" arguments in ordinary life, where, forced to decide upon insufficient evidence, we are sometimes satisfied that we have "nothing to lose and everything to gain" by acting in a certain way. It is characteristic of such arguments (as I have argued in a previ-

---

[12] A "conditional performance procedure" must not be confused with a "decision procedure" in logic. The latter is an *effective* procedure for determining whether a given theorem is or is not a theorem of the logical system in question. On the other hand, if P has been shown to be a conditional performance procedure with respect to T, it is not even known whether following P will lead to the performance of T. And even if T can be performed, and following P does lead to the accomplishment of the task, no upper bound can be supplied in advance for the number of operations that will be needed.

[196]

ous paper [13]) that they use empirical premises. The very nature of the situation arising in an attempted defense of induction by a convinced skeptic excludes such empirical premises. Holding himself to be in a position of absolute and ineradicable ignorance with regard to the truth or probability of all empirical assertions extending beyond the immediate present, the practicalist cannot employ such assertions in his vindication. He is compelled, therefore, to stipulate that the only permissible "vindication" of induction employs no premises at all, i.e., consists in a proof that the conditional adequacy of P *follows* from the definition of T. So, Feigl rightly speaks of "the extreme, degenerate case [of justification with appeal to] logical truths" [14] and says, "The reasoning . . . is purely deductive because of the extreme (degenerate) nature of the question at issue." [15]

In view of this, the formal step of the practicalist's vindication should properly be regarded as a deductive elaboration or an *elucidation* of the goal set by the corresponding task. If the first step is successful, it tells us what we are committed to in pursuing a certain goal, without any consideration of the reasonableness of that goal. Of course, it is misleading to call this step alone a "vindication," as practicalists commonly do, overlooking any need for a further step. If all that was needed to justify a procedure was to show that it could serve some arbitrary goal, "vindication" would be a trifling exercise. Every procedure would then be trivially "vindicated," since it would suffice to invoke whatever goal the procedure in question was fitted to achieve. Slitting one's abdomen would be "vindicated," in this extraordinary sense of that word, as a procedure for committing hara-kiri. Yet this could hardly constitute a good reason for that drastic proceeding, in the absence of further discussion of the desirability of committing suicide. All we have a right to say, so far, is that

[13] Black, *op. cit.,* pp. 182–184.

[14] H. Feigl, "Validation and Vindication," in *Readings in Ethical Theory*, W. Sellars and J. Hospers, eds. (New York, 1952), p. 674.

[15] *Ibid.,* p. 676.

MODELS AND METAPHORS

disembowelment is a reasonable thing to do *if* you want to commit hara-kiri. And corresponding remarks apply to the less gruesome undertakings required for performing inductive tasks.

I do not wish to imply that "deductive elaboration" of a goal can serve no useful purpose. It may be extremely advantageous to know that keeping one's hand in contact with the wall of a maze is a conditional performance procedure for making one's way to an exit.

It is worth noting that a given "goal" or "task" may have *no* associated conditional performance procedure, because the definition of the task is too vague to allow the necessary inference. For example, if we consider *being as healthy as possible* as constituting a "task," we shall be unable to produce a corresponding conditional performance procedure. For the meaning of "being as healthy as possible" does not entail the conditional sufficiency of any correlated policy. Doctors might be able to provide some "practical justification" of measures conducive to health, on the ground that *they* would promote health if anything could. But of course the doctors would have to use empirical premises based upon medical observation and so would not be supplying the "degenerate" type of justification here under examination. We shall see, later, that upon one plausible interpretation of the task of inductive prediction, there can be no conditional performance procedure for that task, so that the proposed vindication breaks down at the formal step.

WHAT IS THE "TASK" OF INDUCTION?

If we are to decide whether a proposed inductive procedure has survived the demands of the "formal step," we must be told what the associated task of induction is taken to be. Feigl has said that the end to be served by adopting an inductive rule is "successful prediction [and] more generally, [reaching] true conclusions of nondemonstrative inference." [16]

16 "De Principiis . . . ," p. 136.

[198]

Elsewhere he says that the goal is "to render the observed phenomena maximally predictable." [17] In much the same vein, Salmon says that the aim of induction is "attaining correct predictions and true conclusions." [18] He also says that the purpose is that of "arriving at true results" (*ibid.*) and, again, that "the standard inductive methods are those best suited to the purpose of arriving at correct beliefs." [19]

We are entitled to conclude, I think, that the envisaged task is that of making predictions that turn out to be true more often than not—or, as I shall say, the aim of achieving a *success ratio* (of predictions) greater than one half.

Let us see how the first step of the vindication works in a typical case of inductive inference.

Suppose, therefore, that we are recording a series of consecutive human births at Ithaca, each manifesting the character of being either a male birth (*M*) or a female birth (*F*). Then the task of rendering "the observed phenomena maximally predictable" can be determinately specified as follows:

(T_1) To continue to predict whether each next Ithaca birth to occur will be male or female, in such a way that the proportion of successful predictions (the "success ratio") shall *eventually* remain greater than one half.

Let us abbreviate this specification by saying that the task is that of *successful prediction in the long run.*

A rule of procedure for this special case that conforms to the practicalist conception runs as follows:

(P_1) So long as the ratio of the number of cases of *M* in the total observed sequence of *n* births (the ratio m/n, say) is equal to or greater than one half, predict that the next

---

[17] H. Feigl, "Scientific Method without Metaphysical Presuppositions," *Philosophical Studies*, 5: 17–28 (1954), p. 24.

[18] "Should We Attempt . . . ," p. 40.   [19] *Ibid.*, p. 41.

birth will be a case of M; otherwise, predict that it will be a case of F.[20]

The formal step in vindicating P_1 in relation to T_1 will consist in satisfying ourselves as to the answer to the question "If T_1 *can* be performed, will P_1 then be a *sufficient* means of achieving the goal stated in T_1?" If and only if the answer is "Yes," will the formal step in P_1's vindication have been successful.

Now attention to the way in which T_1 and P_1 have been formulated will immediately show that the correct answer is "No." We are here assuming that the series of births can be regarded as infinite—an assumption which will be criticized later. If the assumption is accepted, we are able to say that T_1 "*can* be performed," inasmuch as some (indeed infinitely many) series of successive predictions will achieve "successful predictions in the long run" (will attain and thereafter maintain success ratios greater than one half). Since T_1 does not require any particular plan of prediction, any series of predictions successful in the long run counts as achieving T_1. Since we know in advance that the task can be performed, the demand that P_1 shall be sufficient for achieving the task, if it can be achieved, reduces here to the simpler demand that the procedure be sufficient to achieve the aim in question.

But this it certainly is not. Although infinitely many series of predictions would lead to the satisfaction of the conditions specified in T_1, there is no guarantee that P_1 will do so. Indeed, the case is conceivable that P_1 might result in false predictions *every* time and so have a success ratio of zero throughout. Think of the predictor as playing a "zero-sum game" against God: if the divine adversary knows His human opponent's strategy of prediction, He knows the exact order in

[20] This rule might be inferred from Salmon's two "rules of prediction" ("The Short Run," pp. 220, 221): "In any sequence, predict that those events which began more frequently in the long run will happen more frequently in the short run" and "Predict that the relative frequency in the short run approximates, sufficiently for practical purposes, the probability of the events in the total sequence."

[200]

which to produce male and female births so as to win every play. We need not invoke this fiction to see that P_1 may prove hopelessly inadequate to achieve the modest aim of being right more often than not in the long run. Thus, the attempted "vindication" collapses at the first step.

This conclusion generalizes immediately, since there is nothing atypical about the illustration. If the aim of predictive inference is one of "attaining correct predictions," in the weak sense of being right more often than not in the long run, there can be no a priori guarantee that the "standard inductive procedure" is sufficient.

TRANSITION TO A MODIFIED TASK

The practicalists could hardly have failed to notice the difficulty explained above. When Feigl and others think that the formal step in the "vindication" succeeds, they sometimes have in view another and different task. In terms of our illustration, it can be stated as follows:

(T_2) So to predict the characters of successive births that the proportion of successful predictions shall eventually remain greater than one half, *in case the relative frequency* m/n *of male births tends to a limit other than* ½.

It will be noticed that this new version of the inductive task differs from the first only in restricting the intended inferences to cases in which births of one or the other kind eventually continue to predominate.

Since the new task is less ambitious than the old, there is a better prospect of finding a conditional performance procedure. Indeed, the "formal step" in vindicating P_1 in relation to T_2 now succeeds. For if the condition expressed in the italicized clause in the statement of T_2 is fulfilled, the predictor will, sooner or later, be constantly anticipating the occurrence of one and the same character, and in so doing will be right most of the time. If the relative frequency of the eventually more frequent character converges to a limit

[201]

greater than one half, as stipulated, the over-all proportion of successful predictions must converge to the same ratio.

Is there any good reason why T_2, rather than T_1, should be taken to be a proper formulation of the aim of rational prediction? An attempt to render plausible the transition from the latter to the former might run as follows: "If the relative frequencies of occurrence of the two characters (M and F) do not converge to limits, predictions of the characters of subsequent births can have no grounds and are mere guesses. Only if births of one sex ultimately predominate, can we ever be in a position to make *rational* predictions. Now, by following P_1 we ensure that we shall be making rational predictions, if the time ever comes when that will be possible."

This line of thought would be acceptable if it could be shown that *rational* prediction necessarily entailed adoption of the procedure P_1, i.e., if it were self-contradictory to assert that a man was predicting rationally while not following P_1. But this is not so. If a forecaster of births were to find, after repeated trials, that P_1 was generating an unbroken series of wrong predictions because the M-F series was oscillating, it would be the rational thing for him to abandon P_1 in favor of some alternative predictive procedure that would have had a higher success ratio had it been consistently followed from the start.[21]

At any rate, our examination has shown that the first step of the desired vindication *can* succeed, if the task is circumscribed in the manner indicated.

THE NEED FOR DIFFERENTIAL VINDICATION

It is necessary to bear in mind that any useful "vindication" must supply good reasons for preferring one procedure to another. Salmon sees clearly that we have to justify "a

---

[21] Salmon takes me to task ("Should We Attempt . . . ," p. 37) for claiming "that the practicalists have unduly restricted their definition of the aims of cognitive inquiry." But I am unconvinced by his gesture in the direction of Reichenbach's work. At any rate, it seems clear that

choice from among the wide variety of possible inductive rules." [22] This means, in our example, that we have to show either that P_1 is the only conditional performance procedure for T_2—or that it is *superior* in some way to its alternatives.

Now, P_1 is certainly not the only procedure that might lead to the performance of T_2. Reichenbach showed that there will always be an infinite class of "asymptotic rules" [23] that can be justified by the same considerations that linked P_1 with T_2, and Salmon has ably elaborated the point.[24] Consider, for instance, the following alternative to P_1:

(P_2) Predict the occurrence of M for a million consecutive predictions, and then follow the same procedure as for P_1.

If P_1 "works," then P_2 must work, and so must infinitely many other alternatives. Reichenbach's recourse to the "descriptive simplicity" of his preferred inductive rule [25] is unconvincing. For why should the fact, if it is a fact, that P_1 is simpler than P_2 be a good reason for adopting the former? I suppose "simpler" here means the same as "gives less trouble"—hardly an impresssive consideration in favor of an inductive procedure. Nor will it do to say, as Salmon sometimes does, that P_1 "is as good as or better than" its competitors.[26] P_1 and infinitely many alternatives are all equally "good" in the sense of eventually leading to a constant predominance of true over false predictions if certain favorable circum-

---

the practicalist must *somehow* narrow the general task, T_1, if he is to have any hope of showing that P_1 is a conditional performance procedure.

[22] *Ibid.*, p. 33.   [23] *Op. cit.*, p. 446.

[24] Wesley C. Salmon, "The Predictive Inference," *Philosophy of Science*, 24:180–190 (1957), p. 181. Salmon goes beyond Reichenbach by showing that there are infinitely many "regular" asymptotic rules. He adds, quite correctly, that "the variety of such rules is sufficient to make estimates of the limit of the frequency completely arbitrary" (p. 181).

[25] *Op. cit.*, p. 447.

[26] "Should We Attempt . . . ," p. 34.

stances obtain. "In the long run" it will not make any difference—but then the "long run" is what, by definition, never happens, no matter how long we wait. Meanwhile, in the indefinitely extended "short run," the alleged "vindication" is a license to predict in any way we please—provided only that we promise to adapt our procedure *eventually* to fit the case where the limiting frequencies in the series converge to limits.

CRITICISM OF THE "DIRECTIVE STEP" IN THE VINDICATION

Is it reasonable to choose T_2? Feigl simply takes for granted that the goal in question will be affirmed, when he says "a pragmatic justification amounts to showing that something serves as a means toward an end. It thus requires a *prior agreement as to the desiredness of the end.*" [27] He likewise says, "In the. reconstruction of vindication we encounter *ultimate ends or purposes.*" [28] If he thinks it impossible to argue about the ends specified in the vindication of induction, he is mistaken. It can be shown that, given the skeptical assumptions of the practicalist, there is a grave question whether it is reasonable even to attempt such a task as T_2.

I have spoken above as if the tasks T_1 and T_2 could be accomplished, even though the series of predictions envisaged were infinite in both cases. But this was only for the sake of a sympathetic presentation of the practicalist point of view. The truth of the matter is that T_2 is a task that cannot be accomplished. For we know here and now that children will not be born in Ithaca in perpetuity. Hence, any task defined in terms of the supposed existence of an infinite series of Ithaca births (as was the case in our definitions of T_1 and T_2) implies the existence of something that will not occur, and the tasks are impossible. It is as impossible to perform them as it would be to win a supposedly eternal game of chess. Now to attempt a task, knowing it to be impossible, is un-

27 "De Principiis . . . ," p. 152, italics supplied.
28 *Ibid.*, p. 129, italics supplied.

[204]

reasonable. The proposed tasks are unreasonable and so the "directive step" fails.

To the contention that a certain procedure for escaping from prison would be bound to succeed if the prisoner lived forever, a sufficient objection might be that the prisoner is mortal, and so the proposed "solution" must be irrelevant to his problem. Similarly, if I want to know how best to make predictions about human births in Ithaca, it is unhelpful to be offered a procedure depending upon the convergence of the limiting value of relative frequency in an *infinite* series. Since I know that the series that interests me will not be infinite, the recommendation is irrelevant.

Of course, a "conditional" justification for following P_1 can be produced: "If you want to make predictions in such a way that you will be right more often than not in the long run, and on the supposition that births of one kind eventually predominate, it will be sufficient to follow P_1." True enough, since the truth of this statement follows from the meanings of the terms employed in it. But this conditional justification is no more than the banality "If this is what you want to do (T_2), this is a way to do it (P_1)." I call it a banality because the connection between the "task" and the associated procedure is so obvious: it is not as if this deductive elaboration of the task brought to light unexpected modes of performance. In our illustration—and, indeed, in all other cases where predictions are desired about the actual world, and not about some mathematical surrogate—the imputed "task" (T_2) is irrelevant. Since our predictions concern a finite series, any method predicated upon convergence of some magnitude in an infinite series misses the mark. To chase a will-o'-the-wisp may be futile, but not as futile as chasing one that we know to be nonexistent.

THE PLEA THAT IDEALIZATION IS NEEDED

Supporters of pragmatic justification may retort by recalling the need for "idealization" in scientific investigation.

It may be said that even though the series of empirical events cannot continue indefinitely, it is profitable to argue as *if* it did. Well, let us suppose it makes sense to imagine that Ithaca children will continue to be born in perpetuity, and let us even imagine the observer himself immortal. Even so, the proposed task (T_2) will have to be regarded as unreasonable.

For, in the first place, the observer will never be able to know that his adopted inductive policy is working. Even if the series does have limiting frequencies *sub specie aeternitatis*, the observer can never know it. No matter how far an initial segment of the series extends, its character is compatible with any subsequent values of the relative frequencies "in the long run." So, at every stage of his endless task, the observer remains absolutely and invincibly ignorant about his prospects of success. Sooner or later, if conditions are favorable, the success ratio will reach and thereafter maintain values greater than one half. But the observer will never have the least reason for supposing that this favorable point of no return has been reached, or ever will be reached. As to this, he remains, as he began, completely in the dark.

It might be thought that our hypothetical observer at least has the consolation of reflecting upon successes already achieved if luck has favored him in his initial predictions. Might he not preen himself upon the success ratio shown in the initial segment so far observed? Unfortunately, his supposed knowledge of past successes, if we ignore what he remembers directly, is itself based upon inductive argument, and hence inadmissible on skeptical principles. The skeptic ought to admit that knowledge of the past is just as "unattainable" as knowledge of the future. Indeed, the skeptic might well wonder how the predictor is to know even that he is still pursuing the same task he set out to perform.

So the position is this: our supposedly immortal observer sets himself a "task"—if we still want to call it that—of which the following can be said: (1) it is logically impossible to know whether the task can be achieved, (2) and, if it can, that it will be achieved, (3) or that any progress has been made toward achieving it. The immortal predictor is, as it were, always on his way, but to a goal he has no hope of approaching, and with nothing to show whether he is on the right track. Even for an immortal, such a "task" would be unreasonable. But in any case, we are not immortals: and it is hard to imagine why we should conceive our finite tasks of prediction upon so uninviting a model.

TRANSITION TO FINITE PREDICTIVE TASKS

One way of trying to avoid the objections above would be to redefine the task of predictive inference, by converting it into a finite task that might at least have some chance of being performed. In our illustration, the appropriate specification might run as follows:

(T_3) To continue to predict whether each next Ithaca birth to occur will be male or female, in such a way that the proportion of successful predictions (the "success ratio") shall be greater than one half *in some finite number, k, of trials.*

This can be regarded as a finitist variant of T_1 above. We have already seen that P_1 is not a conditional performance procedure for T_1, and it is easy to see that for similar reasons it is not one for T_3 either. If k is a given number, it is possible for a predictor to be right on every forecast—so, a fortiori, task T_3 *can* be performed. On the other hand, P_1 is insufficient to ensure success. For it is easy to construct a series composed of cases of M and cases of F in which P_1 would lead to an unbroken run of failures.

Finally, we might try to produce a finite variant of T_2 in, say, the following form:

(T_4) To continue to predict whether each next Ithaca birth to occur will be male or female, in such a way that the proportion of successful predictions in k trials shall be greater than one half, *in case the relative frequency*

[207]

m/n *of male births continues to be unequal to 1 for a sufficiently long terminal segment of the k trials.*

Here, the italicized clause expresses the adaptation to our example of the notion of a "practical limit." [29]

For this artificially circumscribed task, P_1 is a conditional performance procedure, so that the "formal step" in the vindication of P_1 with respect to T_4 now succeeds. But then the question remains, why should we find it reasonable to adopt *this* task?

Salmon has seen clearly that a pragmatic justification should have some bearing upon prediction of the characters of initial segments ("short runs") of series of observed events. In his ingenious paper "The Short Run" he tries to build one pragmatic justification upon another—arguing, in effect, that we have "nothing to lose" by assuming that "practical convergence" will occur in the finite series of events we shall in fact observe. But in the later paper "The Predictive Inference" he confesses that this attempt was a failure and he can offer no alternative.[30]

The fact is that the task of making predominantly correct predictions in a finite number of trials is, on practicalist principles, insoluble. Of no strategy for the finite task can it be said, along "pragmatic" lines: "Pursue this strategy and, if there is a solution of the problem you have set yourself, you will eventually arrive sufficiently close to that solution for practical purposes." The skeptical premises accepted by the practicalist yield completely skeptical conclusions concerning the prospects of rational prediction. But this need disturb only those who think there is no reply to skepticism.

[29] Reichenbach, *op. cit.*, p. 447.

[30] Salmon's conclusion is "the treatment of the problem offered in "The Short Run" is totally inadequate. Among the rules justifiable by the arguments there presented we can find one which would justify any consistent prediction whatsoever about the short run. The whole difficulty seems to stem from the introduction of the limit of the relative frequency as a mediator between the finite observed sample and the short run prediction" (pp. 184–185).

XII

Self-supporting
Inductive Arguments

THE USE of inductive rules has often led to true conclusions about matters of fact. Common sense regards this as a good reason for trusting inductive rules in the future, if due precautions are taken against error. Yet an argument from success in the past to probable success in the future itself uses an inductive rule, and therefore seems circular. Nothing would be accomplished by any argument that needed to assume the reliability of an inductive rule in order to establish that rule's reliability.

Suppose that inferences governed by some inductive rule have usually resulted in true conclusions; and let an inference from this fact to the probable reliability of the rule in the future be called a *second-order* inference. So long as the rule by which the second-order inference is governed differs from the rule whose reliability is to be affirmed, there will be no appearance of circularity. But if the second-order inference is governed by the very same rule of inference whose reliability is affirmed in the conclusion, the vicious circularity seems blatant.

Must we, then, reject forthwith every second-order inductive argument purporting to support the very rule of inference by which the argument itself is governed? Contrary to general opinion, a plausible case can be made for saying, "No." [1] Properly constructed and interpreted, such "self-supporting" inferences, as I shall continue to call them, can satisfy all the conditions for legitimate inductive inference:

[1] See Max Black, *Problems of Analysis* (Ithaca, N.Y., 1954), chapter 11, and R. B. Braithwaite, *Scientific Explanation* (Cambridge, 1953), chapter 8.

when an inductive rule has been reliable (has generated true conclusions from true premises more often than not) in the past, a second-order inductive inference governed by the same rule can show that the rule deserves to be trusted in its next application.

The reasons I have given for this contention have recently been sharply criticized by Professor Wesley C. Salmon.[2] In trying to answer his precisely worded objections, I hope to make clearer the view I have been defending and to dispel some lingering misapprehensions.

My original example of a legitimate self-supporting inductive argument was the following:

(a): In most instances of the use of R in arguments with true premises examined in a wide variety of conditions, R has been successful.

Hence (probably):

In the next instance to be encountered of the use of R in an argument with a true premise, R will be successful.[3]

The rule of inductive inference mentioned in the premise and the conclusion of the argument above is:

$R:$ To argue from *Most instances of A's examined in a wide variety of conditions have been B* to (probably) *The next A to be encountered will be B.*

Thus the second-order argument (a) uses the rule R in showing that the same rule will be "successful" (will generate a

---

[2] See Wesley C. Salmon, "Should We Attempt to Justify Induction?" *Philosophical Studies*, Vol. VIII, No. 3 (April, 1957), pp. 45–47.

[3] See *Problems*, page 197, where the argument is called "(a_2)" and the rule by which it is governed "R_2." At that place, I also presented another self-supporting argument with a more sweeping conclusion of the *general* reliability of the corresponding rule. But since I was unable to accept the premise of that argument, or the reliability of the rule it employed, I shall follow Salmon in discussing only the argument presented above.

[210]

true conclusion from a true premise [4]) in the next encountered instance of its use.

The rule, R, stated above is not intended to be a "supreme rule" of induction, from which all other inductive rules can be derived; nor is it claimed that R, as it stands, is a wholly acceptable rule for inductive inference. The unsolved problem of a satisfactory formulation of canons of inductive inference will arise only incidentally in the present discussion. The rule R and the associated argument (a) are to serve merely to illustrate the logical problems that arise in connection with self-supporting arguments: the considerations to be adduced in defense of (a) could be adapted to fit many other self-supporting arguments.

The proposed exculpation of the self-supporting argument (a) from the charge of vicious circularity is linked to a feature of the corresponding rule R that must be carefully noted. Inductive arguments governed by R vary in "strength" [5] according to the number and variety of the favorable instances reported in the premise. So, although R permits us to assert a certain conclusion categorically, it is to be understood throughout that the strength of the assertion fluctuates with the character of the evidence. If only a small number of instances have been examined and the relative frequency of favorable instances (A's that are B) is little better than a half, the strength of the argument may be close to zero; while a vast predominance of favorable instances in a very large sample of observations justifies a conclusion affirmed with nearly maximal strength. The presence of the word "probably" in

[4] Here and throughout this discussion, I assume for simplicity that all the premises of any argument or inference considered have been conjoined into a single statement.

[5] In *Problems*, page 193, I spoke, with the same intention, of the "degree of support" given to the conclusion by the premise. If the latter has the form "m/n A's examined in a wide variety of conditions have been B," it is natural to suppose that the strength of the argument increases as m increases, and also as m/n increases. A plausible formula for the "strength" of the argument might be $(1 - e^{-m})(2m/n - 1)$.

[211]

the original formulation of R indicates the variability of strength of the corresponding argument; in more refined substitutes for R, provision might be made for some precise measure of the associated degree of strength.

Variability in strength is an important respect in which inductive arguments differ sharply from deductive ones. If a deductive argument is not valid, it must be *invalid*, no intermediate cases being conceivable; but a legitimate inductive argument, whose conclusion may properly be affirmed on the evidence supplied, may still be very weak. Appraisal of an inductive argument admits of degrees.

Similar remarks apply to inductive rules, as contrasted with deductive ones. A deductive rule is either valid or invalid—*tertium non datur;* but at any time in the history of the employment of an inductive rule, it has what may be called a *degree of reliability* depending upon its ratio of successes in previous applications. A legitimate or correct inductive rule may still be a weak one: appraisal of an inductive rule admits of degrees.

Now in claiming that the second-order argument (a) *supports* the rule R, I am claiming that the argument raises the degree of reliability of the rule, and hence the strength of the arguments in which it will be used; I have no intention of claiming that the self-supporting argument can definitively establish or demonstrate that the rule is correct. Indeed, I do not know what an outright demonstration of the correctness or legitimacy of an inductive rule would be like. My attempted rebuttal of Salmon's objections will turn upon the possibility of raising the degree of reliability of an inductive rule, as already explained.

The contribution made by the second-order argument (a) to strengthening the rule R by which it is governed can be made plain by a hypothetical illustration. Suppose evidence is available that $\frac{4}{5}$ of the A's so far examined have been B, and it is proposed, by an application of the rule R, to draw the inference that the next A to be encountered will be B. For the sake of simplicity the proposed argument may be taken to have a strength of $\frac{4}{5}$.[6] Before accepting the conclusion about the next A, we may wish to consider the available evidence about past successes of the rule R. Suppose, for the sake of argument, that we know R to have been successful in $\frac{9}{10}$ of the cases in which it has been previously used. If so, the second-order argument affirms with strength $\frac{9}{10}$ that R will be successful in the next instance of its use. But the "next instance" is before us, as the argument whose premise is that $\frac{4}{5}$ of the A's have been B. For R to be "successful" in this instance is for the conclusion of the first-order argument to be true; the strength of the second-order argument is therefore immediately transferred to the first-order argument. Before invoking the second-order argument, we were entitled to affirm the conclusion of the first-order argument with a strength of no better than $\frac{4}{5}$, but we are now able to raise the strength to $\frac{9}{10}$. Conversely, if the second-order argument had shown R to have been unsuccessful in less than $\frac{4}{5}$ of its previous uses, our confidence in the proposed conclusion of the first-order argument would have been diminished.

There is no mystery about the transfer of strength from the second-order argument to the first-order argument: the evidence cited in the former amplifies the evidence immediately relevant to the latter. Evidence concerning the proportion of A's found to have been B permits the direct inference, with strength $\frac{4}{5}$, that the next A to be encountered will be B. It is, however, permissible to view the situation in another aspect as concerned with the extrapolation of an already observed statistical association between true premises of a certain sort and a corresponding conclusion. The evidence takes the form: In 9 cases out of 10, the truth of a statement of the form "m/n X's have been found to be Y's" has been found associated in a wide variety of cases with the

---

[6] This means taking m/n as the measure of strength, rather than some more complicated formula like the one suggested in footnote 5 above. The argument does not depend upon the exact form of the measure of strength.

truth of the statement "The next X to be encountered was Y." [7] This is better evidence than that cited in the premise of the original first-order argument: it is therefore to be expected that the strength of the conclusion shall be raised.

It should be noticed that the evidence cited in the second-order argument is not merely greater in amount than the evidence cited in the first-order argument. If R has been successfully used for drawing conclusions about fish, neutrons, planets, and so on (the "wide variety of conditions" mentioned in the premise of the second-order argument), it would be illegitimate to coalesce such heterogeneous kinds of objects into a single class for the sake of a more extensive *first-order* argument. Proceeding to "second-order" considerations allows us to combine the results of previous inductive inquiries in a way which would not otherwise be possible.

Nothing in this conception of inductive method requires us to remain satisfied with the second-order argument. If circumstances warrant, and suitable evidence can be found, we might be led to formulate third- or even higher-order arguments. These might conceivably result in lowering the measures of strength we at present attach to certain arguments in which R is used. But if this were to happen, we would not have been shown to have been mistaken in previously attaching these measures of strength. Nor is it required that a first-order argument be checked against a corresponding second-order argument before the former can properly be used. If we have no reason to think that R is unsuccessful most of the time, or is objectionable on some logical grounds, that is enough to make our employment of it so far reasonable. The function of higher-order arguments in the tangled web of inductive method is to permit us to progress from relatively imprecise and uncritical methods to methods whose degrees of reliability and limits of applica-

---

[7] We might wish to restrict the second-order argument to cases in which the ratio m/n was close to ⅚. Other refinements readily suggest themselves.

[214]

bility have themselves been checked by inductive investigations. It is in this way that inductive method becomes self-regulating and, if all goes well, self-supporting.

Salmon's objections to the foregoing conception are summarized by him as follows:

The so-called self-supporting arguments are . . . circular in the following precise sense: the conclusiveness of the argument cannot be established without assuming the truth of the conclusion. It happens, in this case, that the assumption of the truth of the conclusion is required to establish the correctness of the rules of inference used rather than the truth of the premises, but that makes the argument no less viciously circular. The circularity lies in regarding the facts stated in the premises as *evidence* for the conclusion, rather than as evidence against the conclusion or as no evidence either positive or negative. To regard the facts in the premises as evidence for the conclusion is to assume that the rule of inference used in the argument is a correct one. And this is precisely what is to be proved. If the conclusion is denied, then the facts stated in the premises are no longer evidence for the conclusion.[8]

I shall reply by making three points. (1) Salmon's reference to "conclusiveness" smacks too much of the appraisal of deductive argument. An inductive argument is not required to be "conclusive" if that means that its conclusion is entailed or logically implied by its premises; it is, of course, required to be correct or legitimate, but that means only that the rule of inductive inference shall be reliable—shall usually lead from true premises to true conclusions. The correctness of an inductive argument could only depend upon the truth of its conclusion if the latter asserted the reliability of the rule by which the argument was governed. But this was not the case in our argument (*a*). The conclusion there was that *R* would be successful in the next instance of its use: this might very well prove to be false without impugning the reliability of *R*. Salmon was plainly mistaken

[8] Salmon, *loc. cit.*, p. 47.

if he thought that the falsity of (*a*)'s conclusion entails the incorrectness of the rule by which (*a*) is governed.[9]

(2) Can the *correctness* of argument (*a*) be "established without assuming the truth of the conclusion" of (*a*)? Well, if "established" means the same as "proved by a deductive argument," the answer must be that the correctness of (*a*) cannot be established at all. But again, a correct inductive argument in support of the rule governing (*a*) can certainly be constructed without assuming (*a*)'s conclusion. We do not have to assume that *R* will be successful in the next instance in order to argue correctly that the available evidence supports the reliability of *R*.

(3) Salmon says: "To regard the facts in the premises as evidence for the conclusion is to assume that the rule of inference used in the argument is a correct one." In using the rule of inference we certainly *treat* it as correct: we would not use it if we had good reasons for suspecting it to be unreliable. If this is what Salmon means, what he says is right, but not damaging to the correctness of (a). But he would be plainly wrong if he maintained that an assertion of the correctness of (*a*) was an additional premise required by (*a*), or that an argument to the effect that (*a*) was correct must precede the legitimate use of (*a*). For if this last demand were pressed, it would render deductive inference no less than inductive inference logically impossible. If we were never entitled to *use* a correct rule of inference before we had formally argued in support of that rule, the process of inference could never get started.

I shall end by considering an ingenious counterexample provided by Salmon. He asks us to consider the following argument:

[9] I conjecture that Salmon was led into making this mistake by forgetting the conclusion of the argument that he correctly reproduces at the foot of page 45 of his article. It is a sheer blunder to say "A given inductive rule can be established by a self-supporting argument, according to Black" (p. 45)—if "established" means the same as "proved reliable." The self-supporting argument can *strengthen* the rule, and in this way *"support"* it.

[216]

(a'): In most instances of the use of R' in arguments with true premises in a wide variety of conditions, R' has been *un*successful.

Hence (probably):

In the next instance to be encountered of the use of R' in an argument with a true premise, R' will be successful.

The relevant rule is the "counterinductive" one:

R': To argue from *Most instances of A's examined in a wide variety of conditions have not been B* to (probably) *The next A to be encountered will be B.*

Salmon says that while (a') must be regarded as a self-supporting argument by my criteria, the rule here supported, R', is in conflict with R. From the same premises the two rules "will almost always produce contrary conclusions." [10] This must be granted. But Salmon apparently overlooks an important respect in which the "counterinductive" rule R' must be regarded as illegitimate.

In calling an inductive rule "correct," so that it meets the canons of legitimacy of *inductive* rules of inference, we claim at least that the rule is reliable, in the sense of usually leading from true premises to true conclusions. That is part of what we *mean* by a "correct inductive rule." It can easily be shown that R' must fail to meet this condition.

Suppose we were using R' to predict the terms of a series of 1's and o's, of which the first three terms were known to be 1's. Then our first two predictions might be as follows (shown by underlining):

$$1 \quad 1 \quad 1 \quad \underline{0} \quad \underline{0}$$

At this point, suppose R' has been used successfully in each of the two predictions, so that the series is in fact now observed to be 1 1 1 o o. Since 1's still predominate, direct application of the rule calls for o to be predicted next. On the other

[10] Salmon, *loc, cit.,* p. 46.

[217]

hand, the second-order argument shows that R' has been successful each time and therefore demands that it not be trusted next time, i.e., calls for the prediction of 1. So the very definition of R' renders it impossible for the rule to be successful without being *incoherent*.[11] The suggested second-order argument in support of R' could be formulated only if R' were known to be unreliable, and would therefore be worthless. So we have an a priori reason for preferring R to its competitor R'. But it is easy to produce any number of alternative rules of inductive inference, none of which suffers from the fatal defect of R'. The choice between such rules, I suggest, has to be made in the light of experience of their use. I have tried to show in outline how such experience can properly be invoked without logical circularity.

[11] A parallel situation would arise in the use of R in predicting the members of the 1-0 series only if R were to be predominantly *un*-successful. But then we would have the best of reasons for assigning R zero strength, and the second-order argument would be pointless.

XIII

Models and Archetypes

SCIENTISTS often speak of using models but seldom pause to consider the presuppositions and the implications of their practice. I shall find it convenient to distinguish between a number of operations, ranging from the familiar and trivial to the farfetched but important, all of which are sometimes called "the use of models." I hope that even this rapid survey of a vast territory may permit a well-grounded verdict on the value of recourse to cognitive models.

To speak of "models" in connection with a scientific theory already smacks of the metaphorical. Were we called upon to provide a perfectly clear and uncontroversial example of a model, in the literal sense of that word, none of us, I imagine, would think of offering Bohr's model of the atom, or a Keynesian model of an economic system.

Typical examples of models in the literal sense of the word might include: the ship displayed in the showcase of a travel agency ("a model of the *Queen Mary*"), the airplane that emerges from a small boy's construction kit, the Stone Age village in the museum of natural history. That is to say, the standard cases are three-dimensional miniatures, more or less "true to scale," of some existing or imagined material object. It will be convenient to call the real or imaginary thing depicted by a model the *original* of that model.

We also use the word "model" to stand for a type of design (the dress designer's "spring models," the 1959 model Ford) —or to mean some exemplar (a model husband, a model solution of an equation). The senses in which a model is a type of design—or, on the other hand, something worthy of imitation—can usually be ignored in what follows.

It seems arbitrary to restrict the idea of a model to something *smaller* than its original. A natural extension is to

[219]

admit magnification, as in a larger-than-life-size likeness of a mosquito. A further natural extension is to admit proportional change of scale in *any* relevant dimension, such as time.

In all such cases, I shall speak of *scale models*. This label will cover all likenesses of material objects, systems, or processes, whether real or imaginary, that preserve relative proportions. They include experiments in which chemical or biological processes are artificially decelerated ("slow motion experiments") and those in which an attempt is made to imitate social processes in miniature.

The following points about scale models seem uncontroversial:

1. A scale model is always a model *of* something. The notion of a scale model is relational and, indeed, asymmetrically so: If *A* is a scale model of *B*, *B* is not a scale model of *A*.

2. A scale model is designed to serve a purpose, to be a means to some end. It is to show how the ship looks, or how the machine will work, or what law governs the interplay of parts in the original; the model is intended to be enjoyed for its own sake only in the limiting case where the hobbyist indulges a harmless fetishism.

3. A scale model is a representation of the real or imaginary thing for which it stands: its use is for "reading off" properties of the original from the directly presented properties of the model.

4. It follows that some features of the model are irrelevant or unimportant, while others are pertinent and essential, to the representation in question. There is no such thing as a perfectly faithful model; only by being unfaithful in *some* respect can a model represent its original.

5. As with all representations, there are underlying conventions of interpretation—correct ways for "reading" the model.

6. The conventions of interpretation rest upon partial identity of properties coupled with invariance of proportionality. In making a scale model, we try on the one hand

to make it resemble the original by reproduction of some features (the color of the ship's hull, the shape and rigidity of the airfoil) and on the other hand to preserve the *relative* proportions between relevant magnitudes. In Peirce's terminology, the model is an *icon*, literally embodying the features of interest in the original.[1] It says, as it were: "*This* is how the original is."

In making scale models, our purpose is to reproduce, in a relatively manipulable or accessible embodiment, selected features of the "original": we want to see how the new house will look, or to find out how the airplane will fly, or to learn how the chromosome changes occur. We try to bring the remote and the unknown to our own level of middle-sized existence.[2]

There is, however, something self-defeating in this aim, since change of scale must introduce irrelevance and distortion. We are forced to replace living tissue by some inadequate substitute, and sheer change of size may upset the balance of factors in the original. Too small a model of a uranium bomb will fail to explode, too large a reproduction of a housefly will never get off the ground, and the solar system cannot be expected to look like its planetarium model. Inferences from scale model to original are intrinsically precarious and in need of supplementary validation and correction.

---

[1] "An *Icon* is a sign which refers to the Object that it denotes merely by virtue of characters of its own, and which it possesses, just the same, whether any such Object actually exists or not. . . . Anything whatever . . . is an Icon of anything, in so far as it is like that thing and used as a sign of it." *Collected Papers of Charles Sanders Peirce* (Cambridge, Mass., 1931–35), II, 247.

[2] A good example of the experimental use of models is described in Victor P. Starr's article, "The General Circulation of the Atmosphere," *Scientific American*, CXCV (December 1956), 40–45. The atmosphere of one hemisphere is represented by water in a shallow rotating pan, dye being added to make the flow visible. When the perimeter of the pan is heated the resulting patterns confirm the predictions made by recent theories about the atmosphere.

Let us now consider models involving *change of medium*. I am thinking of such examples as hydraulic models of economic systems, or the use of electrical circuits in computers. In such cases I propose to speak of *analogue models*.

An analogue model is some material object, system, or process designed to reproduce as faithfully as possible in some new medium the *structure* or web of relationships in an original. Many of our previous comments about scale models also apply to the new case. The analogue model, like the scale model, is a symbolic representation of some real or imaginary original, subject to rules of interpretation for making accurate inferences from the relevant features of the model.

The crucial difference between the two types of models is in the corresponding methods of interpretation. Scale models, as we have seen, rely markedly upon identity: their aim is to imitate the original, except where the need for manipulability enforces a departure from sheer reproduction. And when this happens the deviation is held to a minimum, as it were: geometrical magnitudes in the original are still *reproduced,* though with a constant change of ratio. On the other hand, the making of analogue models is guided by the more abstract aim of reproducing the *structure* of the original.

An adequate analogue model will manifest a point-by-point correspondence between the relations *it* embodies and those embodied in the original: every incidence of a relation in the original must be echoed by a corresponding incidence of a correlated relation in the analogue model. To put the matter in another way: there must be rules for translating the terminology applicable to the model in such a way as to conserve truth value.

Thus, the dominating principle of the analogue model is what mathematicians call "isomorphism." [3] We can, if we please, regard the analogue model as iconic of its original,

[3] For a more precise account of isomorphism, see for instance Rudolf Carnap, *Introduction to Symbolic Logic and Its Applications* (New York, 1958), p. 75.

as we did in the case of the scale model, but if we do so we must remember that the former is "iconic" in a more abstract way than the latter. The analogue model shares with its original not a set of features or an identical proportionality of magnitudes but, more abstractly, the same structure or pattern of relationships. Now identity of structure is compatible with the widest variety of content—hence the possibilities for construction of analogue models are endless.

The remarkable fact that the same pattern of relationships, the same structure, can be embodied in an endless variety of different media makes a powerful and a dangerous thing of the analogue model. The risks of fallacious inference from inevitable irrelevancies and distortions in the model are now present in aggravated measure. Any would-be scientific use of an analogue model demands independent confirmation. Analogue models furnish plausible hypotheses, not proofs.

I now make something of a digression to consider "mathematical models." [4] This expression has become very popular among social scientists, who will characteristically speak of "mapping" an "object system" upon one or another of a number of "mathematical systems or models."

When used unemphatically, "model" in such contexts is often no more than a pretentious substitute for "theory" or "mathematical treatment." Usually, however, there are at least the following three additional suggestions: The original field is thought of as "projected" upon the abstract domain of sets, functions, and the like that is the subject matter of the correlated mathematical theory; thus social forces are said to be "modeled" by relations between mathematical entities. The "model" is conceived to be *simpler* and *more abstract* than the original. Often there is a suggestion of the model's being a kind of ethereal analogue model, as if the mathematical equations referred to an invisible mechanism whose

[4] There is now a considerable literature on this subject. See Kenneth J. Arrow, "Mathematical Models in the Social Sciences," in D. Lerner, ed., *The Policy Sciences* (Stanford, Calif., 1951), pp. 129–154.

[223]

operation illustrates or even partially explains the operation of the original social system under investigation. This last suggestion must be rejected as an illusion.

The procedures involved in using a "mathematical model" seem to be the following:

1. In some original field of investigation, a number of relevant variables are identified, either on the basis of common sense or by reason of more sophisticated theoretical considerations. (For example, in the study of population growth we may decide that variation of population with time depends upon the number of individuals born in that time, the number dying, the number entering the area, and the number leaving.[5] I suppose these choices of variables are made at the level of common sense.)

2. Empirical hypotheses are framed concerning the imputed relations between the selected variables. (In population theory, common sense, supported by statistics, suggests that the numbers of births and deaths during any brief period of time are proportional both to that time and to the initial size of the population.)

3. Simplifications, often drastic, are introduced for the sake of facilitating mathematical formulation and manipulation of the variables. (Changes in a population are treated as if they were continuous; the simplest differential equations consonant with the original empirical data are adopted.)

4. An effort is now made to solve the resulting mathematical equations—or, failing that, to study the *global* features of the mathematical systems constructed. (The mathematical equations of population theory yield the so-called "logistic function," whose properties can be specified completely. More commonly, the mathematical treatment of social data leads at best to "plausible topology," to use Kenneth Boulding's happy phrase;[6] i.e., qualitative conclusions con-

[5] Further details may be found conveniently in V. A. Kostitsyn, *Mathematical Biology* (London, 1939).

[6] "Economics as a Social Science," in *The Social Sciences at Mid-*

cerning distributions of maxima, minima, and so forth. This result is connected with the fact that the original data are in most cases at best *ordinal* in character.)

5. An effort is made to extrapolate to testable consequences in the original field. (Thus the prediction can be made that an isolated population tends toward a limiting size independent of the initial size of that population.)

6. Removing some of the initial restrictions imposed upon the component functions in the interest of simplicity (e.g., their linearity) may lead to some increase in generality of the theory.

The advantages of the foregoing procedures are those usually arising from the introduction of mathematical analysis into any domain of empirical investigation, among them precision in formulating relations, ease of inference via mathematical calculation, and intuitive grasp of the structures revealed (e.g., the emergence of the "logistic function" as an organizing and mnemonic device).

The attendant dangers are equally obvious. The drastic simplifications demanded for success of the mathematical analysis entail a serious risk of confusing accuracy of the mathematics with strength of empirical verification in the original field. Especially important is it to remember that the mathematical treatment furnishes no *explanations*. Mathematics can be expected to do no more than draw consequences from the original empirical assumptions. If the functions and equations have a familiar form, there may be a background of pure mathematical research readily applicable to the illustration at hand. We may say, if we like, that the pure mathematics provides the *form* of an explanation, by showing what *kinds* of function would approximately fit the known data. But *causal* explanations must be sought elsewhere. In their inability to suggest explanations, "mathe-

Century: Essays in Honor of Guy Stanton Ford (Minneapolis, 1952), p. 73.

matical models" differ markedly from the theoretical models now to be discussed.[7]

In order now to form a clear conception of the scientific use of "theoretical models," I shall take as my paradigm Clerk Maxwell's celebrated representation of an electrical field in terms of the properties of an imaginary incompressible fluid. In this instance we can draw upon the articulate reflections of the scientist himself. Here is Maxwell's own account of his procedure:

> The first process therefore in the effectual study of the science must be one of simplification and reduction of the results of previous investigation to a form in which the mind can grasp them. The results of this simplification may take the form of a purely mathematical formula or of a physical hypothesis. In the first case we entirely lose sight of the phenomena to be explained; and though we may trace out the consequences of given laws, we can never obtain more extended views of the connexions of the subject. If, on the other hand, we adopt a physical hypothesis, we see the phenomena only through a medium, and are liable to that blindness to facts and rashness in assumption which a partial explanation encourages. We must therefore discover some method of investigation which allows the mind at every step to lay hold of a clear physical conception, without being committed to any theory founded on the physical science from which that conception is borrowed, so that it is neither drawn aside from the subject in pursuit of analytical subtleties, nor carried beyond the truth by a favourite hypothesis.[8]

Later comments of Maxwell's explain what he has in mind:

> By referring everything to the purely geometrical idea of the motion of an imaginary fluid, I hope to attain generality and precision, and to avoid the dangers arising from a premature

---

[7] It is perhaps worth noting that nowadays logicians use "model" to stand for an "interpretation" or "realization" of a formal axiom system. See John G. Kemeny, "Models of Logical Systems," *Journal of Symbolic Logic*, XIII (March 1948), 16–30.

[8] *The Scientific Papers of James Clerk Maxwell* (Cambridge University Press, 1890), I, 155–156.

theory professing to explain the cause of the phenomena. . . .
The substance here treated of . . . is not even a hypothetical
fluid which is introduced to explain actual phenomena. It is
merely a collection of imaginary properties which may be employed for establishing certain theorems in pure mathematics in
a way more intelligible to many minds and more applicable to
physical problems than that in which algebraic symbols alone are
used.[9]

Points that deserve special notice are Maxwell's emphasis
upon obtaining a "clear physical conception" that is both
"intelligible" and "applicable to physical problems," his
desire to abstain from "premature theory," and, above all,
his insistence upon the "imaginary" character of the fluid
invoked in his investigations. In his later elaboration of the
procedure sketched above, the fluid seems at first to play the
part merely of a mnemonic device for grasping mathematical
relations more precisely expressed by algebraic equations
held in reserve. The "exact mental image" [10] he professes to
be seeking seems little more than a surrogate for facility with
algebraic symbols.

Before long, however, Maxwell advances much farther toward ontological commitment. In his paper on action at a
distance, he speaks of the "wonderful medium" filling all
space and no longer regards Faraday's lines of force as "purely
geometrical conceptions." [11] Now he says forthrightly that
they "must not be regarded as mere mathematical abstractions.
They are the directions in which the medium is exerting a
tension like that of a rope, or rather, like that of our own
muscles." [12] Certainly this is no way to talk about a collocation
of imaginary properties. The purely geometrical medium has
become very substantial.

A great contemporary of Maxwell is still more firmly committed to the realistic idiom. We find Lord Kelvin saying:

We must not listen to any suggestion that we are to look upon
the luminiferous ether as an ideal way of putting the thing. A

---

[9] *Ibid.,* I, 159–160. [10] *Ibid.,* II, 360. [11] *Ibid.,* II, 322.
[12] *Ibid.,* II, 323.

real matter between us and the remotest stars I believe there is, and that light consists of real motions of that matter. . . . We know the luminiferous ether better than we know any other kind of matter in some particulars. We know it for its elasticity; we know it in respect to the constancy of the velocity of propagation of light for different periods. . . . Luminiferous ether must be a substance of most extreme simplicity. We might imagine it to be a material whose ultimate property is to be incompressible; to have a definite rigidity for vibrations in times less than a certain limit, and yet to have the absolutely yielding character that we recognize in wax-like bodies when the force is continued for a sufficient time.[13]

There is certainly a vast difference between treating the ether as a mere heuristic convenience, as Maxwell's first remarks require, and treating it in Kelvin's fashion as "real matter" having definite—though, to be sure, paradoxical— properties independent of our imagination. The difference is between thinking of the electrical field *as if* it were filled with a material medium, and thinking of it *as being* such a medium. One approach uses a detached comparison reminiscent of simile and argument from analogy; the other requires an identification typical of metaphor.

In *as if* thinking there is a willing suspension of ontological unbelief, and the price paid, as Maxwell insists, is absence of explanatory power. Here we might speak of the use of models as *heuristic fictions*. In risking existential statements, however, we reap the advantages of an explanation but are exposed to the dangers of self-deception by myths (as the subsequent history of the ether [14] sufficiently illustrates).

The *existential use of models* seems to me characteristic of the practice of the great theorists in physics. Whether we

[13] Sir William Thomson, *Baltimore Lectures* (London, 1904), pp. 8–12.

[14] See Sir Edmund Whittaker, *A History of the Theories of Aether and Electricity* (2nd ed.; London, 1951), I, especially chapter 9: "Models of the Aether." For further discussion of Maxwell's position, see Joseph Turner, "Maxwell on the Method of Physical Analogy," *British Journal for the Philosophy of Science*, VI (1955–56), 226–238.

consider Kelvin's "rude mechanical models," [15] Rutherford's solar system, or Bohr's model of the atom, we can hardly avoid concluding that these physicists conceived themselves to be describing the atom *as it is,* and not merely offering mathematical formulas in fancy dress. In using theoretical models, they were not comparing two domains from a position neutral to both. They used language appropriate to the model in thinking about the domain of application: they worked not *by* analogy, but *through* and by means of an underlying analogy. Their models were conceived to be more than expository or heuristic devices.

Whether the fictitious or the existential interpretation be adopted, there is one crucial respect in which the sense of "model" here in question sharply diverges from those previously discussed in this paper. Scale models and analogue models must be actually put together: a merely "hypothetical" architect's model is nothing at all, and imaginary analogue models will never show us how things work in the large. But theoretical models (whether treated as real or fictitious) are not literally constructed: the heart of the method consists in *talking* in a certain way.

It is therefore plausible to say, as some writers do, that the use of theoretical models consists in introducing a new language or dialect, suggested by a familiar theory but extended to a new domain of application. Yet this suggestion overlooks the point that the new idiom is always a description of some definite object or system (the model itself). If there is a change in manner of expression and representation, there is also the alleged depiction of a specific object or system, inviting further investigation.

The theoretical model need not be built; it is enough that it be *described.* But freedom to describe has its own liabilities. The inventor of a theoretical model is undistracted by accidental and irrelevant properties of the model object, which must have just the properties he assigns to it; but he is deprived of the controls enforced by the attempt at actual construction.

[15] Thomson, *op. cit.,* p. 12.

[229]

Even the elementary demand for self-consistency may be violated in subtle ways unless independent tests are available; and what is to be meant by the reality of the model becomes mysterious.

Although the theoretical model is described but not constructed, the sense of "model" concerned is continuous with the senses previously examined. This becomes clear as soon as we list the conditions for the use of a theoretical model.

1. We have an original field of investigation in which *some* facts and regularities have been established (in any form, ranging from disconnected items and crude generalizations to precise laws, possibly organized by a relatively well-articulated theory).

2. A need is felt, either for explaining the given facts and regularities, or for understanding the basic terms applying to the original domain, or for extending the original corpus of knowledge and conjecture, or for connecting it with hitherto disparate bodies of knowledge—in short, a need is felt for further scientific mastery of the original domain.

3. We describe some entities (objects, materials, mechanisms, systems, structures) belonging to a relatively unproblematic, more familiar, or better-organized secondary domain. The postulated properties of these entities are described in whatever detail seems likely to prove profitable.

4. Explicit or implicit rules of correlation are available for translating statements about the secondary field into corresponding statements about the original field.

5. Inferences from the assumptions made in the secondary field are translated by means of the rules of correlation and then independently checked against known or predicted data in the primary domain.

The relations between the "described model" and the original domain are like those between an analogue model and its original. Here, as in the earlier case, the key to understanding the entire transaction is the identity of structure that in favorable cases permits assertions made about the secondary domain to yield insight into the original field of interest.

Reliance upon theoretical models may well seem a devious and artificial procedure. Although the history of science has often shown that the right way to success is to "go round about" (as the Boyg advised Peer Gynt), one may well wonder whether the detour need be as great as it is in the use of models. Is the leap from the domain of primary interest to an altogether different domain really necessary? Must we really go to the trouble of using half-understood metaphors? Are the attendant risks of mystification and conceptual confusion unavoidable? And does not recourse to models smack too much of philosophical fable and literary allegory to be acceptable in a rational search for the truth? I shall try to show that such natural misgivings can be allayed.

The severest critic of the method will have to concede that recourse to models yields results. To become convinced of this, it is unnecessary to examine the great classical instances of large-scale work with models. The pragmatic utility of the method can be understood even more clearly in the simpler examples.

Consider, for instance, a recently published account of investigations in pure mathematics.[16] The problem to be solved was that of finding some method for dissecting any rectangle into a set of unequal squares—a problem of no practical importance, to be sure, and likely to interest only those who enjoy playing with "mathematical recreations." According to the authors' own account of their investigations, the direct path seemed to lead nowhere: trial and error (or "experiment," as they call it) and straightforward computation produced no results. The decisive breakthrough came when the investigators began to "go round about." As they put the matter: "In the next stage of the research we

[16] Martin Gardner (ed.), "Mathematical Games," *Scientific American,* CXCIX (November 1958), 136–142. The mathematicians were William T. Tutte, C. A. B. Smith, Arthur H. Stone, and R. L. Brooks.

abandoned experiment for theory. We tried to represent rectangles by diagrams of different kinds. The last of these diagrams . . . suddenly made our problem part of the theory of electrical networks." [17]

Here we notice the deliberate introduction of a point-for-point model. Geometrical lines in the original figure were replaced by electrical terminals, squares by connecting wires through which electrical currents are imagined to flow. By suitable choices of the resistances in the wires and the strengths of the currents flowing through them, a circuit was described conforming to known electrical principles (Kirchoff's Laws). In this way, the resources of a well-mastered theory of electrical networks became applicable to the original geometrical problem. "The discovery of this electrical analogy," our authors say, "was important to us because it linked our problem with an established theory. We could now borrow from the theory of electrical networks and obtain formulas for the currents . . . and the sizes of the corresponding component squares." [18] This fascinating episode strikingly illustrates the usefulness of theoretical models.

It is sometimes said that the virtue of working with models is the replacement of abstractions and mathematical formulas by *pictures*, or any other form of representation that is readily visualized. But the example just mentioned shows that this view emphasizes the wrong thing. It is not easier to visualize a network of electrical currents than to visualize a rectangle dissected into component squares: the point of thinking about the electric currents is not that we can see or imagine them more easily, but rather that their properties are *better known* than those of their intended field of application. (And thus it makes perfectly good sense to treat something abstract, even a mathematical calculus, as a theoretical model of something relatively concrete.) To make good use of a model, we usually need intuitive grasp ("Gestalt knowledge") of its capacities, but so long as we can freely *draw inferences* from the model, its picturability is of no

[17] *Ibid.*, p. 136. [18] *Ibid.*, p. 138.

importance. Whereas Maxwell turned away from the electrical field to represent it by a better-known model, subsequent progress in electrical theory now permits us to use the electrical field itself as a model for something else relatively unknown and problematical.

It has been said that the model must belong to a more "familiar" realm than the system to which it is applied. This is true enough, if familiarity is taken to mean belonging to a well-established and thoroughly explored theory. But the model need not belong to a realm of common experience. It may be as recondite as we please, provided we know how to use it. A promising model is one with implications rich enough to suggest novel hypotheses and speculations in the primary field of investigation. "Intuitive grasp" of the model means a ready control of such implications, a capacity to pass freely from one aspect of the model to another, and has very little to do with whether the model can literally be seen or imagined.

The case for the use of theoretical models is that the conditions favoring their success are sometimes satisfied; that sometimes it does prove feasible to invent models "better known" than the original subject matter they are intended to illuminate; and that it is often hard to conceive how the research in question could have been brought to fruition without recourse to the model. But there is also a formidable case against the use of theoretical models, which must now be heard.

Nobody has attacked the use of models more eloquently or more savagely than the great French physicist Pierre Duhem. Here is a characteristic criticism:

The French or German physicist conceives, in the space separating two conductors, abstract lines of force having no thickness or real existence, the English physicist materializes these lines and thickens them to the dimensions of a tube which he will fill with vulcanized rubber. In place of a family of ideal forces, conceivable only by reason, he will have a bundle of elastic strings, visible and tangible, firmly glued at both ends to the surfaces of

[233]

the two conductors, and, when stretched, trying both to contract and to expand. When the two conductors approach each other, he sees the elastic strings drawing closer together; then he sees each of them bunch up and grow large. Such is the famous model of electro-static action designed by Faraday and admired as a work of genius by Maxwell and the whole English school.[19]

Behind such passages as this is a conviction that the nineteenth-century English physicists were corrupting the ideals of science by abandoning clear definitions and a taut system of principles in logical array. "Theory is for him [the English physicist] neither an explanation nor a rational classification, but a model of these laws, a model not built for the satisfying of reason but for the pleasure of the imagination. Hence, it escapes the domination of logic." [20] Duhem might have tolerated, with a grimace, "those disparities, those incoherencies," [21] he disliked in the work of his English contemporaries could he have believed that models were fruitful. But he held them to be useless.

Oddly enough, Duhem applauds "the use of physical analogues" as "an infinitely valuable thing" and an altogether respectable "method of discovery." He is able to reconcile this approval with his strictures against models by purging reliance upon analogy of all its imaginative power. The two domains to be brought into relation by analogy must *antecedently* have been formulated as "abstract systems," and then, as he says, the demonstration of "an exact correspondence" will involve nothing "that can astonish the most rigorous logician." [22]

This is a myopic conception of scientific method; if much in scientific investigation offends the "rigorous logician,"

[19] *The Aim and Structure of Physical Theory*, trans. Philip P. Wiener (Princeton University Press, 1954), p. 70.

[20] *Ibid.*, p. 81.

[21] *Ibid.* Duhem took preference for working with models to be an expression of the English character. He thought the English, unlike the French, typically manifested "l'esprit de finesse" rather than "l'esprit géométrique."

[22] *Ibid.*, pp. 96–97.

[234]

the truth may be that the rigor is out of place. To impose upon the exercise of scientific imagination the canons of a codified and well-ordered logical system is to run the risk of stifling research. Duhem's allegations of lack of coherence and clarity in the physical theories he was attacking must not be taken lightly. But this does not require us to treat the use of models as an aberration of minds too feeble to think about abstractions without visual aids.

It is instructive to compare Duhem's intemperate polemic with the more measured treatment of the same topic by a recent writer. In his valuable book, *Scientific Explanation*, Professor R. B. Braithwaite allows that "there are great advantages in thinking about a scientific theory through the medium of thinking about a model for it," but at once adds as his reason that "to do this avoids the complications and difficulties involved in having to think explicitly about the language or other form of symbolism by which the theory is represented." [23] That is to say that he regards the use of models as a *substitute* for the available alternative of taking the scientific theory "straight." The dominating notion in Braithwaite's conception of scientific theory is that of a "deductive scientific system" defined as "a set of hypotheses . . . arranged in such a way that from some of the hypotheses as premises all the other hypotheses logically follow." [24] The ideal form of scientific theory, for Braithwaite as for Duhem, is essentially that of Euclid's *Elements*—or, rather, Euclid as reformed by Hilbert. It is natural, accordingly, for Braithwaite to agree with Duhem in attaching little value to the use of models in science.

Braithwaite says that "the price of the employment of models is eternal vigilance"; [25] yet as much could be said for the employment of deductive systems or anything else. The crucial issue is whether the employment of models is to be regarded as a prop for feeble minds (as Duhem thought) or a convenient short cut to the consideration of deductive

[23] *Scientific Explanation* (Cambridge, 1953), p. 92.
[24] *Ibid.*, p. 12.   [25] *Ibid.*, p. 93.

systems (as Braithwaite seems to think)—in short, as surrogate for some other procedure—or as a rational method having its own canons and principles. Should we think of the use of models as belonging to psychology—like doodles in a margin—or as having its proper place in the logic of scientific investigation? I have been arguing that models are sometimes not epiphenomena of research, but play a distinctive and irreplaceable part in scientific investigation: models are not disreputable understudies for mathematical formulas.

It may be useful to consider this central issue from another point of view. To many, the use of models in science has strongly resembled the use of metaphors. One writer says, "We are forced to employ models when, for one reason or another, we cannot give a direct and complete description in the language we normally use. Ordinarily, when words fail us, we have recourse to analogy and metaphor. The model functions as a more general kind of *metaphor*." [26]

Certainly there is some similarity between the use of a model and the use of metaphor—perhaps we should say, of a sustained and systematic metaphor. And the crucial question about the autonomy of the method of models is paralleled by an ancient dispute about the translatability of metaphors. Those who see a model as a mere crutch are like those who consider metaphor a mere decoration or ornament. But there are powerful and irreplaceable uses of metaphor not adequately described by the old formula of "saying one thing and meaning another." [27]

A memorable metaphor has the power to bring two separate domains into cognitive and emotional relation by using language directly appropriate to the one as a lens for seeing the other; the implications, suggestions, and supporting values entwined with the literal use of the metaphorical expression enable us to see a new subject matter in a new

[26] E. H. Hutten, "The Role of Models in Physics," *British Journal for the Philosophy of Science*, IV (1953-54), 289.

[27] For elaboration of this and related points, see Chapter III above.

way. The extended meanings that result, the relations between initially disparate realms created, can neither be
antecedently predicted nor subsequently paraphrased in
prose. We can comment *upon* the metaphor, but the metaphor itself neither needs nor invites explanation and paraphrase. Metaphorical thought is a distinctive mode of achieving insight, not to be construed as an ornamental substitute
for plain thought.

Much the same can be said about the role of models in
scientific research. If the model were invoked *after* the work
of abstract formulation had already been accomplished, it
would be at best a convenience of exposition. But the memorable models of science are "speculative instruments," to
borrow I. A. Richards' happy title.[28] They, too, bring about
a wedding of disparate subjects, by a distinctive operation
of transfer of the *implications* of relatively well-organized
cognitive fields. And as with other weddings, their outcomes
are unpredictable. Use of a particular model may amount
to nothing more than a strained and artificial description of
a domain sufficiently known otherwise. But it may also help
us to notice what otherwise would be overlooked, to shift
the relative emphasis attached to details—in short, to *see
new connections.*

A dissenting critic might be willing to agree that models
are useful in the ways I have stated, and yet still harbor
reservations about their rationality. "You have compared the
use of models in science to the use of metaphors," I imagine
him saying, "yet you cannot seriously contend that scientific
investigation *requires* metaphorical language. That a model
may lead to insight not otherwise attainable is just a fact
of psychology. The *content* of the theory that finally emerges
is wholly and adequately expressed by mathematical equations, supplemented by rules for co-ordination with the
physical world. To count the model as an intrinsic part of
the investigation is as plausible as including pencil sharpen-

[28] *Speculative Instruments* (London, 1955).

[237]

ing in scientific research. Your inflated claims threaten to debase the hard-won standards of scientific clarity and accuracy."

This objection treats the relation between the model and the formal theory by which it is eventually replaced as *causal;* it claims that the model is no more than a *de facto* contrivance for leading scientists to a deductive system. I cannot accept this view of the relation between model and theory. We have seen that the successful model must be isomorphic with its domain of application. So there is a rational basis for using the model. In stretching the language by which the model is described in such a way as to fit the new domain, we pin our hopes upon the existence of a common structure in both fields. If the hope is fulfilled, there will have been an objective ground for the analogical transfer. For we call a mode of investigation rational when it has a rationale, that is to say, when we can find reasons which justify what we do and that allow for articulate appraisal and criticism. The putative isomorphism between model and field of application provides such a rationale and yields such standards of critical judgment. We can determine the validity of a given model by checking the extent of its isomorphism with its intended application. In appraising models as good or bad, we need not rely on the sheerly pragmatic test of fruitfulness in discovery; we can, in principle at least, determine the "goodness" of their "fit."

We may deal with any residual qualms about the propriety of condoning metaphorical description in scientific research by stressing the limitations of any comparison between model and metaphor. The term "metaphor" is best restricted to relatively brief statements, and if we wished to draw upon the traditional terms of rhetoric we might better compare use of models with allegory or fable. But none of these comparisons will stand much strain.

Use of theoretical models resembles the use of metaphors in requiring analogical transfer of a vocabulary. Metaphor and model-making reveal new relationships; both are at-

[238]

tempts to pour new content into old bottles. But a metaphor operates largely with *commonplace* implications. You need only proverbial knowledge, as it were, to have your metaphor understood; but the maker of a scientific model must have prior control of a well-knit scientific theory if he is to do more than hang an attractive picture on an algebraic formula. Systematic complexity of the source of the model and capacity for analogical development are of the essence. As Stephen Toulmin says:

It is in fact a great virtue of a good model that it does suggest further questions, taking us beyond the phenomena from which we began, and tempts us to formulate hypotheses which turn out to be experimentally fertile. . . . Certainly it is this suggestiveness, and systematic deployability, that makes a good model something more than a simple metaphor.[29]

I have tried to consider various senses of "model" in a systematic order, proceeding from the familiar construction of miniatures to the making of scale models in a more generalized way, and then to "analogue models" and "mathematical models," until we reached the impressive but mysterious uses of "theoretical models," where mere description of an imaginary but possible structure sufficed to facilitate scientific research. Now I propose to take one last step by considering cases where we have, as it were, an implicit or submerged model operating in a writer's thought. What I have in mind is close to what Stephen C. Pepper meant by "root metaphors." This is his explanation of the notion:

The method in principle seems to be this: A man desiring to understand the world looks about for a clue to its comprehension. He pitches upon some area of common-sense fact and tries if he cannot understand other areas in terms of this one. The original area becomes then his basic analogy or root metaphor. He describes as best he can the characteristics of this area, or, if you will, discriminates its structure. A list of its structural characteristics becomes his basic concepts of explanation and description.

[29] *The Philosophy of Science* (London, 1953), pp. 38–39.

We call them a set of categories. In terms of these categories he proceeds to study all other areas of fact whether uncriticized or previously criticized. He undertakes to interpret all facts in terms of these categories. As a result of the impact of these other facts upon his categories, he may qualify and readjust the categories, so that a set of categories commonly changes and develops. Since the basic analogy or root metaphor normally (and probably at least in part necessarily) arises out of common sense, a great deal of development and refinement of a set of categories is required if they are to prove adequate for a hypothesis of unlimited scope. Some root metaphors prove more fertile than others, have greater power of expansion and adjustment. These survive in comparison with the others and generate the relatively adequate world theories.[30]

Pepper is talking about how metaphysical systems ("world hypotheses," as he calls them) arise; but his remarks have wider application. Use of a dominating system of concepts to describe a new realm of application by analogical extension seems typical of much theorizing:

Any area for investigation, so long as it lacks prior concepts to give it structure and an express terminology with which it can be managed, appears to the inquiring mind inchoate—either a blank, or an elusive and tantalizing confusion. Our usual recourse is, more or less deliberately, to cast about for objects which offer parallels to dimly sensed aspects of the new situation, to use the better known to elucidate the less known, to discuss the intangible in terms of the tangible. This analogical procedure seems characteristic of much intellectual enterprise. There is a deal of wisdom in the popular locution for "what is its nature?" namely: "What's it *like?*" We tend to describe the nature of something in similes and metaphors, and the vehicles of these recurrent figures, when analyzed, often turn out to be the attributes of an implicit analogue through which we are viewing the object we describe.[31]

Here no *specific* structure or system is postulated by the theorist—there is not even a suppressed or implicit model.

[30] *World Hypotheses* (University of California Press, 1942), pp. 91–92.

[31] M. H. Abrams, *The Mirror and the Lamp* (Oxford University Press, 1953), pp. 31–32.

A system of concepts is used analogically, but there is no question of a definite explanation of given phenomena or laws. For reasons already given, I shall not follow Pepper in speaking of "metaphors." For want of a better term, I shall speak of "conceptual archetypes" or, more briefly, of "archetypes." [32] Others have perhaps had a similar idea in mind when they spoke of "ultimate frames of reference" or "ultimate presuppositions."

By an *archetype* I mean a systematic repertoire of ideas by means of which a given thinker describes, by *analogical extension*, some domain to which those ideas do not immediately and literally apply. Thus, a detailed account of a particular archetype would require a list of key words and expressions, with statements of their interconnections and their paradigmatic meanings in the field from which they were originally drawn. This might then be supplemented by analysis of the ways in which the original meanings become extended in their analogical uses.

A striking illustration of the influence of an archetype upon a theorist's work is to be found in the writings of Kurt Lewin. Ironically enough, he formally disclaims any intention of using models. "We have tried," he says, "to avoid developing elaborate 'models'; instead we have tried to represent the dynamic relations between the psychological facts by mathematical constructs at a sufficient level of generality." [33] Well, there may be no specific models envisaged; yet any reader of Lewin's papers must be impressed by the degree to which he employs a vocabulary indigenous to *physical* theory. We repeatedly encounter such words as "field," "vector," "phase-space," "tension," "force," "boundary," "fluidity"—visible symptoms of a massive archetype awaiting to be reconstructed by a sufficiently patient critic.

[32] The term is used in a rather different sense by literary critics as, for example, in Maud Bodkin's well-known *Archetypal Patterns in Poetry* (Oxford, 1934).

[33] Kurt Lewin, *Field Theory in Social Science* (New York, 1951), p. 21.

[241]

In this I see nothing to be deplored on the ground of general principles of sound method. Competent specialists must appraise the distinctive strengths and weaknesses of Lewin's theories; but an onlooker may venture to record his impression that Lewin's archetype, confused though it may be in detail, is sufficiently rich in implicative power to be a useful speculative instrument. It is surely no mere coincidence that Lewin's followers have been stimulated into making all manner of interesting empirical investigations that bear the stamp of their master's archetype. Now if an archetype is sufficiently fruitful, we may be confident that logicians and mathematicians will eventually reduce the harvest to order. There will always be competent technicians who, in Lewin's words, can be trusted to build the highways "over which the streamlined vehicles of a highly mechanized logic, fast and efficient, can reach every important point on fixed tracks." [34] But clearing intellectual jungles is also a respectable occupation. Perhaps every science must start with metaphor and end with algebra; and perhaps without the metaphor there would never have been any algebra.

Of course, there is an ever-present and serious risk that the archetype will be used metaphysically, so that its consequences will be permanently insulated from empirical disproof. The more persuasive the archetype, the greater the danger of its becoming a self-certifying myth. But a good archetype can yield to the demands of experience; while it channels its master's thought, it need not do so inflexibly. The imagination must not be confused with a strait jacket.

If I have been on the right track in my diagnosis of the part played in scientific method by models and archetypes, some interesting consequences follow for the relations between the sciences and the humanities. All intellectual pursuits, however different their aims and methods, rely firmly upon such exercises of the imagination as I have been recalling. Similar archetypes may play their parts in different disciplines; a sociologist's pattern of thought may also be

[34] *Ibid.*, p. 3.

[242]

the key to understanding a novel. So perhaps those interested in excavating the presuppositions and latent archetypes of scientists may have something to learn from the industry of literary critics. When the understanding of scientific models and archetypes comes to be regarded as a reputable part of scientific culture, the gap between the sciences and the humanities will have been partly filled. For exercise of the imagination, with all its promise and its dangers, provides a common ground. If I have so much emphasized the importance of scientific models and archetypes, it is because of a conviction that the imaginative aspects of scientific thought have in the past been too much neglected. For science, like the humanities, like literature, is an affair of the imagination.

XIV

Linguistic Relativity: The Views of Benjamin Lee Whorf

THE WELCOME appearance of a collection of Whorf's scattered writings,[1] together with an illuminating memoir and introduction and a fuller bibliography than has hitherto been available, makes it possible to see the work of that remarkable man in something like its astonishing entirety. Few books of equal importance are as interesting: it would take a dull reader to be indifferent to Whorf's views.

Competent experts have praised Whorf's technical contributions to the study of American Indian languages. But these are overshadowed by his remarkable and still controversial pronouncements about the relations between language, culture, and mental process,[2] to which this discussion will be devoted.

The aim of rendering what Whorf called "linguistic relativity" sufficiently precise to be tested and criticized encoun-

[1] *Language, Thought, and Reality: Selected Writings of Benjamin Lee Whorf.* Edited and with an introduction by John B. Carroll. Foreword by Stuart Chase (New York, 1956, x, 278 pp). A valuable feature is the inclusion of a number of Whorf's hitherto unpublished manuscripts.

[2] See, for instance, *Language in Culture,* ed. H. Hoijer (Chicago, 1954), a report of a conference between linguists, anthropologists, and philosophers on Whorf's views. See also Hoijer's "The Relation of Language to Culture" in *Anthropology Today,* by A. L. Kroeber and others (Chicago, 1953) and L. von Bertalanffy, "An Essay on the Relativity of Categories," *Philosophy of Science,* XX (1955), 243–263 (both favorable) and E. H. Lenneberg, "Cognition in Ethnolinguistics," *Language,* XXIX (1953), 463–471, and L. S. Feuer, "Sociological Aspects of the Relations between Language and Philosophy," *Philosophy of Science,* XX (1953), 85–100 (both highly critical). *Language in Culture* contains further lists of secondary sources.

ters formidable obstacles in his writings: variant formulations of the main points are often inconsistent, there is much exaggeration, and a vaporous mysticism blurs perspectives already sufficiently elusive.

The dominating thought is happily expressed in the quotation from Sapir that Whorf himself used as an epigraph for his best essay:

Human beings do not live in the objective world alone, nor alone in the world of social activity as ordinarily understood, but are very much at the mercy of the particular language which has become the medium of expression for their society. It is quite an illusion to imagine that one adjusts to reality essentially without the use of language and that language is merely an incidental means of solving specific problems of communication and reflection. The fact of the matter is that the "real world" is to a large extent unconsciously built up on the language habits of the group.[3]

This has been called the "Sapir-Whorf hypothesis."

I believe Whorf is committed to the following ten propositions, each of which needs elucidation:

(1) Languages embody "integrated fashions of speaking" or *"background linguistic systems,"* consisting of prescribed modes of expressing thought and experience.

(2) A native speaker has a distinctive *"conceptual system"* for "organizing experience," and (3) a distinctive *"world view"* concerning the universe and his relations to it.

(4) The background linguistic system partially determines the associated conceptual system, and (5) partially determines the associated world view.

(6) Reality consists of a "kaleidoscopic flux of impressions."

(7) The "facts" said to be perceived are a function of the language in which they are expressed, and (8) the "nature of the universe" is a function of the language in which it is stated.

[3] *Selected Writings of Edward Sapir,* ed. D. G. Mandelbaum (University of California Press, 1949), p. 162.

(9) Grammar does not reflect reality, but varies arbitrarily with language.

(10) Logic does not reflect reality, but varies arbitrarily with language.

(1) *Languages incorporate "background linguistic systems."* For uses of the quoted expression, see Whorf's *Language, Thought, and Reality*, pages 212, 247, and elsewhere; "integrated fashion of speaking" (p. 158) and "pattern system" (p. 252) are approximate synonyms.

A recurring difficulty is that of distinguishing the "background" from the language itself and so preventing Whorf's main contentions from degenerating into tautology. That a given language imposes an inherited vocabulary and grammar upon its users is too obvious to require mention; but of course Whorf means more than this. The "background" has to be a *sub*system composed of "patterns" that are *meaningful* to the native speaker no less than to the investigating linguist.

To take an illustration, Whorf claims to discover a category of gender in English (pp. 68, 90 ff.) which, unlike gender in Romance languages, is genuinely functional. Here and throughout Whorf recognizes some linguistic categories, but not all, as genuinely having meaning. For him "any scientific grammar is necessarily a deep analysis into relations" (p. 68) and "linguistics is essentially the quest of MEANING" (p. 73, capitals in original).

In isolating *significant* categories, Whorf proceeds as follows: Formal criteria of somewhat heterodox kinds define the linguistic category; the linguistic analyst (Whorf) then searches for the "idea" that "unifies" the category (p. 81), which is then expressed in the linguist's metalanguage. Ideally, some verifiable predictions about admissible constructions in the language should result. A paradigm of the method is Whorf's isolation of three classes of Hopi verbs (pp. 107–109). Although he begins by using nonsemantical criteria, he characteristically presses on until he has satisfied

[246]

himself about three underlying "concepts." There result what Whorf calls "covert categories" or "cryptotypes" (pp. 88, 89, 92), grammatical classes not marked by invariable morphemic tags, but recognizable by the distinctive interactions of their members with the contexts in which they can occur.

This outcome may remind philosophers of "semantical types" or even of Wittgenstein's "depth grammar." Nor need the most tough-minded of professional linguists feel any qualms about the identification of cryptotypes, since the relevant criteria are *formal*.

The chief difficulty lies in the claim that the cryptotypes *have meaning* for the unsophisticated native speaker. Whorf speaks of "a sort of habitual consciousness" (p. 69); of "a submerged, subtle, and elusive meaning" (p. 70); of a "formless idea" (p. 71), a "rising toward fuller consciousness . . . of linkage bonds" (p. 69), and so on. But it is hard to believe that the ordinary speaker is aware of a grammatical classification that takes all the virtuosity of a Whorf to discover. I doubt that the average English speaker realizes that the particle *"un-"* can be prefixed only to transitive verbs of a "covering, enclosing, and surface attaching meaning" (p. 71) that constitute a prototype. Whorf himself must have the concept since he succeeds in expressing it; but the man in the English street simply uses *"un-"* in happy ignorance. Here I think Whorf commits the *linguist's fallacy* of imputing his own sophisticated attitudes to the speakers he is studying. The heuristic value of the notion of a cryptotype is manifested in its capacity to induce verifiable predictions (cf. the discussion of the imaginary verb *to flimmick* at p. 71); the rest is mythical psychology.

(2) *A native speaker has a distinctive "conceptual system" for "organizing experience."* The underlying picture is of an undivided continuum arbitrarily dissected by language. Whorf speaks of the "segmentation of nature" (p. 240) and the "artificial chopping up of the continuous spread and flow of existence" (p. 253); he says "we dissect nature" (pp. 213,

[247]

214) and "cut" it up (p. 213) when we "organize it into concepts" (p. 213), and all this "largely because, through our mother tongue, we are parties to an agreement to do so, not because nature itself is segmented in that way exactly for all to see" (p. 240).

Let us try this out on color words. We have only a poor handful of uncompounded color words for referring to the millions of observably different components of the color solid; and other languages select the color labels in ways strikingly different—Navaho splits our *black* into two colors and lumps *blue* and *green* together. (But the Navaho are just as good at discriminating colors as we are!)

Here is as favorable a case for Whorf's thesis as can be imagined; yet to apply his ways of talking about the undisputed facts would be to engender confusion. The vocabulary of the operating theatre ("cutting," "chopping," "dissecting," "segmenting") is out of place; to speak is not to butcher, *pace* Bergson and other critics of analysis. To dissect a frog is to destroy it, but talk about the rainbow leaves it unchanged. The case would be different if it could be shown that color vocabularies influence the perception of colors, but where is the evidence for that? If we treat Whorf's talk about "segmentation" as excusable rhetoric, there remains only the complaint that classification is arbitrary.

Is the discreteness of our vocabulary to count as a sporadic or a universal defect? When Whorf talks of everybody seeing the constellation Ursa Major in the same way (p. 164), he seems to admit that language is sometimes adequate to reality; but he inclines to treat the case as exceptional, and the Milky Way serves his metaphysics better than the Big Dipper. He subscribes, consciously or not, to the ancient metaphysical lament that to describe is *necessarily* to falsify. The flat unsatisfying answer is that Whorf, like many others, has succumbed to the muddled notion that the function of speech is to *reinstate* reality. Well, the best recipe for apple pie can't be eaten—but it would be odd to regard that as an inadequacy.

How can language generate a "conceptual system"? If we

[248]

were to accept the view that reference to somebody's-having-a-concept-of-something is a compendious way of talking about certain related capacities to distinguish objects, to respond to them differentially, and especially to talk about them,[4] we might agree to regard "thinking as the [a?] function which is largely linguistic" (p. 66). But having-a-concept cannot be straightforwardly identified with ability to use the corresponding word.

We must admit that human beings have far more concepts (distinctive cognitive capacities) than words for expressing them—as the example of colors amply shows. Even if symbolization is essential to thought, a place must be left for *ad hoc* symbols, nonverbal tokens, and other ways of thinking without using dictionary words. Consequently, inferences from vocabulary to cognitive capacities are always precarious. If the presence of a word actively in use suggests the existence of a corresponding concept, absence of a word shows almost nothing. A striking example is provided by Whorf's observation that the Hopi have no name for the kiva (p. 205). Now it is hardly to be supposed that they have no concept of a "structure so highly typical of pueblo culture and so intimately connected with their religion" (*ibid.*).

Were we able, as we are not, to infer from a given vocabulary to corresponding cognitive capacities, a further inferential leap would be needed to show that different languages incorporate different conceptual systems. The admitted possibility of translation from any language into any other renders the supposed relativity of such systems highly dubious.

Whorf is most interested in what might be called *structural concepts*, typically expressed by grammatical features. He makes much of the fact that the statement "It is a dripping spring" (an odd example, by the way) is expressed in Apache by a very different construction, inadequately rendered by "As water, or springs, whiteness moves downwards" (p. 241). Whorf adds: "How utterly unlike our way of thinking!"

---

[4] See H. H. Price, *Thinking and Experience* (London, 1953), especially pp. 337–357.

But what is the evidence that the Apache *thinks* differently? The difficulty is that the hypostatized structural concepts are so bound to the defining grammatical constructions that it becomes hard to conceive of any extralinguistic verification. Having the concept of a predicate, for all except the linguist or the philosopher, is about the same as using a language that insists upon the use of predicates, and Whorf's contention reduces to saying that one cannot speak grammatically without using a particular grammar. It is a far cry to the assumption that to speak grammatically is to mold "reality" into a structure isomorphic with the grammar. Here, again, Whorf commits the "linguist's fallacy."

(3) *A native speaker has a distinctive "world view" concerning the universe and his relations to it.* Or, as we might say, every man is his own metaphysician. Every language crystallizes "the basic postulates of an unformulated philosophy" (p. 61) and "conceals a METAPHYSICS" (p. 58, capitals in the original).[5]

I understand this to mean that every language incorporates a distinctive set of general categories applicable to the universe and a set of ontological propositions involving those categories. In English,[6] according to Whorf, the relevant categories include "time," "space," "substance," and "matter" (p.138). We are said to "see existence through a binomial formula that expresses any existent as a spatial form plus a spatial formless continuum related to the form as contents [*sic*] is related to the outlines of its container. Nonspatial existents are imaginatively spatialized and charged with similar implications of form and continuum" (p. 147). Whorf

[5] "Grammar contains in crystallized form the accumulated and accumulating experience, the Weltanschauung of a people" (D. D. Lee, "Conceptual Implications of an Indian Language," *Philosophy of Science*, V [1938], 89). This article takes a Whorfian approach to the language of the Wintu tribe of California.

[6] He says there are no important differences in metaphysics between the various Indo-European languages that he lumps together as "SAE, or 'Standard Average European'" (p. 138).

may be saying that the dominant categories in English are either substance-plus-property or form-plus-matter—the first literally applicable to a physical body of a definite outline, the second to a tangible container with fluid contents. These categories, he suggests, are then applied by "extension" and "metaphor" to cases where they cannot literally fit, so that all our descriptions tend to be "objectified" and "spatialized." This is no vaguer than Whorf's own account, though occasionally he speaks as if "Newtonian space, time, and matter" (pp. 152, 153) were what he meant by the "form-plus-substance dichotomy" (p. 152).

Consider now the Hopi "metaphysics": Here, we are told, there is no explicit or implicit reference to time, nor are there "our familiar contrasts of time and space" (p. 58); instead, we have "two grand cosmic forms, which as a first approximation in terminology we may call MANIFESTED and MANIFESTING (or, UNMANIFEST) or, again, OBJECTIVE and SUBJECTIVE" (p. 59). The "subjective" realm includes all that is yet to happen, but conceived of as "mental," as something "burgeoning" and "fermenting" in a conative, spiritual activity that embraces natural and animal phenomena as well as human activity (p. 62); the "objective" realm consists of present and past manifestations of this universal spiritual striving (p. 59). The Hopi think of reality mainly in terms of *events* (p. 147): objectively these are constituted by such directly perceptible features as outlines, colors, movements (p. 147), subjectively as "the expression of invisible intensity factors, on which depend their stability and persistence, or their fugitiveness and proclivities" (p. 147). How much of all this would the average Hopi recognize? Perhaps it might leave him as dumbfounded as a Greek peasant reading Aristotle.

So much for the supposed contrast between the metaphysics implicit in the Hopi language and the metaphysics of "standard average Europeans." Now for some comments.

The idea that a given language commits its users to a distinctive philosophy has been memorably expressed by

[251]

Lichtenberg: "Our false philosophy is incorporated in our whole language; we cannot reason without, so to speak, reasoning wrongly. We overlook the fact that speaking, no matter of what, is itself a philosophy." One cannot help feeling that an idea that has appealed to thinkers as diverse as Von Humboldt,[7] Cassirer, and Wittgenstein must have something to be said for it.

An extreme form of the view rejected by Whorf might hold language to be no more than an external representation of an independent content, so that the relation between the two would be like that of a garment to the body it clothes. But this is plainly indefensible: speech is often an integral part of a wider activity, as the much-discussed case of "performatory language" sufficiently demonstrates. So far we must certainly agree with Whorf and Sapir. But the denial that language is a separable garment for an independently existing reality merely announces a program and offers no arguable thesis. Whorf goes much farther in making specific contentions about the "implicit metaphysics" underlying English and other European languages.

Consider a single inference from grammar to underlying metaphysics. Starting from the alleged fact that "our normal sentence" contains a subject before the verb (p. 242), Whorf goes on to say, "We therefore read action into every sentence, even into 'I hold it' " (p. 243). And again, "We think of it [i.e., *holding*] and even see it as an action because language formulates it in the same way as it formulates more numerous expressions, like 'I strike it,' which deal with movements and changes" (p. 243).

But what is it to "read" action into a sentence? Can it be anything more than *using* the transitive verb? One formal mark of an "action" in the narrow sense is the possibility of adding distinctive modifiers: a man may strike (to use Whorf's example) slowly, jerkily, energetically, and so on. Now if

---

[7] Cf. Harold Basilius, "Neo-Humboldtian Ethnolinguistics," *Word*, VIII (1952), 95–105. This useful article contains several references to similar standpoints.

somebody were to attach these adverbs to the verb "to hold" that would be sufficient indication that he was "reading action" into the verb. I suppose a child might say he was holding his hat slowly, and the poet is allowed a similar license; but otherwise the conceptual confusion is too gross to occur.

Still more dubious are Whorf's broader delineations of the unformulated metaphysics. He says that we "objectify" our "awareness of time and cyclicity" and explains: "I call it [our conception of time] OBJECTIFIED, or imaginary, because it is patterned on the OUTER world. It is this that reflects our linguistic usage" (pp. 139–140). And again, "Concepts of time lose contact with the subjective experience of 'becoming later' and are objectified as counted QUANTITIES, especially as lengths, made up of units as a length can be visibly marked off into inches. A 'length of time' is envisioned as a row of similar units, like a row of bottles" (p. 140).

But what is it to "objectify"? Is it more than the fact that we use words like "long" and "short" in connection with time intervals? Objectification is supposed to be shown by our interest in exact records, in calculation, and in history (p. 153). But if so, "objectification" seems to shift its meaning. I doubt if we can even imagine what it would be like to "treat time as if it were space": I doubt whether this phrase has any definite meaning for Whorf or his readers.

Whorf concedes that there is no observable difference in the behavior of speakers of languages having markedly different grammars: "The Hopi language is capable of accounting for and describing correctly, in a pragmatic or operational sense, all observable phenomena of the universe" (p. 58). I suppose therefore that the Hopi can estimate time intervals and supply dates, so that even if Whorf is right in his remarkable statement that their language "contains no reference to 'time,' either explicit or implicit" (p. 58), they may be expected to have pretty much the same concept of time that we have. Of course, much depends on what one means by "implicit": if the Hopi manage to get along without any reference to time, one would like to know their secret.

[253]

The fact is that the metaphysics that Whorf envisages is not the "unformulated and naive world-view" of the layman, but the sophisticated construction of a metaphysician. Shorn of its fanciful appendages, the philosophy that Whorf professes to discern in "standard average European" looks uncommonly like a bowdlerized version of some scholia from Newton's *Principia*. To the contention that this is *the* metaphysics embodied in the Western languages (only awaiting formulation by the analyst) the sufficient answer is that Descartes—another "standard average European"—was led to a metaphysical system radically different. Languages that Hume and Hegel could use with equal fluency can hardly embody a unique philosophy.

(4) *The background linguistic system partially determines the associated conceptual system, and* (5) *partially determines the associated world view.* I have chosen to say "partially determines" in both cases, though it is hard to decide what Whorf's final opinion was about the relation. A much cited passage denies "that there is anything so definite as 'a correlation' between culture and language" (p. 139), and Whorf says emphatically that "there are connections but not correlations or diagnostic correspondences between cultural norms and linguistic patterns" (p. 159). But in these passages Whorf is discussing inferences from linguistic features to specific cultural features such as hunting practices (p. 139) or "the existence of Crier Chiefs" (p. 159). In saying, "The idea of 'correlation' between language and culture, in the generally accepted sense of correlation, is certainly a mistaken one" (p. 139, n. 1), he is referring to culture as a constellation of observable practices and institutions. But in talking about the connection with "habitual thought" he consistently implies a tighter bond: language "imposes" contrasts on us (p. 55), our dominant categories are "creatures" of language (p. 162), our thoughts are "controlled" (p. 252) by "inexorable systems" (p. 257), and similarly in many other places.

I have already argued that Whorf identified the "conceptual

[254]

system" and the "world view" with the language in which they were expressed, while also confusedly thinking of them as distinct. No wonder then that he is led to think of the connection as "inexorable": if "thought" is defined as an aspect of "language," the connection between the two becomes one of logical necessity.

(6) *Reality consists of a kaleidoscopic flux of impressions.* This "flux" (p. 213) is uncommonly like James's "stream of thought." Whorf is under the spell of a conception of "raw experience" (p. 102) that is "more basic than language" (p. 149), where all is in motion and impermanence and even the contrast between past and present has yet to arise: "If we inspect consciousness we find no past, present, future, but a unity embracing consciousness. EVERYTHING is in consciousness, and everything in consciousness Is, and is together" (pp. 143–144). And the "real time" of consciousness is a *becoming*: "Where real time comes in is that all this in consciousness [the global unity of experience] is 'getting later,' changing certain relations in an irreversible manner" (p. 144).

Well, it is futile to argue against this picture: insistence upon the continuity and flow of experience is unexceptionable but empty, since nothing imaginable is being denied; but it is a bold leap to the contention that customary reference to time-intervals and temporal relations involves falsification. When Whorf claims that "if 'ten days' be regarded as a group it must be as an 'imaginary,' mentally constructed group" (p. 139), he must be taking the logic of counting to require the simultaneous existence of the things counted. Perhaps the best to be said for Whorf's metaphysics is that in all its amateurish crudity it is no worse than some philosophical systems that have had a considerable vogue.

Yet Whorf manages after all to express his philosophy. In describing the "deeper process of consciousness" upon which language is "a superficial embroidery" (p. 239) he refutes his own claim that "no individual is free to describe nature with absolute impartiality" (p. 239). Here is the familiar

[255]

paradox that all general theories of the relativity of truth must brand themselves as biased and erroneous. The standard defense of claiming a privileged position for the theory's own promulgator takes the quaint form in Whorf of a hope that the linguist "familiar with very many widely different linguistic systems" (p. 214) may be free from the metaphysical biases of any. But if Whorf's linguistic studies led him to a Bergsonism that he might have read in the French, it is conceivable that a Greek-reading Hopi might have been led to the delighted discovery of Aristotelian substances as the prime reality.

Whorf's own metaphysics supplies him with a supposed "canon of reference for all observers, irrespective of their languages or scientific jargon" (p. 163), that allows him to appraise languages in terms of their relative ontological adequacy. So he is led, surprisingly, to praise a language that "cannot say 'a wave'" as being "closer to reality in this respect" (p. 262), and to suggest that the Hopi language is a better vehicle for physics than the European languages. But if he were to abstain from metaphysics altogether, on the ground of the incurable relativity of all conceptual systems, his own included, his position would hardly suffer. For the desired relativity might still be argued on the basis of intralinguistic comparisons, just as we establish the relativity of geometries without reference to a supposed absolute and nongeometrical knowledge of space. Such intralinguistic comparisons will in any case be needed, since the detour into dubious ontology cannot excuse the theorist from the detailed demonstration of variation of grammatical structure. Abandoning the metaphysical substructure would have the additional advantage of permitting argument between thinkers who will need a good deal of persuasion before they become Bergsonians.

This examination threatens to become tedious and need not be prolonged, since enough has been said to reveal the basic difficulties of Whorf's position. I have been particularly interested throughout in the extent to which Whorf's outlook was controlled by philosophical conceptions. It would have been presumptuous to rush in where so many linguists fear to tread, were not so much philosophy entwined with the linguistics. I do not wish the negative conclusions reached to leave an impression that Whorf's writings are of little value. Often enough in the history of thought the unsoundest views have proved the most suggestive. Whorf's mistakes are more interesting than the carefully hedged commonplaces of more cautious writers.

Additional Notes and References

I. LANGUAGE AND REALITY

Presidential address delivered at the fifty-fifth annual meeting of the Eastern Division of the American Philosophical Association at the University of Vermont, December 28, 1958. Originally published in *Proceedings and Addresses of the American Philosophical Association*, 32 (Antioch Press, Yellow Springs, Ohio, 1959), pp. 5–17.

II. EXPLANATIONS OF MEANING

Read at the Twelfth International Congress of Philosophy, Venice, September 17, 1958.

In this essay I have used the principle that alternative designations of the same thing ought to be grammatically interchangeable. For criticism of my use of the same principle in "Frege on Functions" in *Problems of Analysis* (Cornell University Press, Ithaca, N.Y., 1954), pp. 229–254, see Alonzo Church's review of that essay in *Journal of Symbolic Logic*, 21 (1956), 201–202. See also T. J. Smiley, "Propositional Functions," *Aristotelian Society Proceedings*, supp. vol. 34 (1960), 38–40, for a review of the whole issue.

III. METAPHOR

Originally published in *Proceedings of the Aristotelian Society*, 55 (1954), 273–294.

A useful review of theories about metaphor is contained in Monroe C. Beardsley, *Aesthetics* (Harcourt, Brace, New York, 1958), pp. 134–144, 159–162. He judges my own discussion to be "incomplete in not explaining what it is about the metaphorical attribution that informs us that the modifier is metaphorical rather than literal" (*op. cit.*, p. 161).

IV. PRESUPPOSITION AND IMPLICATION

Originally published in *A Way to the Philosophy of Science*, ed. Seizi Uyeda (Waseda University Press, Tokyo, 1958).

[259]

ADDITIONAL NOTES AND REFERENCES

The best discussion I know of the questions raised in this essay is C. K. Grant, "Pragmatic Implication," *Philosophy*, 33 (1958), 303–324.

For Strawson's later views on presuppositions, see his *Individuals* (Methuen, London, 1959), especially pp. 190–192, 199–204.

V. NECESSARY STATEMENTS AND RULES

Originally published in the *Philosophical Review*, 67 (1958), 313–341. A shorter version of this paper was delivered as a "Special Lecture in Philosophy" at London University, February 1955.

I am grateful to the John Simon Guggenheim Foundation for the award of a fellowship which made it possible for me to write this and the following essay.

VI. THE ANALYSIS OF RULES

Originally published under the title of "Notes on the Meaning of 'Rule' " in *Theoria*, 24 (1958), 107–136, 139–161.

VII. POSSIBILITY

Originally published in the *Journal of Philosophy*, 57 (1960), 117–126.

VIII. MAKING SOMETHING HAPPEN

Originally published in *Determinism and Freedom*, ed. Sidney Hook (New York University Press, New York, 1958).

The appeal to "paradigm cases" made in this essay would be viewed suspiciously by a number of contemporary philosophers. See, for instance, J. W. N. Watkins, "Farewell to the Paradigm-Case Argument," *Analysis*, 18 (1957), 25–33; Antony Flew's "Reply," pp. 34–40; and papers by H. G. Alexander and by H. S. Eveling and G. O. M. Leith in the same volume of *Analysis*. The value of this kind of argument remains controversial.

IX. CAN THE EFFECT PRECEDE THE CAUSE?

Originally published under the title of "Why Cannot an Effect Precede Its Cause?" in *Analysis*, 16 (1955), 49–58.

For further discussion, see Antony Flew, "Effects before Their Causes? Addenda and Corrigenda," *Analysis*, 16 (1955), 104–111 (with specific criticisms of my essay); Michael Scriven, "Randomness and the Causal Order," *Analysis*, 17 (1956), 5–9; D. F. Pears, "The Priority of Causes," *Analysis*, 17 (1956), 54–63; Roderick M. Chisholm and Richard Taylor, *Analysis*, 20 (1959), 73–78; and William Dray, "Taylor and Chisholm on Making Things to Have Happened," *Analysis*, 20 (1959), 79–81.

X. THE "DIRECTION" OF TIME

Originally published (in Japanese with English abstract) in the *Journal of Philosophical Studies* (Kyoto, Japan), 39 (1957), 485–498. Appeared also in *Analysis*, 19 (1958), 54–63.

Some of the considerations I have relied upon in this essay may have been rendered doubtful by physicists' recent rejection of the principle of "conservation of parity." The best popular account I know of this extraordinary discovery is Philip Morrison's "The Overthrow of Parity," *Scientific American*, 196 (April 1957), 45–53. According to Morrison, the celebrated experiments initiated by Lee and Yang in 1956 established that "the nuclei [of cobalt 60 atoms serving as beta-emitters] had an intrinsically left-handed spin. Left could be distinguished from right. Mirror invariance was dead" (*op. cit.*, p. 50). According to another writer, experiments have since confirmed "unequivocally that in weak interactions there is no right-left symmetry. More precisely, the experiments showed that right-polarized neutrinos exist but left-polarized neutrinos do not. On reflecting a neutrino in a mirror one sees nothing" (A. Salam, *Endeavour*, 17 [1958], 103).

Philosophers who find something absurd in the notion that a mirror reflection of the universe could produce a change in the laws of nature may have to pin their hopes upon the possible existence of "anti-matter." According to Geoffrey Burbidge and Fred Hoyle, "It becomes reasonable to ask whether symmetry may be preserved after all by the existence in some other part of the universe of an equal amount of anti-matter with the opposite 'handedness' " (*Scientific American*, 197 [April 1958], 38–39).

XI. CAN INDUCTION BE VINDICATED?

Originally published in *Philosophical Studies*, 10 (1959), 5–16. This essay and the next constitute a sequel to the discussions of "pragmatic justifications" of induction contained in my *Problems of Analysis*.

[261]

It is perhaps worth repeating that I reject the view that induction needs any "justification" or "vindication" in the senses which philosophers have usually attached to these words. Indeed, I hold attempts to find such "justifications" to be misconceived. The point has been well made in Hilary Putnam's review of *Problems* (*Journal of Philosophy*, 57 [1960], 41).

XII. SELF-SUPPORTING INDUCTIVE ARGUMENTS

Originally published in the *Journal of Philosophy*, 55 (1958), 718–725.

XIII. MODELS AND ARCHETYPES

Read at the University of Pennsylvania, December 9, 1958. Originally published in *Both Human and Humane*, ed. C. E. Boewe (University of Pennsylvania Press, Philadelphia, 1960).

For a different conception of models, the reader may consult Patrick Suppes, "A Comparison of the Meaning and Uses of Models in Mathematics and the Empirical Sciences," *Synthese*, 12 (1960), 287–301. Suppes bases his discussion upon a definition of "model" due to Alfred Tarski: "A possible realization in which all valid sentences of a theory T are satisfied is called a model of T" (*Undecidable Theories*, ed. A. Tarski [North-Holland Publishing Co., Amsterdam, 1953], 11. See also A. Tarski, "Contributions to the Theory of Models," *Indagationes Mathematicae*, 16 [1954], 572–588, and 17 [1955], 56–64.

I cannot agree with Suppes that "the meaning of the concept of model is the same in mathematics and the empirical sciences" (*op. cit.*, p. 289). Since Suppes allows for different "uses" of the concept, the difference between us may be a verbal one.

XIV. LINGUISTIC RELATIVITY

Originally published in the *Philosophical Review*, 68 (1959), 228–238. A Japanese translation appeared in *Americana*, 5 (November 1959).

Index

[263]

INDEX

Isomorphism: a principle of models, 222-223, 238; between grammar and reality, 1-16, 250
Isotropy of space and time, 186-193

James, Henry, 26
James, William, 147-149, 255
Johnson, A. E., 7
Johnson, Samuel, 44n

Kafka, F., 27
Kant, 58, 190
Kemeny, J. G., 226n
Keynes, J. M., 194n
King's companion, 75-76
Kirchoff's Laws, 232
Kostitsyn, V. A., 224n
Kroeber, A. L., 244n

Language: defined by rules, 73; ordinary, and Russell's theory of descriptions, 63; ordinary, is imperfect (Frege), 50; performatory, 118, 122, 252; precausal, 158; rules of, 29-30, 64-94; "Standard Average European" (Whorf), 250n, 251, 254
Language in Culture (Hoijer), 244n
Language, Thought and Reality (Whorf), 12, 244-257
Language, Truth and Logic (Ayer), 70
Languages, American Indian, 244; Apache, 249, 250; Hopi, 246, 249, 251, 253, 256; Navaho, 248; Wintu, 250n
Lee and Yang, 260
Lee, D. D., 250n
Leith, G. O. M., 259
Lenneberg, E. H., 244n
Lerner, D., 223n
Lewin, Kurt, 241-242
Lewis, C. I., 58
Lichtenberg, 252
Limit, practical (Reichenbach), 208
Limiting cases, 81-88
Linguistic relativity, 244-257
Linguist's fallacy, 247, 250
Logic: traditional, 6-8; varies with language (Whorf), 246
Logic (Johnson), 7
Logical form, 30
Logical grammar, 1-16, 25, 71, 95,

102, 119, 137, 151, 247; of "command," 104-105
Logical structure, 13-15
Logistic function, 224

Mace, C. A., 6
Mandelbaum, D. G., 245n
Mathematical Biology (Kostitsyn), 224n
Maxwell, J. C., 226-227, 229, 233, 234
Meaning, 17-24, 103; as an object, 23; as a relation, 23; implicit, 58-63
Meaning and Change of Meaning (Stern), 33n, 34n
Meinong, A., 151
Metaphor, 25-47; and models, 228, 231, 236-241; comparison view of, 35-38, 45, 47n; focus of, 28-29, 32, 38-39, 41, 47; frame of, 28, 32, 35, 39, 47; ground of (Richards), 39; identity of, 28; integration theory (Stanford), 38n; interaction view of, 28n, 38-47; root (Pepper), 239-240; substitution view of, 31, 35-36, 38, 45, 47n
Meyerson, E., 182
Mill, J. S., 145n
Mirror and the Lamp, The (Abrams), 240
Models, 219-243; analogue, 222-223, 229, 230, 238, 239; as heuristic fictions, 228-229; conditions for the use of, 230; existential use of, 228-229; familiarity with, 233; mathematical, 223-226, 239; scale, 220-221, 229, 239; theoretical, 226-243
Moral language, connection with causal language, 166-167
Moral rules, 111-112
Morphemic tags, 247
Morphology, 1
Morrison, Philip, 260
Müller, F. Max, 58
Mussolini, 24

Names, 96; general rules for use of, 55-57
Necessary statements: and associated linguistic rules, 64-94; cannot be regarded as tautologies, 86-88; conventionalistic interpretation of, 68-71, 93
Newton, 254

[265]

INDEX